The Secrets of Success

THE SECRETS OF SUCCESS

8 SELF-HELP CLASSICS
That Have Changed The Lives of Millions

Published 2019 by Gildan Media LLC
aka G&D Media
www.GandDmedia.com

THE SECRETS OF SUCCESS. Copyright © 2019 by G&D Media. All rights reserved. *A Message to Garcia* was originally published in 1914; *Acres of Diamonds* was originally published in 1915; *As a Man Thinketh* was originally published in 1903; *Character Building Thought Power* was originally published in 1900; *The Greatest Thing in the World* was originally published in 1891 and 1898 by Fleming H. Revell Company; *The Magic Story* was originally published in 1900; *The Majesty of Calmness* was originally published in 1900; *The Science of Getting Rich* was originally published in 1910.

No part of this book may be reproduced or transmitted in any form, by any means, (electronic, photocopying, recording, or otherwise) without the prior written permission of the author. No liability is assumed with respect to the use of the information contained within. Although every precaution has been taken, the author and publisher assume no liability for errors or omissions. Neither is any liability assumed for damages resulting from the use of the information contained herein.

Front cover design by David Rheinhardt of Pyrographx

Interior design by Meghan Day Healey of Story Horse, LLC

Library of Congress Cataloging-in-Publication Data is available upon request

ISBN: 978-1-7225-0060-3

10 9 8 7 6 5 4 3 2 1

Contents

Introduction 7

A Message to Garcia
ELBERT HUBBARD 11

Acres of Diamonds
RUSSELL H. CONWELL 23

As a Man Thinketh
JAMES ALLEN 71

Character-Building Thought Power
RALPH WALDO TRINE 105

The Greatest Thing in the World
HENRY DRUMMOND 133

The Magic Story
FREDERICK VAN RENSSELAER DEY 243

The Majesty of Calmness
WILLIAM GEORGE JORDAN 267

The Science of Getting Rich
WALLACE D. WATTLES 311

Introduction

In Defense of Self-Help
By Mitch Horowitz

When G&D Media asked me to write the introduction to this collection, *Secrets of Success*, I was favorably inclined—because the term "self-help" appears prominently, and rightly, in its subtitle.

People too often run away from the term self-help. I believe they should embrace it.

Self-help has developed a bit of a dowdy reputation today. To some, it seems naïve or soft-headed. To others, it seems gauche or down-market. I was once corresponding with a successful self-help writer who seemed embarrassed by the term. "I don't see myself as a self-help writer," he wrote. "I think that most self-help is a sham." The same writer later sent me a mass-mailing for a "Magic Income Trick."

I know another writer of popular psychology who rejects the label self-help because, she says, "I don't provide answers."

Why do good writers flee from a label that obviously belongs to them? Probably because they fear it's undignified. I feel the opposite.

To me, self-help is a noble term. Although I write as both a historian and a spiritual seeker, I wear the label proudly. Some of my books have been about finding a definite aim in life or experimenting with the metaphysical properties of the mind or cultivating personal habits that can produce success. If I'm not a self-help writer—what am I?

The term self-help came into popular use in 1859, when British political reformer Samuel Smiles published his landmark work *Self-Help*, which celebrated good character, self-education, and accountability. Tame-sounding ideas today, but I often note that the profundity of simple ideas is revealed only in their application. The individual's struggle—or failure—to apply basic principles can place him before vast questions. Smiles' book became one of the most influential of its time.

Smiles did not coin the phrase self-help. The term originated in Ralph Waldo Emerson's 1841 lecture, "Man the Reformer," a work that Smiles admired. "Can we not learn the lesson of self-help?" Emerson asked. "Society is full of infirm people, who incessantly summon others to serve them."

Emerson was *not* referring to the destitute. But rather to those who clamor for life's luxuries even while producing little themselves. By contrast, Emerson asked: "Can anything be so elegant as to have few wants and to serve them one's self, so as to have somewhat left to give, instead of being always prompt to grab?"

Authentic self-help demands personal excellence; the drive to overcome addiction or crippling habits; and the wish to make life a little better for those who venture near you.

Some of the greatest exponents of self-help include therapist and Holocaust survivor Viktor Frankl; Alcoholics Anonymous founder Bill Wilson; and Emerson himself, who intended his essays as practical philosophy. While the term didn't exist in his day, Benjamin Franklin can be considered a self-help writer for his popular tracts on good conduct. ("Early to bed and early to rise . . .")

As I've written elsewhere, many contemporary studies in cognitive psychology proffer exaggerated or oversold conclusions, the very things that some of the same researchers accuse New Age writers of.* This trend has weakened the current crop of self-help books. But as far as the classics are concerned—by which I mean books that have attained posterity such as *Alcoholics Anonymous* and *Think and Grow Rich*—their practical effectiveness rests chiefly on the passion of the individual seeker.

As an Arab proverb goes: "The way bread tastes depends on how hungry you are." The depth of your hunger for self-change is likely to match the benefit you experience from any legitimate self-help program.

---

* "In Defense of the 'Woo-Peddlers,'" by Mitch Horowitz, Medium.com, Nov. 30, 2015

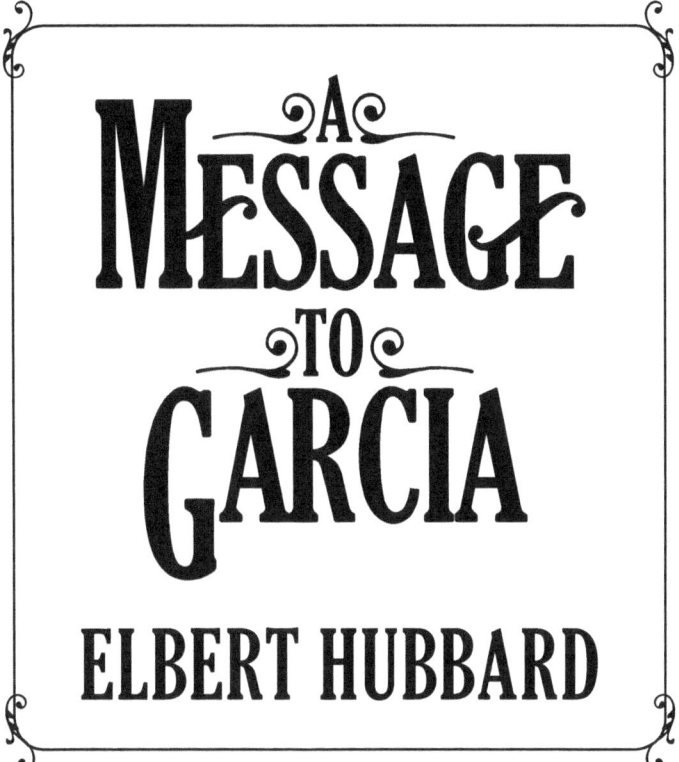

Apologia

Horse Sense

If you work for a man, in Heaven's name work for him. If he pays wages that supply you your bread and butter, work for him, speak well of him, think well of him, and stand by him, and stand by the institution he represents. I think if I worked for a man, I would work for him.

I would not work for him a part of his time, but all of his time. I would give an undivided service or none. If put to the pinch, an ounce of loyalty is worth a pound of cleverness. If you must vilify, condemn, and eternally disparage, why, resign your position, and when you are outside, damn to your heart's content. But, I pray you, so long as you are a part of an institution, do not condemn it. Not that you will injure the institution—not that—but when you disparage the concern of which you are a part, you disparage yourself. And don't forget—"I forgot" won't do in business.

This literary trifle, "A Message to Garcia," was written one evening after supper, in a single hour. It was on the Twenty-second of

February, Eighteen Hundred Ninety-nine, Washington's Birthday, and we were just going to press with the March "Philistine." The thing leaped hot from my heart, written after a trying day, when I had been endeavoring to train some rather delinquent villagers to abjure the comatose state and get radio-active.

The immediate suggestion, though, came from a little argument over the teacups, when my boy Bert suggested that Rowan was the real hero of the Cuban War. Rowan had gone alone and done the thing—carried the message to Garcia.

It came to me like a flash! Yes, the boy is right, the hero is the man who does his work—who carries the message to Garcia. I got up from the table, and wrote "A Message to Garcia." I thought so little of it that we ran it in the Magazine without a heading. The edition went out, and soon orders began to come for extra copies of the March "Philistine," a dozen, fifty, a hundred; and when the American News Company ordered a thousand, I asked one of my helpers which article it was that had stirred up the cosmic dust.

The next day a telegram came from George H. Daniels, of the New York Central Railroad, thus: "Give price on one hundred thousand Rowan article in pamphlet form—Empire State Express advertisement on back—also how soon can ship."

I replied giving price, and stated we could supply the pamphlets in two years. Our facilities were small and a hundred thousand booklets looked like an awful undertaking.

The result was that I gave Mr. Daniels permission to reprint the article in his own way. He issued it in booklet form in editions of half a million. Two or three of these half-million lots were sent out by Mr. Daniels, and in addition the article was reprinted in over two hundred magazines and newspapers. It has been translated into all written languages.

At the time Mr. Daniels was distributing the "Message to Garcia," Prince Hilakoff, Director of Russian Railways, was in this country. He was the guest of the New York Central, and made a tour of the country under the personal direction of Mr. Daniels. The Prince saw the little book and was interested in it, more because Mr. Daniels was putting it out in such big numbers, probably, than otherwise.

In any event, when he got home he had the matter translated into Russian, and a copy of the booklet given to every railroad employee in Russia.

Other countries then took it up, and from Russia it passed into Germany, France, Spain, Turkey, Hindustan and China. During the war between Russia and Japan, every Russian soldier who went to the front was given a copy of the "Message to Garcia."

The Japanese, finding the booklets in possession of the Russian prisoners, concluded that it must be a good thing, and accordingly translated it into Japanese.

And on an order of the Mikado, a copy was given to every man in the employ of the Japanese Government, soldier or civilian. Over forty million copies of "A Message to Garcia" have been printed.

This is said to be a larger circulation than any other literary venture has ever attained during the lifetime of the author, in all history—thanks to a series of lucky accidents!

—E.H.

A Message to Garcia

As the cold of snow in the time of harvest,
so is a faithful messenger to them that send him:
for he refresheth the soul of his masters.
—Proverbs xxv: 13

In all this Cuban business there is one man stands out on the horizon of my memory like Mars at perihelion.

When war broke out between Spain and the United States, it was very necessary to communicate quickly with the leader of the Insurgents.

Garcia was somewhere in the mountain fastnesses of Cuba—no one knew where. No mail or telegraph message could reach him. The President must secure his co-operation, and quickly. What to do!

Some one said to the President, "There is a fellow by the name of Rowan will find Garcia for you, if anybody can."

Rowan was sent for and was given a letter to be delivered to Garcia.

How "the fellow by the name of Rowan" took the letter, sealed it up in an oilskin pouch, strapped it over his heart, in four days landed by night off the coast of Cuba from an open boat, disappeared into the jungle, and in three weeks came out on the other side of the Island, having traversed a hostile country on foot, and delivered his letter to Garcia—are things I have no special desire now to tell in detail.

The point that I wish to make is this: McKinley gave Rowan a letter to be delivered to Garcia; Rowan took the letter and did not ask, "Where is he at?" By the Eternal! there is a man whose form should be cast in deathless bronze and the statue placed in every college of the land.

It is not book-learning young men need, nor instruction about this and that, but a stiffening of the vertebrae which will cause them to be loyal to a trust, to act promptly, concentrate their energies: do the thing—"Carry a message to Garcia."

General Garcia is dead now, but there are other Garcias.

No man who has endeavored to carry out an enterprise where many hands were needed, but has been well-nigh appalled at times by the imbecility of the average man—the inability or unwillingness to concentrate on a thing and do it.

Slipshod assistance, foolish inattention, dowdy indifference, and half-hearted work seem the rule; and no man succeeds, unless by hook or crook or threat he forces or bribes other men to assist him; or mayhap, God in His goodness performs a miracle, and sends him an Angel of Light for an assistant. You, reader, put this matter to a test: You are sitting now in your office—six clerks are within call. Summon any one and make this request: "Please look in the encyclopedia and make a brief memorandum for me concerning the life of Correggio."

Will the clerk quietly say, "Yes, sir," and go do the task?

On your life he will not. He will look at you out of a fishy eye and ask one or more of the following questions:

Who was he?
Which encyclopedia?
Where is the encyclopedia?
Was I hired for that?
Don't you mean Bismarck?

What's the matter with Charlie doing it?
Is he dead?
Is there any hurry?
Shall I bring you the book and let you look it up yourself?
What do you want to know for?

I wasn't hired for that anyway!

And I will lay you ten to one that after you have answered the questions, and explained how to find the information, and why you want it, the clerk will go off and get one of the other clerks to help him try to find Garcia—and then come back and tell you there is no such man. Of course I may lose my bet, but according to the Law of Average I will not.

Now, if you are wise, you will not bother to explain to your "assistant" that Correggio is indexed under the C's, not in the K's, but you will smile very sweetly and say, "Never mind," and go look it up yourself.

And this incapacity for independent action, this moral stupidity, this infirmity of the will, this unwillingness to cheerfully catch hold and lift—these are the things that put pure Socialism so far into the future. If men will not act for themselves, what will they do when the benefit of their effort is for all? A first mate with knotted club seems necessary; and the dread of getting "the bounce" Saturday night holds many a worker to his place.

Advertise for a stenographer, and nine out of ten who apply can neither spell nor punctuate—and do not think it necessary to.

Can such a one write a letter to Garcia?

"You see that bookkeeper," said a foreman to me in a large factory.

"Yes; what about him?"

"Well, he's a fine accountant, but if I'd send him up-town on an errand, he might accomplish the errand all right, and on the other hand, might stop at four saloons on the way, and when he got to Main Street would forget what he had been sent for."

Can such a man be entrusted to carry a message to Garcia?

We have recently been hearing much maudlin sympathy expressed for the "downtrodden denizens of the sweat-shop" and the "homeless wanderer searching for honest employment," and with it all often go many hard words for the men in power.

Nothing is said about the employer who grows old before his time in a vain attempt to get frowsy ne'er-do-wells to do intelligent work; and his long, patient striving with "help" that does nothing but loaf when his back is turned. In every store and factory there is a constant weeding-out process going on. The employer is continually sending away "help" that have shown their incapacity to further the interests of the business, and others are being taken on.

No matter how good times are, this sorting continues: only if times are hard and work is scarce, the sorting is done finer—but out and forever out the incompetent and unworthy go. It is the survival of the fittest. Self-interest prompts every employer to keep the best—those who can carry a message to Garcia.

I know one man of really brilliant parts who has not the ability to manage a business of his own, and yet who is absolutely worthless to any one else, because he carries with him constantly the insane suspicion that his employer is oppressing, or intending to oppress, him. He can not give orders; and he will not receive them. Should a message be given him to take to Garcia, his answer would probably be, "Take it yourself!"

Tonight this man walks the streets looking for work, the wind whistling through his threadbare coat. No one who knows him dare employ him, for he is a regular firebrand of discontent. He is impervious to reason, and the only thing that can impress him is the toe of a thick-soled Number Nine boot.

Of course I know that one so morally deformed is no less to be pitied than a physical cripple; but in our pitying let us drop a tear, too, for the men who are striving to carry on a great enterprise, whose working hours are not limited by the whistle, and whose hair is fast turning white through the struggle to hold in line dowdy indifference, slipshod imbecility, and the heartless ingratitude which, but for their enterprise, would be both hungry and homeless.

Have I put the matter too strongly? Possibly I have; but when all the world has gone a-slumming I wish to speak a word of sympathy for the man who succeeds—the man who, against great odds, has directed the efforts of others, and having succeeded, finds there's nothing in it: nothing but bare board and clothes. I have carried a dinner-pail and worked for day's wages, and I have also been an employer of labor, and I know there is something to be said on both sides. There is no excellence, per se, in poverty; rags are no recommendation; and all employers are not rapacious and high-handed, any more than all poor men are virtuous.

My heart goes out to the man who does his work when the "boss" is away, as well as when he is at home. And the man who, when given a letter for Garcia, quietly takes the missive, without asking any idiotic questions, and with no lurking intention of chucking it into the nearest sewer, or of doing aught else but deliver it, never gets "laid off," nor has to go on a strike for higher wages. Civilization is one long, anxious search for just such individuals. Anything such a man asks shall be granted. His kind is so rare that no employer can afford to let him go. He is wanted in every city, town and village—in every office, shop, store and factory.

The world cries out for such: he is needed, and needed badly—the man who can carry

A MESSAGE TO GARCIA.

* * *

To act in absolute freedom and at the same time know that responsibility is the price of freedom is salvation.

Life In Abundance

The supreme prayer of my heart is not to be learned or "good," but to be Radiant.

I desire to radiate health, cheerfulness, sincerity, calm courage and good-will.

I wish to be simple, honest, natural, frank, clean in mind and clean in body, unaffected—ready to say, "I do not know," if so it be, to meet all men on an absolute equality—to face any obstacle and meet every difficulty unafraid and unabashed.

I wish others to live their lives, too, up to their highest, fullest and best. To that end I pray that I may never meddle, dictate, interfere, give advice that is not wanted, nor assist when my services are not needed. If I can help people I'll do it by giving them a chance to help themselves; and if I can uplift or inspire, let it be by example, inference and suggestion, rather than by injunction and dictation. That is to say, I desire to be Radiant—to Radiate Life.

Acres of Diamonds

Russell H. Conwell

An Appreciation

Though Russell H. Conwell's *Acres of Diamonds* have been spread all over the United States, time and care have made them more valuable, and now that they have been reset in black and white by their discoverer, they are to be laid in the hands of a multitude for their enrichment.

In the same case with these gems there is a fascinating story of the Master Jeweler's life-work which splendidly illustrates the ultimate unit of power by showing what one man can do in one day and what one life is worth to the world.

As his neighbor and intimate friend in Philadelphia for thirty years, I am free to say that Russell H. Conwell's tall, manly figure stands out in the state of Pennsylvania as its first citizen and "The Big Brother" of its seven millions of people.

From the beginning of his career he has been a credible witness in the Court of Public Works to the truth of the strong language of the New Testament Parable where it says, "If ye have faith as a grain of mustard-seed, ye shall say unto this mountain, 'Remove hence to yonder place,' AND IT SHALL REMOVE AND NOTHING SHALL BE IMPOSSIBLE UNTO YOU."

As a student, schoolmaster, lawyer, preacher, organizer, thinker and writer, lecturer, educator, diplomat, and leader of men, he has made his mark on his city and state and the times in which he has lived. A man dies, but his good work lives.

His ideas, ideals, and enthusiasms have inspired tens of thousands of lives. A book full of the energetics of a master workman is just what every young man cares for.

Friends.—This lecture has been delivered under these circumstances: I visit a town or city, and try to arrive there early enough to see the postmaster, the barber, the keeper of the hotel, the principal of the schools, and the ministers of some of the churches, and then go into some of the factories and stores, and talk with the people, and get into sympathy with the local conditions of that town or city and see what has been their history, what opportunities they had, and what they had failed to do—and every town fails to do something—and then go to the lecture and talk to those people about the subjects which applied to their locality. "Acres of Diamonds"—the idea—has continuously been precisely the same. The idea is that in this country of ours every man has the opportunity to make more of himself than he does in his own environment, with his own skill, with his own energy, and with his own friends.

—*Russell H. Conwell.*

Acres Of Diamonds

When going down the Tigris and Euphrates rivers many years ago with a party of English travelers I found myself under the direction of an old Arab guide whom we hired up at Bagdad, and I have often thought how that guide resembled our barbers in certain mental characteristics. He thought that it was not only his duty to guide us down those rivers, and do what he was paid for doing, but also to entertain us with stories curious and weird, ancient and modern, strange and familiar. Many of them I have forgotten, and I am glad I have, but there is one I shall never forget.

The old guide was leading my camel by its halter along the banks of those ancient rivers, and he told me story after story until I grew weary of his story-telling and ceased to listen. I have never been irritated with that guide when he lost his temper as I ceased listening. But I remember that he took off his Turkish cap and swung it in a circle to get my attention. I could see it through the corner of my eye, but I determined not to look straight at him for fear he would tell another story. But although I am not a woman, I did finally look, and as soon as I did he went right into another story.

Said he, "I will tell you a story now which I reserve for my particular friends." When he emphasized the words "particular friends," I listened, and I have ever been glad I did. I really feel devoutly thankful, that there are 1,674 young men who have been carried through college by this lecture who are also glad that I did listen. The old guide told me that there once lived not far from the River Indus an ancient Persian by the name of Ali Hafed. He said that Ali Hafed owned a very large farm, that he had orchards, grain-fields, and gardens; that he had money at interest, and was a wealthy and contented man. He was contented because he was wealthy, and wealthy because he was contented. One day there visited that old Persian farmer one of those ancient Buddhist priests, one of the wise men of the East. He sat down by the fire and told the old farmer how this world of ours was made. He said that this world was once a mere bank of fog, and that the Almighty thrust His finger into this bank of fog, and began slowly to move His finger around, increasing the speed until at last He whirled this bank of fog into a solid ball of fire. Then it went rolling through the universe, burning its way through other banks of fog, and condensed the moisture without, until it fell in floods of rain upon its hot surface, and cooled the outward crust. Then the internal fires bursting outward through the crust threw up the mountains and hills, the valleys, the plains and prairies of this wonderful world of ours. If this internal molten mass came bursting out and cooled very quickly it became granite; less quickly copper, less quickly silver, less quickly gold, and, after gold, diamonds were made.

Said the old priest, "A diamond is a congealed drop of sunlight." Now that is literally scientifically true, that a diamond is an actual deposit of carbon from the sun. The old priest told Ali Hafed that if he had one diamond the size of his thumb he could purchase the county, and if he had a mine of diamonds he could place his children upon thrones through the influence of their great wealth.

Ali Hafed heard all about diamonds, how much they were worth, and went to his bed that night a poor man. He had not lost anything, but he was poor because he was discontented, and discontented because he feared he was poor. He said, "I want a mine of diamonds," and he lay awake all night.

Early in the morning he sought out the priest. I know by experience that a priest is very cross when awakened early in the morning, and when he shook that old priest out of his dreams, Ali Hafed said to him:

"Will you tell me where I can find diamonds?"

"Diamonds! What do you want with diamonds?" "Why, I wish to be immensely rich." "Well, then, go along and find them. That is all you have to do; go and find them, and then you have them." "But I don't know where to go." "Well, if you will find a river that runs through white sands, between high mountains, in those white sands you will always find diamonds." "I don't believe there is any such river." "Oh yes, there are plenty of them. All you have to do is to go and find them, and then you have them." Said Ali Hafed, "I will go."

So he sold his farm, collected his money, left his family in charge of a neighbor, and away he went in search of diamonds. He began his search, very properly to my mind, at the Mountains of the Moon. Afterward he came around into Palestine, then wandered on into Europe, and at last when his money was all spent and he was in rags, wretchedness, and poverty, he stood on the shore of that bay at Barcelona, in Spain, when a great tidal wave came rolling in between the pillars of Hercules, and the poor, afflicted, suffering, dying man could not resist the awful temptation to cast himself into that incoming tide, and he sank beneath its foaming crest, never to rise in this life again.

When that old guide had told me that awfully sad story he stopped the camel I was riding on and went back to fix the baggage that was coming off another camel, and I had an opportunity to muse over his story while he was gone. I remember saying to myself, "Why did he reserve that story for his 'particular friends'?" There seemed to be no beginning, no middle, no end, nothing to it. That was the first story I had ever heard told in my life, and would be the first one I ever read, in which the hero was killed in the first chapter. I had but one chapter of that story, and the hero was dead.

When the guide came back and took up the halter of my camel, he went right ahead with the story, into the second chapter, just as though there had been no break. The man who purchased Ali Hafed's farm one day led his camel into the garden to drink, and as that camel put its nose into the shallow water of that garden brook, Ali Hafed's successor noticed a curious flash of light from the white sands of the stream. He pulled out a black stone having an eye of light reflecting all the hues of the rainbow. He took the pebble into the house and put it on the mantel which covers the central fires, and forgot all about it.

A few days later this same old priest came in to visit Ali Hafed's successor, and the moment he opened that drawing-room door he saw that flash of light on the mantel, and he rushed up to it, and shouted: "Here is a diamond! Has Ali Hafed returned?" "Oh no, Ali Hafed has not returned, and that is not a diamond. That is nothing but a stone we found right out here in our own garden." "But," said the priest, "I tell you I know a diamond when I see it. I know positively that is a diamond."

Then together they rushed out into that old garden and stirred up the white sands with their fingers, and lo! there came up other more beautiful and valuable gems than the first. "Thus," said the guide to me, and, friends, it is historically true, "was discovered the diamond-mine of Golconda, the most magnificent diamond-mine in all the history of mankind, excelling the Kimberly itself. The Kohinoor, and the Orloff of the crown jewels of England and Russia, the largest on earth, came from that mine."

When that old Arab guide told me the second chapter of his story, he then took off his Turkish cap and swung it around in the air again to get my attention to the moral. Those Arab guides have morals to their stories, although they are not always moral. As he swung his hat, he said to me, "Had Ali Hafed remained at home and dug in his own cellar, or underneath his own wheat-fields, or in his own garden, instead of wretchedness, starvation, and death by suicide in a strange land, he would have had 'acres of diamonds.' For every acre of that old farm, yes, every shovelful, afterward revealed gems which since have decorated the crowns of monarchs."

When he had added the moral to his story I saw why he reserved it for "his particular friends." But I did not tell him I could see it. It was that mean old Arab's way of going around a thing like a lawyer, to say indirectly what he did not dare say directly, that "in his private opinion there was a certain young man then traveling down the Tigris River that might better be at home in America." I did not tell him I could see that, but I told him his story reminded me of one, and I told it to him quick, and I think I will tell it to you.

I told him of a man out in California in 1847, who owned a ranch. He heard they had discovered gold in southern California, and so with a passion for gold he sold his ranch to Colonel Sutter, and away he went, never to come back. Colonel Sutter put a mill upon a stream that ran through that ranch, and one day his little girl brought some wet sand from the raceway into their home and sifted it through her fingers before the fire, and in that falling sand a visitor saw the first shining scales of real gold that were ever discovered in California. The man who had owned that ranch wanted gold, and he could have secured it for the mere taking. Indeed, thirty-eight millions of dollars has been taken out of a very few acres since then. About eight years ago I delivered this lecture in a city that stands on that farm, and they told me that a one-third owner for years and years had been getting one hundred and twenty dollars in gold every fifteen minutes, sleeping or waking, without taxation. You and I would enjoy an income like that—if we didn't have to pay an income tax.

But a better illustration really than that occurred here in our own Pennsylvania. If there is anything I enjoy above another on the platform, it is to get one of these German audiences in Pennsylvania before me, and fire that at them, and I enjoy it to-night. There was a man living in Pennsylvania, not unlike some Pennsylvanians you have seen, who owned a farm, and he did with that farm just what I should do with a farm if I owned one in Pennsylvania—he sold it. But before he sold it he decided to secure employment collecting coal-oil for his cousin, who was in the business in Canada, where they first discovered oil on this continent. They dipped it from the running streams at that early time. So this Pennsylvania farmer wrote to his cousin asking for employment. You see, friends, this farmer was not altogether a foolish man. No, he was not. He did not leave his farm until he had something else to do. *Of all the simpletons the stars shine on I don't know of a worse one than the man who leaves one job before he has gotten another.*

That has especial reference to my profession, and has no reference whatever to a man seeking a divorce. When he wrote to his cousin for employment, his cousin replied, "I cannot engage you because you know nothing about the oil business."

Well, then the old farmer said, "I will know," and with most commendable zeal (characteristic of the students of Temple University) he set himself at the study of the whole subject. He began away back at the second day of God's creation when this world was covered thick and deep with that rich vegetation which since has turned to the primitive beds of coal. He studied the subject until he found that the drainings really of those rich beds of coal furnished the coal-oil that was worth pumping, and then he found how it came up with the living springs. He studied until he knew what it looked like, smelled like, tasted like, and how to refine it. Now said he in his letter to his cousin, "I understand the oil business." His cousin answered, "All right, come on."

So he sold his farm, according to the county record, for $833 (even money, "no cents"). He had scarcely gone from that place before the man who purchased the spot went out to arrange for the watering of the cattle. He found the previous owner had gone out years before and put a plank across the brook back of the barn, edgewise into the surface of the water just a few inches. The purpose of that plank at that sharp angle across the brook was to throw over to the other bank a dreadful-looking scum through which the cattle would not put their noses. But with that plank there to throw it all over to one side, the cattle would drink below, and thus that man who had gone to Canada had been himself damming back for twenty-three years a flood of coal-oil which the state geologists of Pennsylvania declared to us ten years later was even then worth a hundred millions of dollars to our state, and four years ago our geologist declared the discovery to be worth to our state a thousand millions of dollars. The man who owned that territory on which the city of Titusville now stands, and those Pleasantville valleys, had studied the subject from the second day of God's creation clear down to the present time. He studied it until he knew all about it, and yet he is said to have sold the whole of it for $833, and again I say, "no sense."

But I need another illustration. I found it in Massachusetts, and I am sorry I did because that is the state I came from. This young man in Massachusetts furnishes just another phase of my thought. He went to Yale College and studied mines and mining, and became such an adept as a mining engineer that he was employed by the authorities of the university to train students who were behind their classes. During his senior year he earned $15 a week for doing that work. When he graduated they raised his pay from $15 to $45 a week, and offered him a professorship, and as soon as they did he went right home to his mother. *If they had raised that boy's pay from $15 to $15.60 he would have stayed and been proud of the place, but when they put it up to $45 at one leap, he said, "Mother, I won't work for $45 a week. The idea of a man with a brain like mine working for $45 a week! Let's go out in California and stake out gold-mines and silver-mines, and be immensely rich."*

Said his mother, "Now, Charlie, it is just as well to be happy as it is to be rich."

"Yes," said Charlie, "but it is just as well to be rich and happy, too." And they were both right about it. As he was an only son and she a widow, of course he had his way. They always do.

They sold out in Massachusetts, and instead of going to California they went to Wisconsin, where he went into the employ of the Superior Copper Mining Company at $15 a week again, but with the proviso in his contract that he should have an interest in any mines he should discover for the company. I don't believe he ever discovered a mine, and if I am looking in the face of any stockholder of that copper company you wish he had discovered something or other. I have friends who are not here because they could not afford a ticket, who did have stock in that company at the time this young man was employed there. This young man went out there, and I have not heard a word from him. I don't know what became of him, and I don't know whether he found any mines or not, but I don't believe he ever did.

But I do know the other end of the line. He had scarcely gotten out of the old homestead before the succeeding owner went out to dig potatoes. The potatoes were already growing in the ground when he bought the farm, and as the old farmer was bringing in a basket of potatoes it hugged very tight between the ends of the stone fence. You know in Massachusetts our farms are nearly all stone wall. There you are obliged to be very economical of front gateways in order to have some place to put the stone. When that basket hugged so tight he set it down on the ground, and then dragged on one side, and pulled on the other side, and as he was dragging that basket through this farmer noticed in the upper and outer corner of that stone wall, right next the gate, a block of native silver eight inches square. That professor of mines, mining, and mineralogy who knew so much about the subject that he would not work for $45 a week, when he sold that homestead in Massachusetts sat right on that silver to make the bargain. He was born on that homestead, was brought up there, and had gone back and forth rubbing the stone with his sleeve until it reflected his countenance, and seemed to say, "Here is a hundred thousand dollars right down here just for the taking." But he would not take it. It was in a home in Newburyport, Massachusetts, and there was no silver there, all away off—well, I don't know where, and he did not, but somewhere else, and he was a professor of mineralogy.

My friends, that mistake is very universally made, and why should we even smile at him. I often wonder what has become of him. I do not know at all, but I will tell you what I "guess" as a Yankee. I guess that he sits out there by his fireside to-night with his friends gathered around him, and he is saying to them something like this: "Do you know that man Conwell who lives in Philadelphia?" "Oh yes, I have heard of him." "Do you know that man Jones that lives in Philadelphia?" "Yes, I have heard of him, too."

Then he begins to laugh, and shakes his sides, and says to his friends, "Well, they have done just the same thing I did, precisely"— and that spoils the whole joke, for you and I have done the same thing he did, and while we sit here and laugh at him he has a better right to sit out there and laugh at us. I know I have made the same mistakes, but, of course, that does not make any difference, because we don't expect the same man to preach and practise, too.

As I come here to-night and look around this audience I am seeing again what through these fifty years I have continually seen—men that are making precisely that same mistake. I often wish I could see the younger people, and would that the Academy had been filled to-night with our high-school scholars and our grammar-school scholars, that I could have them to talk to. While I would have preferred such an audience as that, because they are most susceptible, as they have not grown up into their prejudices as we have, they have not gotten into any custom that they cannot break, they have not met with any failures as we have; and while I could perhaps do such an audience as that more good than I can do grown-up people, yet I will do the best I can with the material

I have. I say to you that you have "acres of diamonds" in Philadelphia right where you now live. "Oh," but you will say, "you cannot know much about your city if you think there are any 'acres of diamonds' here."

I was greatly interested in that account in the newspaper of the young man who found that diamond in North Carolina. It was one of the purest diamonds that has ever been discovered, and it has several predecessors near the same locality. I went to a distinguished professor in mineralogy and asked him where he thought those diamonds came from. The professor secured the map of the geologic formations of our continent, and traced it. He said it went either through the underlying carboniferous strata adapted for such production, westward through Ohio and the Mississippi, or in more probability came eastward through Virginia and up the shore of the Atlantic Ocean. It is a fact that the diamonds were there, for they have been discovered and sold; and that they were carried down there during the drift period, from some northern locality. Now who can say but some person going down with his drill in Philadelphia will find some trace of a diamond-mine yet down here? Oh, friends! you cannot say that you are not over one of the greatest diamond-mines in the world, for such a diamond as that only comes from the most profitable mines that are found on earth.

But it serves simply to illustrate my thought, which I emphasize by saying if you do not have the actual diamond-mines literally you have all that they would be good for to you. Because now that the Queen of England has given the greatest compliment ever conferred upon American woman for her attire because she did not appear with any jewels at all at the late reception in England, it has almost done away with the use of diamonds anyhow. All you would care for would be the few you would wear if you wish to be modest, and the rest you would sell for money.

Now then, I say again that the opportunity to get rich, to attain unto great wealth, is here in Philadelphia now, within the reach of almost every man and woman who hears me speak to-night, and I mean just what I say. I have not come to this platform even under these circumstances to recite something to you. I have come to tell you what in God's sight I believe to be the truth, and if the years of life have been of any value to me in the attainment of common sense, I know I am right; that the men and women sitting here, who found it difficult perhaps to buy a ticket to this lecture or gathering to-night, have within their reach "acres of diamonds," opportunities to get largely wealthy. There never was a place on earth more adapted than the city of Philadelphia to-day, and never in the history of the world did a poor man without capital have such an opportunity to get rich quickly and honestly as he has now in our city. I say it is the truth, and I want you to accept it as such; for if you think I have come to simply recite something, then I would better not be here. I have no time to waste in any such talk, but to say the things I believe, and unless some of you get richer for what I am saying to-night my time is wasted.

I say that you ought to get rich, and it is your duty to get rich. How many of my pious brethren say to me, "Do you, a Christian minister, spend your time going up and down the country advising young people to get rich, to get money?" "Yes, of course I do." They say, "Isn't that awful! Why don't you preach the gospel instead of preaching about man's making money?" "Because to make money honestly is to preach the gospel." That is the reason. The men who get rich may be the most honest men you find in the community.

"Oh," but says some young man here to-night, "I have been told all my life that if a person has money he is very dishonest and dishonorable and mean and contemptible." My friend, that is the reason why you have none, because you have that idea of people. The foundation of your faith is altogether false. Let me say here clearly, and say it briefly, though subject to discussion which I have not time for here, ninety-eight out of one hundred of the rich men of America are honest. That is why they are rich. That is why they are trusted with money. That is why they carry on great enterprises and find plenty of people to work with them. It is because they are honest men.

Says another young man, "I hear sometimes of men that get millions of dollars dishonestly." Yes, of course you do, and so do I. But they are so rare a thing in fact that the newspapers talk about them all the time as a matter of news until you get the idea that all the other rich men got rich dishonestly.

My friend, you take and drive me—if you furnish the auto—out into the suburbs of Philadelphia, and introduce me to the people who own their homes around this great city, those beautiful homes with gardens and flowers, those magnificent homes so lovely in their art, and I will introduce you to the very best people in character as well as in enterprise in our city, and you know I will. A man is not really a true man until he owns his own home, and they that own their homes are made more honorable and honest and pure, and true and economical and careful, by owning the home.

For a man to have money, even in large sums, is not an inconsistent thing. We preach against covetousness, and you know we do, in the pulpit, and oftentimes preach against it so long and use the terms about "filthy lucre" so extremely that Christians get the idea that when we stand in the pulpit we believe it is wicked for any man to have money—until the collection-basket goes around, and then we almost swear at the people because they don't give more money. Oh, the inconsistency of such doctrines as that!

Money is power, and you ought to be reasonably ambitious to have it. You ought because you can do more good with it than you could without it. Money printed your Bible, money builds your churches, money sends your missionaries, and money pays your preachers, and you would not have many of them, either, if you did not pay them. I am always willing that my church should raise my salary, because the church that pays the largest salary always raises it the easiest. You never knew an exception to it in your life. The man who gets the largest salary can do the most good with the power that is furnished to him. Of course he can if his spirit be right to use it for what it is given to him.

I say, then, you ought to have money. If you can honestly attain unto riches in Philadelphia, it is your Christian and godly duty to do so. It is an awful mistake of these pious people to think you must be awfully poor in order to be pious.

Some men say, "Don't you sympathize with the poor people?" Of course I do, or else I would not have been lecturing these years. I won't give in but what I sympathize with the poor, but the number of poor who are to be sympathized with is very small. To sympathize with a man whom God has punished for his sins, thus to help him when God would still continue a just punishment, is to do wrong, no doubt about it, and we do that more than we help those who are deserving. While we should sympathize with God's poor—that is, those who cannot help themselves—let us remember there is not a poor person in the United States who was not made poor by his own shortcomings, or by the shortcomings of some one else.

It is all wrong to be poor, anyhow. Let us give in to that argument and pass that to one side.

A gentleman gets up back there, and says, "Don't you think there are some things in this world that are better than money?" Of course I do, but I am talking about money now. Of course there are some things higher than money. Oh yes, I know by the grave that has left me standing alone that there are some things in this world that are higher and sweeter and purer than money. Well do I know there are some things higher and grander than gold. Love is the grandest thing on God's earth, but fortunate the lover who has plenty of money. Money is power, money is force, money will do good as well as harm. In the hands of good men and women it could accomplish, and it has accomplished, good.

I hate to leave that behind me. I heard a man get up in a prayer-meeting in our city and thank the Lord he was "one of God's poor." Well, I wonder what his wife thinks about that? She earns all the money that comes into that house, and he smokes a part of that on the veranda. I don't want to see any more of the Lord's poor of that kind, and I don't believe the Lord does. And yet there are some people who think in order to be pious you must be awfully poor and awfully dirty. That does not follow at all. While we sympathize with the poor, let us not teach a doctrine like that.

Yet the age is prejudiced against advising a Christian man (or, as a Jew would say, a godly man) from attaining unto wealth. The prejudice is so universal and the years are far enough back, I think, for me to safely mention that years ago up at Temple University there was a young man in our theological school who thought he was the only pious student in that department. He came into my office one evening and sat down by my desk, and said to me: "Mr. President, I think it is my duty sir, to come in and labor with you."

"What has happened now?" Said he, "I heard you say at the Academy, at the Peirce School commencement, that you thought it was an honorable ambition for a young man to desire to have wealth, and that you thought it made him temperate, made him anxious to have a good name, and made him industrious. You spoke about man's ambition to have money helping to make him a good man. Sir, I have come to tell you the Holy Bible says that 'money is the root of all evil.'"

I told him I had never seen it in the Bible, and advised him to go out into the chapel and get the Bible, and show me the place. So out he went for the Bible, and soon he stalked into my office with the Bible open, with all the bigoted pride of the narrow sectarian, or of one who founds his Christianity on some misinterpretation of Scripture. He flung the Bible down on my desk, and fairly squealed into my ear: "There it is, Mr. President; you can read it for yourself." I said to him: "Well, young man, you will learn when you get a little older that you cannot trust another denomination to read the Bible for you. You belong to another denomination. You are taught in the theological school, however, that emphasis is exegesis. Now, will you take that Bible and read it yourself, and give the proper emphasis to it?"

He took the Bible, and proudly read, "'The love of money is the root of all evil.'"

Then he had it right, and when one does quote aright from that same old Book he quotes the absolute truth. I have lived through fifty years of the mightiest battle that old Book has ever fought, and I have lived to see its banners flying free; for never in the history of this world did the great minds of earth so universally agree that the Bible is true—all true—as they do at this very hour.

So I say that when he quoted right, of course he quoted the absolute truth. "The love of money is the root of all evil." He who tries to attain unto it too quickly, or dishonestly, will fall into many snares, no doubt about that. The love of money. What is that? It is making an idol of money, and idolatry pure and simple everywhere is condemned by the Holy Scriptures and by man's common sense. The man that worships the dollar instead of thinking of the purposes for which it ought to be used, the man who idolizes simply money, the miser that hordes his money in the cellar, or hides it in his stocking, or refuses to invest it where it will do the world good, that man who hugs the dollar until the eagle squeals has in him the root of all evil.

I think I will leave that behind me now and answer the question of nearly all of you who are asking, "Is there opportunity to get rich in Philadelphia?" Well, now, how simple a thing it is to see where it is, and the instant you see where it is it is yours. Some old gentleman gets up back there and says, "Mr. Conwell, have you lived in Philadelphia for thirty-one years and don't know that the time has gone by when you can make anything in this city?" "No, I don't think it is." "Yes, it is; I have tried it." "What business are you in?" "I kept a store here for twenty years, and never made over a thousand dollars in the whole twenty years."

"Well, then, you can measure the good you have been to this city by what this city has paid you, because a man can judge very well what he is worth by what he receives; that is, in what he is to the world at this time. If you have not made over a thousand dollars in twenty years in Philadelphia, it would have been better for Philadelphia if they had kicked you out of the city nineteen years and nine months ago. A man has no right to keep a store in Philadelphia twenty years and not make at least five hundred thousand dollars, even though it be a corner grocery up-town." You say, "You cannot make five thousand dollars in a store now." Oh, my friends, if you will just take only four blocks around you, and find out what the people want and what you ought to supply and set them down with your pencil, and figure up the profits you would make if you did supply them, you would very soon see it. There is wealth right within the sound of your voice.

Some one says: "You don't know anything about business. A preacher never knows a thing about business." Well, then, I will have to prove that I am an expert. I don't like to do this, but I have to do it because my testimony will not be taken if I am not an expert. My father kept a country store, and if there is any place under the stars where a man gets all sorts of experience in every kind of mercantile transactions, it is in the country store. I am not proud of my experience, but sometimes when my father was away he would leave me in charge of the store, though fortunately for him that was not very often. But this did occur many times, friends: A man would come in the store, and say to me, "Do you keep jack-knives?" "No, we don't keep jack-knives," and I went off whistling a tune. What did I care about that man, anyhow? Then another farmer would come in and say, "Do you keep jack-knives?" "No, we don't keep jack-knives." Then I went away and whistled another tune. Then a third man came right in the same door and said, "Do you keep jack-knives?" "No. Why is every one around here asking for jack-knives? Do you suppose we are keeping this store to supply the whole neighborhood with jack-knives?" Do you carry on your store like that in Philadelphia? The difficulty was I had not then learned that the foundation of godliness and the foundation principle of success in business are both the same precisely. The man who says,

"I cannot carry my religion into business" advertises himself either as being an imbecile in business, or on the road to bankruptcy, or a thief, one of the three, sure. He will fail within a very few years. He certainly will if he doesn't carry his religion into business. If I had been carrying on my father's store on a Christian plan, godly plan, I would have had a jack-knife for the third man when he called for it. Then I would have actually done him a kindness, and I would have received a reward myself, which it would have been my duty to take.

There are some over-pious Christian people who think if you take any profit on anything you sell that you are an unrighteous man. On the contrary, you would be a criminal to sell goods for less than they cost. You have no right to do that. You cannot trust a man with your money who cannot take care of his own. You cannot trust a man in your family that is not true to his own wife. You cannot trust a man in the world that does not begin with his own heart, his own character, and his own life. It would have been my duty to have furnished a jack-knife to the third man, or the second, and to have sold it to him and actually profited myself. I have no more right to sell goods without making a profit on them than I have to overcharge him dishonestly beyond what they are worth. But I should so sell each bill of goods that the person to whom I sell shall make as much as I make.

To live and let live is the principle of the gospel, and the principle of every-day common sense. Oh, young man, hear me; live as you go along. Do not wait until you have reached my years before you begin to enjoy anything of this life. If I had the millions back, or fifty cents of it, which I have tried to earn in these years, it would not do me anything like the good that it does me now in this almost sacred presence to-night. Oh, yes, I am paid over and over a hundredfold to-night for dividing as I have tried to do in some measure as I went along through the years. I ought not speak that way, it sounds egotistic, but I am old enough now to be excused for that. I should have helped my fellow-men, which I have tried to do, and every one should try to do, and get the happiness of it. The man who goes home with the sense that he has stolen a dollar that day, that he has robbed a man of what was his honest due, is not going to sweet rest. He arises tired in the morning, and goes with an unclean conscience to his work the next day. He is not a successful man at all, although he may have laid up millions. But the man who has gone through life dividing always with his fellow-men, making and demanding his own rights and his own profits, and giving to every other man his rights and profits, lives every day, and not only that, but it is the royal road to great wealth. The history of the thousands of millionaires shows that to be the case.

The man over there who said he could not make anything in a store in Philadelphia has been carrying on his store on the wrong principle. Suppose I go into your store to-morrow morning and ask, "Do you know neighbor A, who lives one square away, at house No. 1240?" "Oh yes, I have met him. He deals here at the corner store." "Where did he come from?" "I don't know." "How many does he have in his family?" "I don't know." "What ticket does he vote?" "I don't know." "What church does he go to?" "I don't know, and don't care. What are you asking all these questions for?"

If you had a store in Philadelphia would you answer me like that? If so, then you are conducting your business just as I carried on my father's business in Worthington, Massachusetts. You don't know where your neighbor came from when he moved to Philadelphia, and you don't care. If you had cared you would be a rich man now. If you had cared enough about him to take an interest in his affairs, to find out what he needed, you would have been rich. But you go through the world saying, "No opportunity to get rich," and there is the fault right at your own door.

But another young man gets up over there and says, "I cannot take up the mercantile business." (While I am talking of trade it applies to every occupation.) "Why can't you go into the mercantile business?" "Because I haven't any capital." Oh, the weak and dudish creature that can't see over its collar! It makes a person weak to see these little dudes standing around the corners and saying, "Oh, if I had plenty of capital, how rich I would get." "Young man, do you think you are going to get rich on capital?" "Certainly." Well, I say, "Certainly not." If your mother has plenty of money, and she will set you up in business, you will "set her up in business," supplying you with capital.

The moment a young man or woman gets more money than he or she has grown to by practical experience, that moment he has gotten a curse. It is no help to a young man or woman to inherit money. It is no help to your children to leave them money, but if you leave them education, if you leave them Christian and noble character, if you leave them a wide circle of friends, if you leave them an honorable name, it is far better than that they should have money. It would be worse for them, worse for the nation, that they should have any money at all. Oh, young man, if you have inherited money, don't regard it as a help. It will curse you through your years, and deprive you of the very best things of human life. There is no class of people to be pitied so much as the inexperienced sons and daughters of the rich of our generation. I pity the rich man's son. He can never know the best things in life.

One of the best things in our life is when a young man has earned his own living, and when he becomes engaged to some lovely young woman, and makes up his mind to have a home of his own. Then with that same love comes also that divine inspiration toward better things, and he begins to save his money. He begins to leave off his bad habits and put money in the bank. When he has a few hundred dollars he goes out in the suburbs to look for a home. He goes to the savings-bank, perhaps, for half of the value, and then goes for his wife, and when he takes his bride over the threshold of that door for the first time he says in words of eloquence my voice can never touch: "I have earned this home myself. It is all mine, and I divide with thee." That is the grandest moment a human heart may ever know.

But a rich man's son can never know that. He takes his bride into a finer mansion, it may be, but he is obliged to go all the way through it and say to his wife, "My mother gave me that, my mother gave me that, and my mother gave me this," until his wife wishes she had married his mother. I pity the rich man's son.

The statistics of Massachusetts showed that not one rich man's son out of seventeen ever dies rich. I pity the rich man's sons unless they have the good sense of the elder Vanderbilt, which sometimes happens. He went to his father and said, "Did you earn all your money?" "I did, my son. I began to work on a ferry-boat for twenty-five cents a day." "Then," said his son, "I will have none of your money," and he, too, tried to get employment on a ferry-boat that Saturday night. He could not get one there, but he did get a place for three dollars a week. Of course, if a rich man's son will do that, he will get the discipline of a poor boy that is worth more than a university education to any man. He would then be able to take care of the millions of his father. But as a rule the rich men will not let their sons do the very thing that made them great. As a rule, the rich man will not allow his son to work—and his mother?

Why, she would think it was a social disgrace if her poor, weak, little lily-fingered, sissy sort of a boy had to earn his living with honest toil. I have no pity for such rich men's sons.

I remember one at Niagara Falls. I think I remember one a great deal nearer. I think there are gentlemen present who were at a great banquet, and I beg pardon of his friends. At a banquet here in Philadelphia there sat beside me a kind-hearted young man, and he said, "Mr. Conwell, you have been sick for two or three years. When you go out, take my limousine, and it will take you up to your house on Broad Street." I thanked him very much, and perhaps I ought not to mention the incident in this way, but I follow the facts. I got on to the seat with the driver of that limousine, outside, and when we were going up I asked the driver, "How much did this limousine cost?" "Six thousand eight hundred, and he had to pay the duty on it." "Well," I said, "does the owner of this machine ever drive it himself?" At that the chauffeur laughed so heartily that he lost control of his machine. He was so surprised at the question that he ran up on the sidewalk, and around a corner lamp-post out into the street again. And when he got out into the street he laughed till the whole machine trembled. He said: "He drive this machine! Oh, he would be lucky if he knew enough to get out when we get there."

I must tell you about a rich man's son at Niagara Palls. I came in from the lecture to the hotel, and as I approached the desk of the clerk there stood a millionaire's son from New York. He was an indescribable specimen of anthropologic potency. He had a skull-cap on one side of his head, with a gold tassel in the top of it, and a gold-headed cane under his arm with more in it than in his head. It is a very difficult thing to describe that young man. He wore an eye-glass that he could not see through, patent-leather boots that he could not walk in, and pants that he could not sit down in—

dressed like a grasshopper. This human cricket came up to the clerk's desk just as I entered, adjusted his unseeing eye-glass, and spake in this wise to the clerk. You see, he thought it was "Hinglish, you know," to lisp. "Thir, will you have the kindness to supply me with thome papah and enwelophs!" The hotel clerk measured that man quick, and he pulled the envelopes and paper out of a drawer, threw them across the counter toward the young man, and then turned away to his books. You should have seen that young man when those envelopes came across that counter. He swelled up like a gobbler turkey, adjusted his unseeing eye-glass, and yelled: "Come right back here. Now thir, will you order a thervant to take that papah and enwelophs to yondah dethk." Oh, the poor, miserable, contemptible American monkey! He could not carry paper and envelopes twenty feet. I suppose he could not get his arms down to do it. I have no pity for such travesties upon human nature. If you have not capital, young man, I am glad of it. What you need is common sense, not copper cents.

The best thing I can do is to illustrate by actual facts well-known to you all. A. T. Stewart, a poor boy in New York, had $1.50 to begin life on. He lost 87-½ cents of that on the very first venture. How fortunate that young man who loses the first time he gambles. That boy said, "I will never gamble again in business," and he never did. How came he to lose 87-½ cents? You probably all know the story how he lost it—because he bought some needles, threads, and buttons to sell which people did not want, and had them left on his hands, a dead loss. Said the boy, "I will not lose any more money in that way." Then he went around first to the doors and asked the people what they did want. Then when he had found out what they wanted he invested his 62-½ cents to supply a known demand. Study it wherever you choose—in business, in your profession, in your housekeeping, whatever your life, that one thing is the secret of success. You must first know the demand. You must first know what people need, and then invest yourself where you are most needed. A. T. Stewart went on that principle until he was worth what amounted afterward to forty millions of dollars, owning the very store in which Mr. Wanamaker carries on his great work in New York. His fortune was made by his losing something, which taught him the great lesson that he must only invest himself or his money in something that people need. When will you salesmen learn it? When will you manufacturers learn that you must know the changing needs of humanity if you would succeed in life? Apply yourselves, all you Christian people, as manufacturers or merchants or workmen to supply that human need. It is a great principle as broad as humanity and as deep as the Scripture itself.

The best illustration I ever heard was of John Jacob Astor. You know that he made the money of the Astor family when he lived in New York. He came across the sea in debt for his fare. But that poor boy with nothing in his pocket made the fortune of the Astor family on one principle. Some young man here to-night will say, "Well, they could make those fortunes over in New York, but they could not do it in Philadelphia!" My friends, did you ever read that wonderful book of Riis (his memory is sweet to us because of his recent death), wherein is given his statistical account of the records taken in 1889 of 107 millionaires of New York. If you read the account you will see that out of the 107 millionaires only seven made their money in New York. Out of the 107 millionaires worth ten million dollars in real estate then, 67 of them made their money in towns of less than 3,500 inhabitants. The richest man in this country to-day, if you read the real-estate values, has never moved away from a town of 3,500 inhabitants. It makes not so much difference where you are as who you are. But if you cannot get rich in Philadelphia you certainly cannot do it in New York.

Now John Jacob Astor illustrated what can be done anywhere. He had a mortgage once on a millinery-store, and they could not sell bonnets enough to pay the interest on his money. So he foreclosed that mortgage, took possession of the store, and went into partnership with the very same people, in the same store, with the same capital. He did not give them a dollar of capital. They had to sell goods to get any money. Then he left them alone in the store just as they had been before, and he went out and sat down on a bench in the park in the shade. What was John Jacob Astor doing out there, and in partnership with people who had failed on his own hands? He had the most important and, to my mind, the most pleasant part of that partnership on his hands. For as John Jacob Astor sat on that bench he was watching the ladies as they went by; and where is the man who would not get rich at that business? As he sat on the bench if a lady passed him with her shoulders back and head up, and looked straight to the front, as if she did not care if all the world did gaze on her, then he studied her bonnet, and by the time it was out of sight he knew the shape of the frame, the color of the trimmings, and the crinklings in the feather. I sometimes try to describe a bonnet, but not always. I would not try to describe a modern bonnet. Where is the man that could describe one? This aggregation of all sorts of driftwood stuck on the back of the head, or the side of the neck, like a rooster with only one tail feather left. But in John Jacob Astor's day there was some art about the millinery business, and he went to the millinery-store and said to them: "Now put into the show-window just such a bonnet as I describe to you, because I have already seen a lady who likes such a bonnet. Don't make up any more until

I come back." Then he went out and sat down again, and another lady passed him of a different form, of different complexion, with a different shape and color of bonnet. "Now," said he, "put such a bonnet as that in the show-window." He did not fill his show-window up-town with a lot of hats and bonnets to drive people away, and then sit on the back stairs and bawl because people went to Wanamaker's to trade. He did not have a hat or a bonnet in that show-window but what some lady liked before it was made up. The tide of custom began immediately to turn in, and that has been the foundation of the greatest store in New York in that line, and still exists as one of three stores. Its fortune was made by John Jacob Astor after they had failed in business, not by giving them any more money, but by finding out what the ladies liked for bonnets before they wasted any material in making them up. I tell you if a man could foresee the millinery business he could foresee anything under heaven!

Suppose I were to go through this audience to-night and ask you in this great manufacturing city if there are not opportunities to get rich in manufacturing. "Oh yes," some young man says, "there are opportunities here still if you build with some trust and if you have two or three millions of dollars to begin with as capital." Young man, the history of the breaking up of the trusts by that attack upon "big business" is only illustrating what is now the opportunity of the smaller man. The time never came in the history of the world when you could get rich so quickly manufacturing without capital as you can now.

But you will say, "You cannot do anything of the kind. You cannot start without capital." Young man, let me illustrate for a moment. I must do it. It is my duty to every young man and woman, because we are all going into business very soon on the same plan.

Young man, remember if you know what people need you have gotten more knowledge of a fortune than any amount of capital can give you.

There was a poor man out of work living in Hingham, Massachusetts. He lounged around the house until one day his wife told him to get out and work, and, as he lived in Massachusetts, he obeyed his wife. He went out and sat down on the shore of the bay, and whittled a soaked shingle into a wooden chain. His children that evening quarreled over it, and he whittled a second one to keep peace. While he was whittling the second one a neighbor came in and said: "Why don't you whittle toys and sell them? You could make money at that." "Oh," he said, "I would not know what to make." "Why don't you ask your own children right here in your own house what to make?" "What is the use of trying that?" said the carpenter. "My children are different from other people's children." (I used to see people like that when I taught school.) But he acted upon the hint, and the next morning when Mary came down the stairway, he asked, "What do you want for a toy?" She began to tell him she would like a doll's bed, a doll's washstand, a doll's carriage, a little doll's umbrella, and went on with a list of things that would take him a lifetime to supply. So, consulting his own children, in his own house, he took the firewood, for he had no money to buy lumber, and whittled those strong, unpainted Hingham toys that were for so many years known all over the world. That man began to make those toys for his own children, and then made copies and sold them through the boot-and-shoe store next door. He began to make a little money, and then a little more, and Mr. Lawson, in his *Frenzied Finance* says that man is the richest man in old Massachusetts, and I think it is the truth. And that man is worth a hundred millions of dollars to-day, and has been only thirty-four years making it on that one principle—that one must judge that what his own children like at home other people's children would like in their homes, too; to judge the human heart by oneself, by one's wife or by one's children. It is the royal road to success in manufacturing. "Oh," but you say, "didn't he have any capital?" Yes, a penknife, but I don't know that he had paid for that.

I spoke thus to an audience in New Britain, Connecticut, and a lady four seats back went home and tried to take off her collar, and the collar-button stuck in the buttonhole. She threw it out and said, "I am going to get up something better than that to put on collars." Her husband said: "After what Conwell said to-night, you see there is a need of an improved collar-fastener that is easier to handle. There is a human need; there is a great fortune. Now, then, get up a collar-button and get rich." He made fun of her, and consequently made fun of me, and that is one of the saddest things which comes over me like a deep cloud of midnight sometimes—although I have worked so hard for more than half a century, yet how little I have ever really done. Notwithstanding the greatness and the handsomeness of your compliment to-night, I do not believe there is one in ten of you that is going to make a million of dollars because you are here to-night; but it is not my fault, it is yours. I say that sincerely. What is the use of my talking if people never do what I advise them to do? When her husband ridiculed her, she made up her mind she would make a better collar-button, and when a woman makes up her mind "she will," and does not say anything about it, she does it. It was that New England woman who invented the snap button which you can find anywhere now. It was first a collar-button with a spring cap attached to the outer side. Any of you who wear modern waterproofs know the button that simply pushes together, and when you unbutton it you simply pull it apart. That is the button to which I refer, and which she invented. She afterward invented several other buttons, and then invested in more, and then was taken into partnership with great factories. Now that woman goes over the sea every summer in her private steamship—yes, and takes her husband with her! If her husband were to die, she would have money enough left now to buy a foreign duke or count or some such title as that at the latest quotations.

Now what is my lesson in that incident? It is this: I told her then, though I did not know her, what I now say to you, "Your wealth is too near to you. You are looking right over it"; and she had to look over it because it was right under her chin.

I have read in the newspaper that a woman never invented anything. Well, that newspaper ought to begin again. Of course, I do not refer to gossip—I refer to machines—and if I did I might better include the men. That newspaper could never appear if women had not invented something. Friends, think. Ye women, think! You say you cannot make a fortune because you are in some laundry, or running a sewing-machine, it may be, or walking before some loom, and yet you can be a millionaire if you will but follow this almost infallible direction.

When you say a woman doesn't invent anything, I ask, Who invented the Jacquard loom that wove every stitch you wear? Mrs. Jacquard. The printer's roller, the printing-press, were invented by farmers' wives. Who invented the cotton-gin of the South that enriched our country so amazingly? Mrs. General Greene invented the cotton-gin and showed the idea to Mr. Whitney, and he, like a man, seized it. Who was it that invented the sewing-machine? If I would go to school to-morrow and ask your children they would say, "Elias Howe."

He was in the Civil War with me, and often in my tent, and I often heard him say that he worked fourteen years to get up that sewing-machine. But his wife made up her mind one day that they would starve to death if there wasn't something or other invented pretty soon, and so in two hours she invented the sewing-machine. Of course he took out the patent in his name. Men always do that. Who was it that invented the mower and the reaper? According to Mr. McCormick's confidential communication, so recently published, it was a West Virginia woman, who, after his father and he had failed altogether in making a reaper and gave it up, took a lot of shears and nailed them together on the edge of a board, with one shaft of each pair loose, and then wired them so that when she pulled the wire one way it closed them, and when she pulled the wire the other way it opened them, and there she had the principle of the mowing-machine. If you look at a mowing-machine, you will see it is nothing but a lot of shears. If a woman can invent a mowing-machine, if a woman can invent a Jacquard loom, if a woman can invent a cotton-gin, if a woman can invent a trolley switch—as she did and made the trolleys possible; if a woman can invent, as Mr. Carnegie said, the great iron squeezers that laid the foundation of all the steel millions of the United States, "we men" can invent anything under the stars! I say that for the encouragement of the men.

Who are the great inventors of the world? Again this lesson comes before us. The great inventor sits next to you, or you are the person yourself. "Oh," but you will say, "I have never invented anything in my life." Neither did the great inventors until they discovered one great secret. Do you think it is a man with a head like a bushel measure or a man like a stroke of lightning? It is neither. The really great man is a plain, straightforward, every-day, common-sense man. You would not dream that he was a great inventor if you did not see something he had actually done. His neighbors do not regard him so great. You never see anything great over your back fence. You say there is no greatness among your neighbors. It is all away off somewhere else. Their greatness is ever so simple, so plain, so earnest, so practical, that the neighbors and friends never recognize it.

True greatness is often unrecognized. That is sure. You do not know anything about the greatest men and women. I went out to write the life of General Garfield, and a neighbor, knowing I was in a hurry, and as there was a great crowd around the front door, took me around to General Garfield's back door and shouted, "Jim! Jim!" And very soon "Jim" came to the door and let me in, and I wrote the biography of one of the grandest men of the nation, and yet he was just the same old "Jim" to his neighbor. If you know a great man in Philadelphia and you should meet him to-morrow, you would say, "How are you, Sam?" or "Good morning, Jim." Of course you would. That is just what you would do.

One of my soldiers in the Civil War had been sentenced to death, and I went up to the White House in Washington—sent there for the first time in my life—to see the President. I went into the waiting-room and sat down with a lot of others on the benches, and the secretary asked one after another to tell him what they wanted. After the secretary had been through the line, he went in, and then came back to the door and motioned for me. I went up to that anteroom, and the secretary said: "That is the President's door right over there. Just rap on it and go right in." I never was so taken aback, friends, in all my life, never. The secretary himself made it worse for me, because he had told me how to go in and then went out another door to the left and shut that. There I was, in the hallway by myself before the President of the United States of America's door. I had been on fields of battle, where the shells did sometimes shriek and the bullets did sometimes hit me, but I always wanted to run. I have no sympathy with the old man who says, "I would just as soon march up to the cannon's mouth as eat my dinner." I have no faith in a man who doesn't know enough to be afraid when he is being shot at. I never was so afraid when the shells came around us at Antietam as I was when I went into that room that day; but I finally mustered the courage—I don't know how I ever did—and at arm's length tapped on the door. The man inside did not help me at all, but yelled out, "Come in and sit down!"

Well, I went in and sat down on the edge of a chair, and wished I were in Europe, and the man at the table did not look up. He was one of the world's greatest men, and was made great by one single rule. Oh, that all the young people of Philadelphia were before me now and I could say just this one thing, and that they would remember it. I would give a lifetime for the effect it would have on our city and on civilization. Abraham Lincoln's principle for greatness can be adopted by nearly all. This was his rule: Whatsoever he had to do at all, he put his whole mind into it and held it all there until that was all done. That makes men great almost anywhere. He stuck to those papers at that table and did not look up at me, and I sat there trembling. Finally, when he had put the string around his papers, he pushed them over to one side and looked over to me, and a smile came over his worn face. He said: "I am a very busy man and have only a few minutes to spare. Now tell me in the fewest words what it is you want." I began to tell him, and mentioned the case, and he said: "I have heard all about it and you do not need to say any more. Mr. Stanton was talking to me only a few days ago about that. You can go to the hotel and rest assured that the President never did sign an order to shoot a boy under twenty years of age, and never will. You can say that to his mother anyhow."

Then he said to me, "How is it going in the field?" I said, "We sometimes get discouraged." And he said: "It is all right. We are going to win out now. We are getting very near the light. No man ought to wish to be President of the United States, and I will be glad when I get through; then Tad and I are going out to Springfield, Illinois. I have bought a farm out there and I don't care if I again earn only twenty-five cents a day. Tad has a mule team, and we are going to plant onions."

Then he asked me, "Were you brought up on a farm?" I said, "Yes; in the Berkshire Hills of Massachusetts." He then threw his leg over the corner of the big chair and said, "I have heard many a time, ever since I was young, that up there in those hills you have to sharpen the noses of the sheep in order to get down to the grass between the rocks." He was so familiar, so every-day, so farmer-like, that I felt right at home with him at once.

He then took hold of another roll of paper, and looked up at me and said, "Good morning." I took the hint then and got up and went out. After I had gotten out I could not realize I had seen the President of the United States at all. But a few days later, when still in the city, I saw the crowd pass through the East Room by the coffin of Abraham Lincoln, and when I looked at the upturned face of the murdered President I felt then that the man I had seen such a short time before, who, so simple a man, so plain a man, was one of the greatest men that God ever raised up to lead a nation on to ultimate liberty. Yet he was only "Old Abe" to his neighbors. When they had the second funeral, I was invited among others, and went out to see that same coffin put back in the tomb at Springfield.

Around the tomb stood Lincoln's old neighbors, to whom he was just "Old Abe." Of course that is all they would say.

Did you ever see a man who struts around altogether too large to notice an ordinary working mechanic? Do you think he is great? He is nothing but a puffed-up balloon, held down by his big feet. There is no greatness there.

Who are the great men and women? My attention was called the other day to the history of a very little thing that made the fortune of a very poor man. It was an awful thing, and yet because of that experience he—not a great inventor or genius—invented the pin that now is called the safety-pin, and out of that safety-pin made the fortune of one of the great aristocratic families of this nation.

A poor man in Massachusetts who had worked in the nail-works was injured at thirty-eight, and he could earn but little money. He was employed in the office to rub out the marks on the bills made by pencil memorandums, and he used a rubber until his hand grew tired. He then tied a piece of rubber on the end of a stick and worked it like a plane. His little girl came and said, "Why, you have a patent, haven't you?" The father said afterward, "My daughter told me when I took that stick and put the rubber on the end that there was a patent, and that was the first thought of that." He went to Boston and applied for his patent, and every one of you that has a rubber-tipped pencil in your pocket is now paying tribute to the millionaire. No capital, not a penny did he invest in it. All was income, all the way up into the millions.

But let me hasten to one other greater thought. "Show me the great men and women who live in Philadelphia." A gentleman over there will get up and say: "We don't have any great men in Philadelphia. They don't live here. They live away off in Rome or St.

Petersburg or London or Manayunk, or anywhere else but here in our town." I have come now to the apex of my thought. I have come now to the heart of the whole matter and to the center of my struggle: Why isn't Philadelphia a greater city in its greater wealth? Why does New York excel Philadelphia? People say, "Because of her harbor." Why do many other cities of the United States get ahead of Philadelphia now? There is only one answer, and that is because our own people talk down their own city. If there ever was a community on earth that has to be forced ahead, it is the city of Philadelphia. If we are to have a boulevard, talk it down; if we are going to have better schools, talk them down; if you wish to have wise legislation, talk it down; talk all the proposed improvements down. That is the only great wrong that I can lay at the feet of the magnificent Philadelphia that has been so universally kind to me. I say it is time we turn around in our city and begin to talk up the things that are in our city, and begin to set them before the world as the people of Chicago, New York, St. Louis, and San Francisco do. Oh, if we only could get that spirit out among our people, that we can do things in Philadelphia and do them well!

Arise, ye millions of Philadelphians, trust in God and man, and believe in the great opportunities that are right here—not over in New York or Boston, but here—for business, for everything that is worth living for on earth. There was never an opportunity greater. Let us talk up our own city.

But there are two other young men here to-night, and that is all I will venture to say, because it is too late. One over there gets up and says, "There is going to be a great man in Philadelphia, but never was one." "Oh, is that so? When are you going to be great?" "When I am elected to some political office." Young man, won't you learn a lesson in the primer of politics that it is a *prima facie* evidence of littleness to hold office under our form of government? Great men get into office sometimes, but what this country needs is men that will do what we tell them to do. This nation—where the people rule—is governed by the people, for the people, and so long as it is, then the office-holder is but the servant of the people, and the Bible says the servant cannot be greater than the master. The Bible says, "He that is sent cannot be greater than Him who sent Him." The people rule, or should rule, and if they do, we do not need the greater men in office. If the great men in America took our offices, we would change to an empire in the next ten years.

I know of a great many young women, now that woman's suffrage is coming, who say, "I am going to be President of the United States some day." I believe in woman's suffrage, and there is no doubt but what it is coming, and I am getting out of the way, anyhow. I may want an office by and by myself; but if the ambition for an office influences the women in their desire to vote, I want to say right here what I say to the young men, that if you only get the privilege of casting one vote, you don't get anything that is worth while. Unless you can control more than one vote, you will be unknown, and your influence so dissipated as practically not to be felt. This country is not run by votes. Do you think it is? It is governed by influence. It is governed by the ambitions and the enterprises which control votes. The young woman that thinks she is going to vote for the sake of holding an office is making an awful blunder.

That other young man gets up and says, "There are going to be great men in this country and in Philadelphia." "Is that so? When?" "When there comes a great war, when we get into difficulty through watchful waiting in Mexico; when we get into war with England over some frivolous deed, or with Japan or China or New Jersey or some distant country. Then I will march up to the cannon's mouth; I will sweep up among the glistening bayonets; I will leap into the arena and tear down the flag and bear it away in triumph. I will come home with stars on my shoulder, and hold every office in the gift of the nation, and I will be great." No, you won't. You think you are going to be made great by an office, but remember that if you are not great before you get the office, you won't be great when you secure it. It will only be a burlesque in that shape.

We had a Peace Jubilee here after the Spanish War. Out West they don't believe this, because they said, "Philadelphia would not have heard of any Spanish War until fifty years hence." Some of you saw the procession go up Broad Street. I was away, but the family wrote to me that the tally-ho coach with Lieutenant Hobson upon it stopped right at the front door and the people shouted, "Hurrah for Hobson!" and if I had been there I would have yelled too, because he deserves much more of his country than he has ever received. But suppose I go into school and say, "Who sunk the *Merrimac* at Santiago?" and if the boys answer me, "Hobson," they will tell me seven-eighths of a lie. There were seven other heroes on that steamer, and they, by virtue of their position, were continually exposed to the Spanish fire, while Hobson, as an officer, might reasonably be behind the smoke-stack. You have gathered in this house your most intelligent people, and yet, perhaps, not one here can name the other seven men.

We ought not to so teach history. We ought to teach that, however humble a man's station may be, if he does his full duty in that place he is just as much entitled to the American people's honor as is the king upon his throne. But we do not so teach. We are now teaching everywhere that the generals do all the fighting.

I remember that, after the war, I went down to see General Robert E. Lee, that magnificent Christian gentleman of whom both North and South are now proud as one of our great Americans. The general told me about his servant, "Rastus," who was an enlisted colored soldier. He called him in one day to make fun of him, and said, "Rastus, I hear that all the rest of your company are killed, and why are you not killed?" Rastus winked at him and said, "'Cause when there is any fightin' goin' on I stay back with the generals."

I remember another illustration. I would leave it out but for the fact that when you go to the library to read this lecture, you will find this has been printed in it for twenty-five years. I shut my eyes—shut them close—and lo! I see the faces of my youth. Yes, they sometimes say to me, "Your hair is not white; you are working night and day without seeming ever to stop; you can't be old." But when I shut my eyes, like any other man of my years, oh, then come trooping back the faces of the loved and lost of long ago, and I know, whatever men may say, it is evening-time.

I shut my eyes now and look back to my native town in Massachusetts, and I see the cattle-show ground on the mountain-top; I can see the horse-sheds there. I can see the Congregational church; see the town hall and mountaineers' cottages; see a great assembly of people turning out, dressed resplendently, and I can see flags flying and handkerchiefs waving and hear bands playing. I can see that company of soldiers that had re-enlisted marching up on that cattle-show ground. I was but a boy, but I was captain of that company and puffed out with pride. A cambric needle would have burst me all to pieces. Then I thought it was the greatest event that ever came to man on earth. If you have ever thought you would like to be a king or queen, you go and be received by the mayor.

The bands played, and all the people turned out to receive us. I marched up that Common so proud at the head of my troops, and we turned down into the town hall. Then they seated my soldiers down the center aisle and I sat down on the front seat. A great assembly of people—a hundred or two—came in to fill the town hall, so that they stood up all around. Then the town officers came in and formed a half-circle. The mayor of the town sat in the middle of the platform. He was a man who had never held office before; but he was a good man, and his friends have told me that I might use this without giving them offense. He was a good man, but he thought an office made a man great. He came up and took his seat, adjusted his powerful spectacles, and looked around, when he suddenly spied me sitting there on the front seat. He came right forward on the platform and invited me up to sit with the town officers. No town officer ever took any notice of me before I went to war, except to advise the teacher to thrash me, and now I was invited up on the stand with the town officers. Oh my! the town mayor was then the emperor, the king of our day and our time. As I came up on the platform they gave me a chair about this far, I would say, from the front.

When I had got seated, the chairman of the Selectmen arose and came forward to the table, and we all supposed he would introduce the Congregational minister, who was the only orator in town, and that he would give the oration to the returning soldiers. But, friends, you should have seen the surprise which ran over the audience when they discovered that the old fellow was going to deliver that speech himself. He had never made a speech in his life, but he fell into the same error that hundreds of other men have fallen into. It seems so strange that a man won't learn he must speak his piece as a boy if he intends to be an orator when he is grown, but he seems to think all he has to do is to hold an office to be a great orator.

So he came up to the front, and brought with him a speech which he had learned by heart walking up and down the pasture, where he had frightened the cattle. He brought the manuscript with him and spread it out on the table so as to be sure he might see it. He adjusted his spectacles and leaned over it for a moment and marched back on that platform, and then came forward like this— tramp, tramp, tramp. He must have studied the subject a great deal, when you come to think of it, because he assumed an "elocutionary" attitude. He rested heavily upon his left heel, threw back his shoulders, slightly advanced the right foot, opened the organs of speech, and advanced his right foot at an angle of forty-five. As he stood in that elocutionary attitude, friends, this is just the way that speech went. Some people say to me, "Don't you exaggerate?" That would be impossible. But I am here for the lesson and not for the story, and this is the way it went:

"Fellow-citizens—" As soon as he heard his voice his fingers began to go like that, his knees began to shake, and then he trembled all over. He choked and swallowed and came around to the table to look at the manuscript. Then he gathered himself up with clenched fists and came back: "Fellow-citizens, we are—Fellow-citizens, we are—we are—we are—we are—we are—we are very happy—we are very happy—we are very happy. We are very happy to welcome back to their native town these soldiers who have fought and bled—and come back again to their native town. We are especially—we are especially—we are especially. We are especially pleased to see with us to-day this young hero" (that meant me)—"this young hero who in imagination" (friends, remember he said that; if he had not said "in imagination" I would not be egotistic enough to refer to it at all)—"this young hero who in imagination we have seen leading—we have seen leading—leading. We have seen leading his troops on to the deadly breach. We have seen his shining—we have seen his shining—his shining—his shining sword—flashing. Flashing in the sunlight, as he shouted to his troops, 'Come on'!"

Oh dear, dear, dear! how little that good man knew about war. If he had known anything about war at all he ought to have known what any of my G. A. R. comrades here to-night will tell you is true, that it is next to a crime for an officer of infantry ever in time of danger to go ahead of his men. "I, with my shining sword flashing in the sunlight, shouting to my troops, 'Come on'!" I never did it. Do you suppose I would get in front of my men to be shot in front by the enemy and in the back by my own men? That is no place for an officer. The place for the officer in actual battle is behind the line. How often, as a staff officer, I rode down the line, when our men were suddenly called to the line of battle, and the Rebel yells were coming out of the woods, and shouted: "Officers to the rear! Officers to the rear!" Then every officer gets behind the line of private soldiers, and the higher the officer's rank the farther behind he goes. Not because he is any the less brave, but because the laws of war require that. And yet he shouted, "I, with my shining sword—" In that house there sat the company of my soldiers who had carried that boy across the Carolina rivers that he might not wet his feet. Some of them had gone far out to get a pig or a chicken. Some of them had gone to death under the shell-swept pines in the mountains of Tennessee, yet in the good man's speech they were scarcely known. He did refer to them, but only incidentally. The hero of the hour was this boy. Did the nation owe him anything? No, nothing then and nothing now. Why was he the hero? Simply because that man fell into that same human error—that this boy was great because he was an officer and these were only private soldiers.

Oh, I learned the lesson then that I will never forget so long as the tongue of the bell of time continues to swing for me. Greatness consists not in the holding of some future office, but really consists in doing great deeds with little means and the accomplishment of vast purposes from the private ranks of life. To be great at all one must be great here, now, in Philadelphia. He who can give to this city better streets and better sidewalks, better schools and more colleges, more happiness and more civilization, more of God, he will be great anywhere. Let every man or woman here, if you never hear me again, remember this, that if you wish to be great at all, you must begin where you are and what you are, in Philadelphia, now. He that can give to his city any blessing, he who can be a good citizen while he lives here, he that can make better homes, he that can be a blessing whether he works in the shop or sits behind the counter or keeps house, whatever be his life, he who would be great anywhere must first be great in his own Philadelphia.*

---

* Transcriber's Note: The following paragraph appears at the bottom of page 3 in the original: This is the most recent and complete form of the lecture. It happened to be delivered in Philadelphia, Dr. Conwell's home city. When he says "right here in Philadelphia," he means the home city, town, or village of every reader of this book, just as he would use the name of it if delivering the lecture there, instead of doing it through the pages which follow.

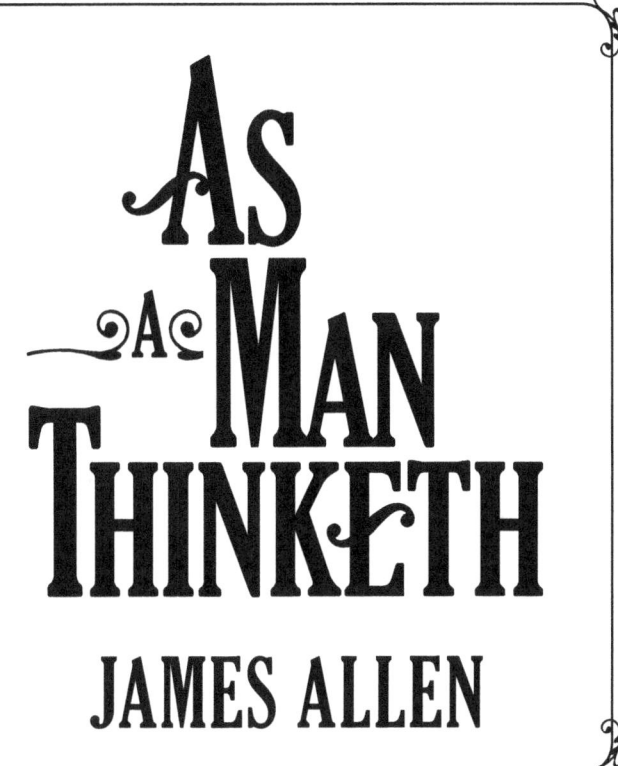

Contents

Foreword 75

Thought and Character 76

Effect of Thought on Circumstances 79

Effect of Thought on Health and the Body 89

Thought and Purpose 92

The Thought-Factor In Achievement 95

Visions and Ideals 99

Serenity 103

Foreword

This little volume (the result of meditation and experience) is not intended as an exhaustive treatise on the much-written-upon subject of the power of thought. It is suggestive rather than explanatory, its object being to stimulate men and women to the discovery and perception of the truth that—

"They themselves are makers of themselves."

by virtue of the thoughts, which they choose and encourage; that mind is the master-weaver, both of the inner garment of character and the outer garment of circumstance, and that, as they may have hitherto woven in ignorance and pain they may now weave in enlightenment and happiness.

JAMES ALLEN.
BROAD PARK AVENUE,
ILFRACOMBE,
ENGLAND

Thought and Character

The aphorism, "As a man thinketh in his heart so is he," not only embraces the whole of a man's being, but is so comprehensive as to reach out to every condition and circumstance of his life. A man is literally what he thinks, his character being the complete sum of all his thoughts.

As the plant springs from, and could not be without, the seed, so every act of a man springs from the hidden seeds of thought, and could not have appeared without them. This applies equally to those acts called "spontaneous" and "unpremeditated" as to those, which are deliberately executed.

Act is the blossom of thought, and joy and suffering are its fruits; thus does a man garner in the sweet and bitter fruitage of his own husbandry.

"Thought in the mind hath made us, What we are
By thought was wrought and built. If a man's mind
Hath evil thoughts, pain comes on him as comes
The wheel the ox behind . . .
. . . If one endure

In purity of thought, joy follows him

As his own shadow—sure."

Man is a growth by law, and not a creation by artifice, and cause and effect is as absolute and undeviating in the hidden realm of thought as in the world of visible and material things. A noble and Godlike character is not a thing of favour or chance, but is the natural result of continued effort in right thinking, the effect of long-cherished association with Godlike thoughts. An ignoble and bestial character, by the same process, is the result of the continued harbouring of grovelling thoughts.

Man is made or unmade by himself; in the armoury of thought he forges the weapons by which he destroys himself; he also fashions the tools with which he builds for himself heavenly mansions of joy and strength and peace. By the right choice and true application of thought, man ascends to the Divine Perfection; by the abuse and wrong application of thought, he descends below the level of the beast. Between these two extremes are all the grades of character, and man is their maker and master.

Of all the beautiful truths pertaining to the soul which have been restored and brought to light in this age, none is more gladdening or fruitful of divine promise and confidence than this—that man is the master of thought, the moulder of character, and the maker and shaper of condition, environment, and destiny.

As a being of Power, Intelligence, and Love, and the lord of his own thoughts, man holds the key to every situation, and contains within himself that transforming and regenerative agency by which he may make himself what he wills.

Man is always the master, even in his weaker and most abandoned state; but in his weakness and degradation he is the foolish master who misgoverns his "household." When he begins to reflect upon his condition, and to search diligently for the Law upon which his being is established, he then becomes the wise master, directing his energies with intelligence, and fashioning his thoughts to fruitful issues. Such is the conscious master, and man can only thus become by discovering within himself the laws of thought; which discovery is totally a matter of application, self analysis, and experience.

Only by much searching and mining, are gold and diamonds obtained, and man can find every truth connected with his being, if he will dig deep into the mine of his soul; and that he is the maker of his character, the moulder of his life, and the builder of his destiny, he may unerringly prove, if he will watch, control, and alter his thoughts, tracing their effects upon himself, upon others, and upon his life and circumstances, linking cause and effect by patient practice and investigation, and utilizing his every experience, even to the most trivial, everyday occurrence, as a means of obtaining that knowledge of himself which is Understanding, Wisdom, Power. In this direction, as in no other, is the law absolute that "He that seeketh findeth; and to him that knocketh it shall be opened;" for only by patience, practice, and ceaseless importunity can a man enter the Door of the Temple of Knowledge.

Effect of Thought on Circumstances

Man's mind may be likened to a garden, which may be intelligently cultivated or allowed to run wild; but whether cultivated or neglected, it must, and will, bring forth. If no useful seeds are put into it, then an abundance of useless weed-seeds will fall therein, and will continue to produce their kind.

Just as a gardener cultivates his plot, keeping it free from weeds, and growing the flowers and fruits which he requires, so may a man tend the garden of his mind, weeding out all the wrong, useless, and impure thoughts, and cultivating toward perfection the flowers and fruits of right, useful, and pure thoughts. By pursuing this process, a man sooner or later discovers that he is the master-gardener of his soul, the director of his life. He also reveals, within himself, the laws of thought, and understands, with ever-increasing accuracy, how the thought-forces and mind elements operate in the shaping of his character, circumstances, and destiny.

Thought and character are one, and as character can only manifest and discover itself through environment and circumstance, the outer conditions of a person's life will always be found to be harmoniously related to his inner state. This does not mean that a man's circumstances at any given time are an indication of his entire character, but that those circumstances are so intimately connected with some vital thought-element within himself that, for the time being, they are indispensable to his development.

Every man is where he is by the law of his being; the thoughts which he has built into his character have brought him there, and in the arrangement of his life there is no element of chance, but all is the result of a law which cannot err. This is just as true of those who feel "out of harmony" with their surroundings as of those who are contented with them.

As a progressive and evolving being, man is where he is that he may learn that he may grow; and as he learns the spiritual lesson which any circumstance contains for him, it passes away and gives place to other circumstances.

Man is buffeted by circumstances so long as he believes himself to be the creature of outside conditions, but when he realizes that he is a creative power, and that he may command the hidden soil and seeds of his being out of which circumstances grow, he then becomes the rightful master of himself.

That circumstances grow out of thought every man knows who has for any length of time practised self-control and self-purification, for he will have noticed that the alteration in his circumstances has been in exact ratio with his altered mental condition. So true is this that when a man earnestly applies himself to remedy the defects in his character, and makes swift and marked progress, he passes rapidly through a succession of vicissitudes.

The soul attracts that which it secretly harbours; that which it loves, and also that which it fears; it reaches the height of its cherished aspirations; it falls to the level of its unchastened desires,—and circumstances are the means by which the soul receives its own.

Every thought-seed sown or allowed to fall into the mind, and to take root there, produces its own, blossoming sooner or later into act, and bearing its own fruitage of opportunity and circumstance. Good thoughts bear good fruit, bad thoughts bad fruit.

The outer world of circumstance shapes itself to the inner world of thought, and both pleasant and unpleasant external conditions are factors, which make for the ultimate good of the individual. As the reaper of his own harvest, man learns both by suffering and bliss.

Following the inmost desires, aspirations, thoughts, by which he allows himself to be dominated, (pursuing the will-o'-the-wisps of impure imaginings or steadfastly walking the highway of strong and high endeavour), a man at last arrives at their fruition and fulfilment in the outer conditions of his life. The laws of growth and adjustment everywhere obtains.

A man does not come to the almshouse or the jail by the tyranny of fate or circumstance, but by the pathway of grovelling thoughts and base desires. Nor does a pure-minded man fall suddenly into crime by stress of any mere external force; the criminal thought had long been secretly fostered in the heart, and the hour of opportunity revealed its gathered power. Circumstance does not make the man; it reveals him to himself No such conditions can exist as descending into vice and its attendant sufferings apart from vicious inclinations, or ascending into virtue and its pure happiness without the continued cultivation of virtuous aspirations; and man, therefore, as the lord and master of thought, is the maker of himself the shaper and author of environment. Even at birth the soul comes to its own and through every step of its earthly pilgrimage it attracts those combinations of conditions which reveal itself, which are the reflections of its own purity and, impurity, its strength and weakness.

Men do not attract that which they want, but that which they are. Their whims, fancies, and ambitions are thwarted at every step, but their inmost thoughts and desires are fed with their own food, be it foul or clean. The "divinity that shapes our ends" is in ourselves; it is our very self. Only himself manacles man: thought and action are the gaolers of Fate—they imprison, being base; they are also the angels of Freedom—they liberate, being noble. Not what he wishes and prays for does a man get, but what he justly earns. His wishes and prayers are only gratified and answered when they harmonize with his thoughts and actions.

In the light of this truth, what, then, is the meaning of "fighting against circumstances?" It means that a man is continually revolting against an effect without, while all the time he is nourishing and preserving its cause in his heart. That cause may take the form of a conscious vice or an unconscious weakness; but whatever it is, it stubbornly retards the efforts of its possessor, and thus calls aloud for remedy.

Men are anxious to improve their circumstances, but are unwilling to improve themselves; they therefore remain bound. The man who does not shrink from self-crucifixion can never fail to accomplish the object upon which his heart is set. This is as true of earthly as of heavenly things. Even the man whose sole object is to acquire wealth must be prepared to make great personal sacrifices before he can accomplish his object; and how much more so he who would realize a strong and well-poised life?

Here is a man who is wretchedly poor. He is extremely anxious that his surroundings and home comforts should be improved, yet all the time he shirks his work, and considers he is justified in trying to deceive his employer on the ground of the insufficiency of his wages. Such a man does not understand the simplest rudiments of those principles which are the basis of true prosperity, and is not only totally unfitted to rise out of his wretchedness, but is actually attracting to himself a still deeper wretchedness by dwelling in, and acting out, indolent, deceptive, and unmanly thoughts.

Here is a rich man who is the victim of a painful and persistent disease as the result of gluttony. He is willing to give large sums of money to get rid of it, but he will not sacrifice his gluttonous desires. He wants to gratify his taste for rich and unnatural viands and have his health as well. Such a man is totally unfit to have health, because he has not yet learned the first principles of a healthy life.

Here is an employer of labour who adopts crooked measures to avoid paying the regulation wage, and, in the hope of making larger profits, reduces the wages of his workpeople. Such a man is altogether unfitted for prosperity, and when he finds himself bankrupt, both as regards reputation and riches, he blames circumstances, not knowing that he is the sole author of his condition.

I have introduced these three cases merely as illustrative of the truth that man is the causer (though nearly always is unconsciously) of his circumstances, and that, whilst aiming at a good end, he is continually frustrating its accomplishment by encouraging thoughts and desires which cannot possibly harmonize with that end. Such cases could be multiplied and varied almost indefinitely, but this is not necessary, as the reader can, if he so resolves, trace the action of the laws of thought in his own mind and life, and until this is done, mere external facts cannot serve as a ground of reasoning.

Circumstances, however, are so complicated, thought is so deeply rooted, and the conditions of happiness vary so, vastly with individuals, that a man's entire soul-condition (although it may be known to himself) cannot be judged by another from the external aspect of his life alone. A man may be honest in certain directions, yet suffer privations; a man may be dishonest in certain directions, yet acquire wealth; but the conclusion usually formed that the one man fails because of his particular honesty, and that the other prospers because of his particular dishonesty, is the result of a superficial judgment, which assumes that the dishonest man is almost totally corrupt, and the honest man almost entirely virtuous. In the light of a deeper knowledge and wider experience such judgment is found to be erroneous. The dishonest man may have some admirable virtues, which the other does, not possess; and the honest man obnoxious vices which are absent in the other. The honest man reaps the good results of his honest thoughts and acts; he also brings upon himself the sufferings, which his vices produce. The dishonest man likewise garners his own suffering and happiness.

It is pleasing to human vanity to believe that one suffers because of one's virtue; but not until a man has extirpated every sickly, bitter, and impure thought from his mind, and washed every sinful stain from his soul, can he be in a position to know and declare that his sufferings are the result of his good, and not of his bad qualities; and on the way to, yet long before he has reached, that supreme perfection, he will have found, working in his mind and life, the Great Law which is absolutely just, and which cannot, therefore, give good for evil, evil for good. Possessed of such knowledge, he will then know, looking back upon his past ignorance and blindness, that his life is, and always was, justly ordered, and that all his past experiences, good and bad, were the equitable outworking of his evolving, yet unevolved self.

Good thoughts and actions can never produce bad results; bad thoughts and actions can never produce good results. This is but saying that nothing can come from corn but corn, nothing from nettles but nettles. Men understand this law in the natural world, and work with it; but few understand it in the mental and moral world (though its operation there is just as simple and undeviating), and they, therefore, do not co-operate with it.

Suffering is always the effect of wrong thought in some direction. It is an indication that the individual is out of harmony with himself, with the Law of his being. The sole and supreme use of suffering is to purify, to burn out all that is useless and impure. Suffering ceases for him who is pure. There could be no object in burning gold after the dross had been removed, and a perfectly pure and enlightened being could not suffer.

The circumstances, which a man encounters with suffering, are the result of his own mental in harmony. The circumstances, which a man encounters with blessedness, are the result of his own mental harmony. Blessedness, not material possessions, is the measure of right thought; wretchedness, not lack of material possessions, is the measure of wrong thought. A man may be cursed and rich; he may be blessed and poor. Blessedness and riches are only joined together when the riches are rightly and wisely used; and the poor man only descends into wretchedness when he regards his lot as a burden unjustly imposed.

Indigence and indulgence are the two extremes of wretchedness. They are both equally unnatural and the result of mental disorder. A man is not rightly conditioned until he is a happy, healthy, and prosperous being; and happiness, health, and prosperity are the result of a harmonious adjustment of the inner with the outer, of the man with his surroundings.

A man only begins to be a man when he ceases to whine and revile, and commences to search for the hidden justice which regulates his life. And as he adapts his mind to that regulating factor, he ceases to accuse others as the cause of his condition, and builds himself up in strong and noble thoughts; ceases to kick against circumstances, but begins to use them as aids to his more rapid progress, and as a means of discovering the hidden powers and possibilities within himself.

Law, not confusion, is the dominating principle in the universe; justice, not injustice, is the soul and substance of life; and righteousness, not corruption, is the moulding and moving force in the spiritual government of the world. This being so, man has but to right himself to find that the universe is right; and during the process of putting himself right he will find that as he alters his thoughts towards things and other people, things and other people will alter towards him.

The proof of this truth is in every person, and it therefore admits of easy investigation by systematic introspection and self-analysis. Let a man radically alter his thoughts, and he will be astonished at the rapid transformation it will effect in the material conditions of his life. Men imagine that thought can be kept secret, but it cannot; it rapidly crystallizes into habit, and habit solidifies into circumstance. Bestial thoughts crystallize into habits of drunkenness and sensuality, which solidify into circumstances of destitution and disease: impure thoughts of every kind crystallize into enervating and confusing habits, which solidify into distracting and adverse circumstances: thoughts of fear, doubt, and indecision crystallize into weak, unmanly, and irresolute habits, which solidify into circumstances of failure, indigence, and slavish dependence: lazy thoughts crystallize into habits of uncleanliness and dishonesty, which solidify into circumstances of foulness and beggary: hateful and condemnatory thoughts crystallize into habits of accusation and violence, which solidify into circumstances of injury and persecution: selfish thoughts of all kinds crystallize into habits of self-seeking, which solidify into circumstances more or less distressing. On the other hand, beautiful thoughts of all kinds crystallize into habits of grace and kindliness, which solidify into genial and sunny circumstances: pure thoughts crystallize into habits of temperance and self-control, which solidify into circumstances of repose and peace: thoughts of courage, self-reliance, and decision crystallize into manly habits, which solidify into circumstances of success, plenty, and freedom: energetic thoughts crystallize into habits of cleanliness and industry, which solidify into circumstances of pleasantness: gentle and forgiving thoughts crystallize into habits of gentleness, which solidify into protective and preservative circumstances: loving and unselfish thoughts crystallize into habits of self-forgetfulness for others, which solidify into circumstances of sure and abiding prosperity and true riches.

A particular train of thought persisted in, be it good or bad, cannot fail to produce its results on the character and circumstances. A man cannot directly choose his circumstances, but he can choose his thoughts, and so indirectly, yet surely, shape his circumstances.

Nature helps every man to the gratification of the thoughts, which he most encourages, and opportunities are presented which will most speedily bring to the surface both the good and evil thoughts.

Let a man cease from his sinful thoughts, and all the world will soften towards him, and be ready to help him; let him put away his weakly and sickly thoughts, and lo, opportunities will spring up on every hand to aid his strong resolves; let him encourage good thoughts, and no hard fate shall bind him down to wretchedness and shame. The world is your kaleidoscope, and the varying combinations of colours, which at every succeeding moment it presents to you are the exquisitely adjusted pictures of your ever-moving thoughts.

> *"So You will be what you will to be;*
> *Let failure find its false content*
> *In that poor word, 'environment,'*
> *But spirit scorns it, and is free.*
> *"It masters time, it conquers space;*
> *It cowes that boastful trickster, Chance,*
> *And bids the tyrant Circumstance*
> *Uncrown, and fill a servant's place.*
> *"The human Will, that force unseen,*
> *The offspring of a deathless Soul,*
> *Can hew a way to any goal,*
> *Though walls of granite intervene.*
> *"Be not impatient in delays*
> *But wait as one who understands;*
> *When spirit rises and commands*
> *The gods are ready to obey."*

Effect of Thought on Health and the Body

The body is the servant of the mind. It obeys the operations of the mind, whether they be deliberately chosen or automatically expressed. At the bidding of unlawful thoughts the body sinks rapidly into disease and decay; at the command of glad and beautiful thoughts it becomes clothed with youthfulness and beauty.

Disease and health, like circumstances, are rooted in thought. Sickly thoughts will express themselves through a sickly body. Thoughts of fear have been known to kill a man as speedily as a bullet, and they are continually killing thousands of people just as surely though less rapidly. The people who live in fear of disease are the people who get it. Anxiety quickly demoralizes the whole body, and lays it open to the entrance of disease; while impure thoughts, even if not physically indulged, will soon shatter the nervous system.

Strong, pure, and happy thoughts build up the body in vigour and grace. The body is a delicate and plastic instrument, which responds readily to the thoughts by which it is impressed, and habits of thought will produce their own effects, good or bad, upon it.

Men will continue to have impure and poisoned blood, so long as they propagate unclean thoughts. Out of a clean heart comes a clean life and a clean body. Out of a defiled mind proceeds a defiled life and a corrupt body. Thought is the fount of action, life, and manifestation; make the fountain pure, and all will be pure.

Change of diet will not help a man who will not change his thoughts. When a man makes his thoughts pure, he no longer desires impure food.

Clean thoughts make clean habits. The so-called saint who does not wash his body is not a saint. He who has strengthened and purified his thoughts does not need to consider the malevolent microbe.

If you would protect your body, guard your mind. If you would renew your body, beautify your mind. Thoughts of malice, envy, disappointment, despondency, rob the body of its health and grace. A sour face does not come by chance; it is made by sour thoughts. Wrinkles that mar are drawn by folly, passion, and pride.

I know a woman of ninety-six who has the bright, innocent face of a girl. I know a man well under middle age whose face is drawn into inharmonious contours. The one is the result of a sweet and sunny disposition; the other is the outcome of passion and discontent.

As you cannot have a sweet and wholesome abode unless you admit the air and sunshine freely into your rooms, so a strong body and a bright, happy, or serene countenance can only result from the free admittance into the mind of thoughts of joy and goodwill and serenity.

On the faces of the aged there are wrinkles made by sympathy, others by strong and pure thought, and others are carved by passion: who cannot distinguish them? With those who have lived righteously, age is calm, peaceful, and softly mellowed, like the setting sun. I have recently seen a philosopher on his deathbed. He was not old except in years. He died as sweetly and peacefully as he had lived.

There is no physician like cheerful thought for dissipating the ills of the body; there is no comforter to compare with goodwill for dispersing the shadows of grief and sorrow. To live continually in thoughts of ill will, cynicism, suspicion, and envy, is to be confined in a self made prison-hole. But to think well of all, to be cheerful with all, to patiently learn to find the good in all—such unselfish thoughts are the very portals of heaven; and to dwell day by day in thoughts of peace toward every creature will bring abounding peace to their possessor.

Thought and Purpose

Until thought is linked with purpose there is no intelligent accomplishment. With the majority the bark of thought is allowed to "drift" upon the ocean of life. Aimlessness is a vice, and such drifting must not continue for him who would steer clear of catastrophe and destruction.

They who have no central purpose in their life fall an easy prey to petty worries, fears, troubles, and self-pityings, all of which are indications of weakness, which lead, just as surely as deliberately planned sins (though by a different route), to failure, unhappiness, and loss, for weakness cannot persist in a power evolving universe.

A man should conceive of a legitimate purpose in his heart, and set out to accomplish it. He should make this purpose the centralizing point of his thoughts. It may take the form of a spiritual ideal, or it may be a worldly object, according to his nature at the time being; but whichever it is, he should steadily focus his thought-forces upon the object, which he has set before him. He should make this purpose his supreme duty, and should devote himself to its attainment, not allowing his thoughts to wander away into ephemeral fancies, longings, and imaginings. This is the royal road to self-control and true concentration of thought. Even if he fails again and again to accomplish his purpose (as he necessarily must until weakness is overcome), the strength of character gained will be the measure of his true success, and this will form a new starting-point for future power and triumph.

Those who are not prepared for the apprehension of a great purpose should fix the thoughts upon the faultless performance of their duty, no matter how insignificant their task may appear. Only in this way can the thoughts be gathered and focussed, and resolution and energy be developed, which being done, there is nothing which may not be accomplished.

The weakest soul, knowing its own weakness, and believing this truth that strength can only be developed by effort and practice, will, thus believing, at once begin to exert itself, and, adding effort to effort, patience to patience, and strength to strength, will never cease to develop, and will at last grow divinely strong.

As the physically weak man can make himself strong by careful and patient training, so the man of weak thoughts can make them strong by exercising himself in right thinking.

To put away aimlessness and weakness, and to begin to think with purpose, is to enter the ranks of those strong ones who only recognize failure as one of the pathways to attainment; who make all conditions serve them, and who think strongly, attempt fearlessly, and accomplish masterfully.

Having conceived of his purpose, a man should mentally mark out a straight pathway to its achievement, looking neither to the right nor the left. Doubts and fears should be rigorously excluded; they are disintegrating elements, which break up the straight line of effort, rendering it crooked, ineffectual, useless. Thoughts of doubt and fear never accomplished anything, and never can. They always lead to failure. Purpose, energy, power to do, and all strong thoughts cease when doubt and fear creep in.

The will to do springs from the knowledge that we can do. Doubt and fear are the great enemies of knowledge, and he who encourages them, who does not slay them, thwarts himself at every step.

He who has conquered doubt and fear has conquered failure. His every thought is allied with power, and all difficulties are bravely met and wisely overcome. His purposes are seasonably planted, and they bloom and bring forth fruit, which does not fall prematurely to the ground.

Thought allied fearlessly to purpose becomes creative force: he who knows this is ready to become something higher and stronger than a mere bundle of wavering thoughts and fluctuating sensations; he who does this has become the conscious and intelligent wielder of his mental powers.

The Thought-Factor in Achievement

All that a man achieves and all that he fails to achieve is the direct result of his own thoughts. In a justly ordered universe, where loss of equipoise would mean total destruction, individual responsibility must be absolute. A man's weakness and strength, purity and impurity, are his own, and not another man's; they are brought about by himself, and not by another; and they can only be altered by himself, never by another. His condition is also his own, and not another man's. His suffering and his happiness are evolved from within. As he thinks, so he is; as he continues to think, so he remains.

A strong man cannot help a weaker unless that weaker is willing to be helped, and even then the weak man must become strong of himself; he must, by his own efforts, develop the strength which he admires in another. None but himself can alter his condition.

It has been usual for men to think and to say, "Many men are slaves because one is an oppressor; let us hate the oppressor." Now, however, there is amongst an increasing few a tendency to reverse this judgment, and to say, "One man is an oppressor because many are slaves; let us despise the slaves."

The truth is that oppressor and slave are co-operators in ignorance, and, while seeming to afflict each other, are in reality afflicting themselves. A perfect Knowledge perceives the action of law in the weakness of the oppressed and the misapplied power of the oppressor; a perfect Love, seeing the suffering, which both states entail, condemns neither; a perfect Compassion embraces both oppressor and oppressed.

He who has conquered weakness, and has put away all selfish thoughts, belongs neither to oppressor nor oppressed. He is free.

A man can only rise, conquer, and achieve by lifting up his thoughts. He can only remain weak, and abject, and miserable by refusing to lift up his thoughts.

Before a man can achieve anything, even in worldly things, he must lift his thoughts above slavish animal indulgence. He may not, in order to succeed, give up all animality and selfishness, by any means; but a portion of it must, at least, be sacrificed. A man whose first thought is bestial indulgence could neither think clearly nor plan methodically; he could not find and develop his latent resources, and would fail in any undertaking. Not having commenced to manfully control his thoughts, he is not in a position to control affairs and to adopt serious responsibilities. He is not fit to act independently and stand alone. But he is limited only by the thoughts, which he chooses.

There can be no progress, no achievement without sacrifice, and a man's worldly success will be in the measure that he sacrifices his confused animal thoughts, and fixes his mind on the development of his plans, and the strengthening of his resolution and self-reliance. And the higher he lifts his thoughts, the more manly, upright, and righteous he becomes, the greater will be his success, the more blessed and enduring will be his achievements.

The universe does not favour the greedy, the dishonest, the vicious, although on the mere surface it may sometimes appear to do so; it helps the honest, the magnanimous, the virtuous. All the great Teachers of the ages have declared this in varying forms, and to prove and know it a man has but to persist in making himself more and more virtuous by lifting up his thoughts.

Intellectual achievements are the result of thought consecrated to the search for knowledge, or for the beautiful and true in life and nature. Such achievements may be sometimes connected with vanity and ambition, but they are not the outcome of those characteristics; they are the natural outgrowth of long and arduous effort, and of pure and unselfish thoughts.

Spiritual achievements are the consummation of holy aspirations. He who lives constantly in the conception of noble and lofty thoughts, who dwells upon all that is pure and unselfish, will, as surely as the sun reaches its zenith and the moon its full, become wise and noble in character, and rise into a position of influence and blessedness.

Achievement, of whatever kind, is the crown of effort, the diadem of thought. By the aid of self-control, resolution, purity, righteousness, and well-directed thought a man ascends; by the aid of animality, indolence, impurity, corruption, and confusion of thought a man descends.

A man may rise to high success in the world, and even to lofty altitudes in the spiritual realm, and again descend into weakness and wretchedness by allowing arrogant, selfish, and corrupt thoughts to take possession of him.

Victories attained by right thought can only be maintained by watchfulness. Many give way when success is assured, and rapidly fall back into failure.

All achievements, whether in the business, intellectual, or spiritual world, are the result of definitely directed thought, are governed by the same law and are of the same method; the only difference lies in the object of attainment.

He who would accomplish little must sacrifice little; he who would achieve much must sacrifice much; he who would attain highly must sacrifice greatly.

Visions and Ideals

The dreamers are the saviours of the world. As the visible world is sustained by the invisible, so men, through all their trials and sins and sordid vocations, are nourished by the beautiful visions of their solitary dreamers. Humanity cannot forget its dreamers; it cannot let their ideals fade and die; it lives in them; it knows them as the realities which it shall one day see and know.

Composer, sculptor, painter, poet, prophet, sage, these are the makers of the after-world, the architects of heaven. The world is beautiful because they have lived; without them, labouring humanity would perish.

He who cherishes a beautiful vision, a lofty ideal in his heart, will one day realize it. Columbus cherished a vision of another world, and he discovered it; Copernicus fostered the vision of a multiplicity of worlds and a wider universe, and he revealed it; Buddha beheld the vision of a spiritual world of stainless beauty and perfect peace, and he entered into it.

Cherish your visions; cherish your ideals; cherish the music that stirs in your heart, the beauty that forms in your mind, the loveliness that drapes your purest thoughts, for out of them will grow all delightful conditions, all, heavenly environment; of these, if you but remain true to them, your world will at last be built.

To desire is to obtain; to aspire is to, achieve. Shall man's basest desires receive the fullest measure of gratification, and his purest aspirations starve for lack of sustenance? Such is not the Law: such a condition of things can never obtain: "ask and receive."

Dream lofty dreams, and as you dream, so shall you become. Your Vision is the promise of what you shall one day be; your Ideal is the prophecy of what you shall at last unveil.

The greatest achievement was at first and for a time a dream. The oak sleeps in the acorn; the bird waits in the egg; and in the highest vision of the soul a waking angel stirs. Dreams are the seedlings of realities.

Your circumstances may be uncongenial, but they shall not long remain so if you but perceive an Ideal and strive to reach it. You cannot travel within and stand still without. Here is a youth hard pressed by poverty and labour; confined long hours in an unhealthy workshop; unschooled, and lacking all the arts of refinement. But he dreams of better things; he thinks of intelligence, of refinement, of grace and beauty. He conceives of, mentally builds up, an ideal condition of life; the vision of a wider liberty and a larger scope takes possession of him; unrest urges him to action, and he utilizes all his spare time and means, small though they are, to the development of his latent powers and resources. Very soon so altered has his mind become that the workshop can no longer hold him. It has become so out of harmony with his mentality that it falls out of his life as a garment is cast aside, and, with the growth of opportunities, which fit the scope of his expanding powers, he passes out of it forever. Years later we see this youth as a full-grown man. We find him a master of certain forces of the mind, which he wields with worldwide influence and almost unequalled power. In his hands he holds the cords of gigantic responsibilities; he speaks, and lo, lives are changed; men and women hang upon his words and remould their characters, and, sunlike, he becomes the fixed and luminous centre round which innumerable destinies revolve. He has realized the Vision of his youth. He has become one with his Ideal.

And you, too, youthful reader, will realize the Vision (not the idle wish) of your heart, be it base or beautiful, or a mixture of both, for you will always gravitate toward that which you, secretly, most love. Into your hands will be placed the exact results of your own thoughts; you will receive that which you earn; no more, no less. Whatever your present environment may be, you will fall, remain, or rise with your thoughts, your Vision, your Ideal. You will become as small as your controlling desire; as great as your dominant aspiration: in the beautiful words of Stanton Kirkham Davis, "You may be keeping accounts, and presently you shall walk out of the door that for so long has seemed to you the barrier of your ideals, and shall find yourself before an audience—the pen still behind your ear, the ink stains on your fingers and then and there shall pour out the torrent of your inspiration. You may be driving sheep, and you shall wander to the city-bucolic and open-mouthed; shall wander under the intrepid guidance of the spirit into the studio of the master, and after a time he shall say, 'I have nothing more to teach you.' And now you have become the master, who did so recently dream of great things while driving sheep. You shall lay down the saw and the plane to take upon yourself the regeneration of the world."

The thoughtless, the ignorant, and the indolent, seeing only the apparent effects of things and not the things themselves, talk of luck, of fortune, and chance. Seeing a man grow rich, they say, "How lucky he is!" Observing another become intellectual, they exclaim, "How highly favoured he is!" And noting the saintly character and wide influence of another, they remark, "How chance aids him at every turn!" They do not see the trials and failures and struggles which these men have voluntarily encountered in order to gain their experience; have no knowledge of the sacrifices they have made, of the undaunted efforts they have put forth, of the faith they have exercised, that they might overcome the apparently insurmountable, and realize the Vision of their heart. They do not know the darkness and the heartaches; they only see the light and joy, and call it "luck". They do not see the long and arduous journey, but only behold the pleasant goal, and call it "good fortune," do not understand the process, but only perceive the result, and call it chance.

In all human affairs there are efforts, and there are results, and the strength of the effort is the measure of the result. Chance is not. Gifts, powers, material, intellectual, and spiritual possessions are the fruits of effort; they are thoughts completed, objects accomplished, visions realized.

The Vision that you glorify in your mind, the Ideal that you enthrone in your heart—this you will build your life by, this you will become.

Serenity

Calmness of mind is one of the beautiful jewels of wisdom. It is the result of long and patient effort in self-control. Its presence is an indication of ripened experience, and of a more than ordinary knowledge of the laws and operations of thought.

A man becomes calm in the measure that he understands himself as a thought evolved being, for such knowledge necessitates the understanding of others as the result of thought, and as he develops a right understanding, and sees more and more clearly the internal relations of things by the action of cause and effect he ceases to fuss and fume and worry and grieve, and remains poised, steadfast, serene.

The calm man, having learned how to govern himself, knows how to adapt himself to others; and they, in turn, reverence his spiritual strength, and feel that they can learn of him and rely upon him. The more tranquil a man becomes, the greater is his success, his influence, his power for good. Even the ordinary trader will find his business prosperity increase as he develops a greater self-control and equanimity, for people will always prefer to deal with a man whose demeanour is strongly equable.

The strong, calm man is always loved and revered. He is like a shade-giving tree in a thirsty land, or a sheltering rock in a storm. "Who does not love a tranquil heart, a sweet-tempered, balanced life? It does not matter whether it rains or shines, or what changes come to those possessing these blessings, for they are always sweet, serene, and calm. That exquisite poise of character, which we call serenity is the last lesson of culture, the fruitage of the soul. It is precious as wisdom, more to be desired than gold—yea, than even fine gold. How insignificant mere money seeking looks in comparison with a serene life—a life that dwells in the ocean of Truth, beneath the waves, beyond the reach of tempests, in the Eternal Calm!

"How many people we know who sour their lives, who ruin all that is sweet and beautiful by explosive tempers, who destroy their poise of character, and make bad blood! It is a question whether the great majority of people do not ruin their lives and mar their happiness by lack of self-control. How few people we meet in life who are well balanced, who have that exquisite poise which is characteristic of the finished character!

Yes, humanity surges with uncontrolled passion, is tumultuous with ungoverned grief, is blown about by anxiety and doubt only the wise man, only he whose thoughts are controlled and purified, makes the winds and the storms of the soul obey him.

Tempest-tossed souls, wherever ye may be, under whatsoever conditions ye may live, know this in the ocean of life the isles of Blessedness are smiling, and the sunny shore of your ideal awaits your coming. Keep your hand firmly upon the helm of thought. In the bark of your soul reclines the commanding Master; He does but sleep: wake Him. Self-control is strength; Right Thought is mastery; Calmness is power. Say unto your heart, "Peace, be still!"

Character-Building Thought Power

Ralph Waldo Trine

The Book

Unconsciously we are forming habits every moment of our lives. Some are habits of a desirable nature; some are those of a most undesirable nature. Some, though not so bad in themselves, are exceedingly bad in their cumulative effects, and cause us at times much loss, much pain and anguish, while their opposites would, on the contrary, bring as much peace and joy, as well as a continually increasing power. Have we it within our power to determine at all times what types of habits shall take form in our lives? In other words, is habit-forming, character-building, a matter of mere chance, or have we it within our own control? We have, entirely and absolutely. "I will be what I will to be," can be said and should be said by every human soul.

After this has been bravely and determinedly said, and not only said, but fully inwardly realized, something yet remains. Something remains to be said regarding the great law underlying habit-forming, character-building; for there is a simple, natural, and thoroughly scientific method that all should know. A method whereby old, undesirable, earth-binding habits can be broken, and new, desirable, heaven lifting habits can be acquired, a method whereby life in part or in its totality can be changed, provided one is sufficiently in earnest to know and, knowing it, to apply the law.

Thought is the force underlying all. And what do we mean by this? Simply this: Your every act—every conscious act—is preceded by a thought. Your dominating thoughts determine your dominating actions. In the realm of our own minds we have absolute control, or we should have, and if at any time we have not, then there is a method by which we can gain control, and in the realm of the mind become thorough masters. In order to get to the very foundation of the matter, let us look to this for a moment. For if thought is always parent to our acts, habits, character, life, then it is first necessary that we know fully how to control our thoughts.

Here let us refer to that law of the mind which is the same as is the law in Connection with the reflex nerve system of the body, the law which says that whenever one does a certain thing in a certain way it is easier to do the same thing in the same way the next time, and still easier the next, and the next, and the next, until in time it comes to pass that no effort is required, or no effort worth speaking of; but on the opposite would require the effort. The mind carries with it the power that perpetuates its own type of thought, the same as the body carries with it through the reflex nerve system the power which perpetuates and makes continually easier its own particular acts. Thus a simple effort to control one's thoughts, a simple setting about it, even if at first failure is the result, and even if for a time failure seems to be about the only result, will in time, sooner or later, bring him to the point of easy, full, and complete control. Each one, then, can grow the power of determining, controlling his thought, the power of determining what types of thought he shall and what types he shall not entertain. For let us never part in mind with this fact, that every earnest effort along any line makes the end aimed at just a little easier for each succeeding effort, even if, as has been said, apparent failure is the result of the earlier efforts. This is a case where even failure is success, for the failure is not in the effort, and every earnest effort adds an increment of power that will eventually accomplish the end aimed at. We can, then, gain the full and complete power of determining what character, what type of thoughts we entertain.

Shall we now give attention to some two or three concrete cases? Here is a man, the cashier of a large mercantile establishment, or cashier of a bank. In his morning paper he reads of a man who has become suddenly rich, has made a fortune of half a million or a million dollars in a few hours through speculation on the stock market. Perhaps he has seen an account of another man who has done practically the same thing lately. He is not quite wise enough, however, to comprehend the fact that when he reads of one or two cases of this kind he could find, were he to look into the matter carefully, one or two hundred cases of men who have lost all they had in the same way. He thinks, however, that he will be one of the fortunate ones. He does not fully realize that there are no short cuts to wealth honestly made. He takes a part of his savings, and as is true in practically all cases of this kind, he loses all that he has put in, Thinking now that he sees why he lost, and that had he more money he would be able to get back what he has lost, and perhaps make a handsome sum in addition, and make it quickly, the thought comes to him to use some of the funds he has charge of. In nine cases out of ten, if not ten cases in every ten, the results that inevitably follow this are known sufficiently well to make it unnecessary to follow him farther.

Where is the man's safety in the light of what we have been considering? Simply this: the moment the thought of using for his own purpose funds belonging to others enters his mind, if he is wise he will instantly put the thought from his mind. If he is a fool he will entertain it. In the degree in which he entertains it, it will grow upon him; it will become the absorbing thought in his mind; it will finally become master of his will power, and through rapidly succeeding steps, dishonor, shame, degradation, penitentiary, remorse will be his. It is easy for him to put the thought from his mind when it first enters; but as he entertains it, it grows into such proportions that it becomes more and more difficult for him to put it from his mind; and by and by it becomes practically impossible for him to do it. The light of the match, which but a little effort of the breath would have extinguished at first, has imparted a flame that is raging through the entire building, and now it is almost if not quite impossible to conquer it.

Shall we notice another concrete case? A trite case, perhaps, but one in which we can see how habit is formed, and also how the same habit can be unformed. Here is a young man, he may be the son of poor parents, or he may be the son of rich parents; one in the ordinary ranks of life, or one of high social standing, whatever that means. He is good hearted, one of good impulses generally speaking, a good fellow. He is out with some companions, companions of the same general type. They are out for a pleasant evening, out for a good time. They are apt at times to be thoughtless, even careless. The suggestion is made by one of the company, not that they get drunk, no, not at all; but merely that they go and have something to drink together. The young man whom we first mentioned, wanting to be genial, scarcely listens to the suggestion that comes into his inner consciousness that it will be better for him not to fall in with the others in this. He does not stop long enough to realize the fact that the greatest strength and nobility of character lies always in taking a firm stand on the aide of the right, and allow himself to be influenced by nothing that will weaken this stand. He goes, therefore, with his companions to the drinking place. With the same or with other companions this is repeated now and then; and each time it is repeated his power of saying "No" is gradually decreasing. In this way he has grown a little liking for intoxicants, and takes them perhaps now and then by himself. He does not dream, or in the slightest degree realize, what way he is tending, until there comes a day when he awakens to the consciousness of the fact that he hasn't the power nor even the impulse to resist the taste which has gradually grown into a minor form of craving for intoxicants. Thinking, however, that he will be able to stop when he is really in danger of getting into the drink habit, he goes thoughtlessly and carelessly on. We will pass over the various intervening steps and come to the time when we find him a confirmed drunkard. It is simply the same old story told a thousand or even a million times over.

He finally awakens to his true condition; and through the shame, the anguish, the degradation, and the want that comes upon him he longs for a return of the days when he was a free man. But hope has almost gone from his life. It would have been easier for him never to have begun, and easier for him to have stopped before he reached his present condition; but even in his present condition, be it the lowest and the most helpless and hopeless that can be imagined, he has the power to get out of it and be a free man once again. Let us see. The desire for drink comes upon him again. If he entertains the thought, the desire, he is lost again.

His only hope, his only means of escape is this: the moment, aye, the very instant the thought comes to him, if he will put it out of his mind he will thereby put out the little flame of the match. If he entertains the thought the little flame will communicate itself until almost before he is aware of it a consuming fire is raging, and then effort is almost useless. The thought must be banished from the mind the instant it enters; dalliance with it means failure and defeat, or a fight that will be indescribably fiercer than it would be if the thought is ejected at the beginning.

And here we must say a word regarding a certain great law that we may call the "law of indirectness." A thought can be put out of the mind easier and more successfully, not by dwelling upon it, not by, attempting to put it out directly, but by throwing the mind on to some other object by putting some other object of thought into the mind. This may be, for example, the ideal of full and perfect self-mastery, or it may be something of a nature entirely distinct from the thought which presents itself, something to which the mind goes easily and naturally. This will in time become the absorbing thought in the mind, and the danger is past. This same course of action repeated will gradually grow the power of putting more readily out of mind the thought of drink as it presents itself, and will gradually grow the power of putting into the mind those objects of thought one most desires. The result will be that as time passes the thought of drink will present itself less and less, and when it does present itself it can be put out of the mind more easily each succeeding time, until the time comes when it can be put out without difficulty, and eventually the time will come when the thought will enter the mind no more at all.

Still another case. You may be more or less of an irritable nature naturally, perhaps, provoked easily to anger. Someone says something or does something that you dislike, and your first impulse is to show resentment and possibly to give way to anger. In the degree that you allow this resentment to display itself, that you allow yourself to give way to anger, in that degree will it become easier to do the same thing when any cause, even a very slight cause, presents itself. It will, moreover, become continually harder for you to refrain from it, until resentment, anger, and possibly even hatred and revenge become characteristics of your nature, robbing it of its sunniness, its charm, and its brightness for all with whom you come in contact.

If, however, the instant the impulse to resentment and anger arises, you check it then and there, and throw the mind on to some other object of thought, the power will gradually grow itself of doing this same thing more readily, more easily, as succeeding like causes present themselves, until by and by the time will come when there will be scarcely anything that can irritate you, and nothing that can impel you to anger; until by and by a matchless brightness and charm of nature and disposition will become habitually yours, a brightness and charm you would scarcely think possible today. And so we might take up case after case, characteristic after characteristic, habit after habit. The habit of faultfinding and its opposite are grown in identically the same way; the characteristic of jealousy and its opposite; the characteristic of fear and its opposite. In this same way we grow either love or hatred; in this way we come to take a gloomy, pessimistic view of life, which objectifies itself in a nature, a disposition of this type, or we grow that sunny, hopeful, cheerful, buoyant nature that brings with it so much joy and beauty and power for ourselves, as well as so much hope and inspiration and joy for all the world.

There is nothing more true in connection with human life than that we grow into the likeness of those things we contemplate. Literally and scientifically and necessarily true is it that "as a man thinketh in his heart, so is he." The "is" part is his character. His character is the sum total of his habits. His habits have been formed by his conscious acts; but every conscious act is, as we have found, preceded by a thought. And so we have it—thought on the one hand, character, life, and destiny on the other. And simple it becomes when we bear in mind that it is simply the thought of the present moment, and the next moment when it is upon us, and then the next, and so on through all time.

One can in this way attain to whatever ideals he would attain to. Two steps are necessary: first, as the days pass, to form one's ideals; and second, to follow them continually, whatever may arise, wherever they may lead him. Always remember that the great and strong character is the one who is ever ready to sacrifice the present pleasure for the future good. He who will thus follow his highest ideals as they present themselves to him day after day, year after year, will find that as Dante, following his beloved from world to world, finally found her at the gates of Paradise, so he will find himself eventually at the same gates. Life is not, we may say, for mere passing pleasure, but for the highest unfoldment that one can attain to, the noblest character that one can grow, and for the greatest service that one can render to all mankind. In this, however, we will find the highest pleasure, for in this the only real pleasure lies. He who would find it by any short cuts, or by entering upon any other paths, will inevitably find that his last state is always worse than his first; and if he proceed upon paths other than these he will find that he will never find real and lasting pleasure at all.

The question is not, "What are the conditions in our lives?" but, "How do we meet the conditions that we find there?" And whatever the conditions are, it is unwise and profitless to look upon them, even if they are conditions that we would have otherwise, in the attitude of complaint, for complaint will bring depression, and depression will weaken and possibly even kill the spirit that would engender the power that would enable us to bring into our lives an entirely new set of conditions.

In order to be concrete, even at the risk of being personal, I will say that in my own experience there have come at various times into my life circumstances and conditions that I gladly would have run from at the time—conditions that caused at the time humiliation and shame and anguish of spirit. But invariably, as sufficient time has passed, I have been able to look back and see clearly the part that every experience of the type just mentioned had to play in my life. I have seen the lessons it was essential for me to learn; and the result is that now I would not drop a single one of these experiences from my life, humiliating and hard to bear as they were at the time; no, not for the world. And here is also a lesson I have learned: whatever conditions are in my life today that are not the easiest and most agreeable, and whatever conditions of this type all coming time may bring, I will take them just as they come, without complaint, without depression, and meet them in the wisest possible way; knowing that they are the best possible conditions that could be in my life at the time, or otherwise they would not be there; realizing the fact that, although I may not at the time see why they are in my life, although I may not see just what part they have to play, the time will come, and when it comes I will see it all, and thank God for every condition just as it came.

Each one is so apt to think that his own conditions, his own trials or troubles or sorrows, or his own struggles, as the case may be, are greater than those of the great mass of mankind, or possibly greater than those of any one else in the world. He forgets that each one has his own peculiar trials or troubles or sorrows to bear, or struggles in habits to overcome, and that his is but the common lot of all the human race. We are apt to make the mistake in this—in that we see and feel keenly our own trials, or adverse conditions, or characteristics to be overcome, while those of others we do not see so clearly, and hence we are apt to think that they are not at all equal to our own. Each has his own problems to work out. Each must work out his own problems. Each must grow the insight that will enable him to see what the causes are that have brought the unfavorable conditions into his life; each must grow the strength that will enable him to face these conditions, and to set into operation forces that will bring about a different set of conditions. We may be of aid to one another by way of suggestion, by way of bringing to one another a knowledge of certain higher laws and forces—laws and forces that will make it easier to do that which we would do. The doing, however, must be done by each one for himself. And so the way to get out of any conditioning we have got into, either knowingly or inadvertently, either intentionally or unintentionally, is to take time to look the conditions squarely in the face, and to find the law whereby they have come about. And when we have discovered the law, the thing to do is not to rebel against it, not to resist it, but to go with it by working in harmony with it. If we work in harmony with it, it will work for our highest good, and will take us wheresoever we desire. If we oppose it, if we resist it, if we fail to work in harmony with it, it will eventually break us to pieces. The law is immutable in its workings. Go with it, and it brings all things our way; resist it, and it brings suffering, pain, loss, and desolation.

But a few days ago I was talking with a lady, a most estimable lady living on a little New England farm of some five or six acres. Her husband died a few years ago, a good-hearted, industrious man, but one who spent practically all of his earnings in drink. When he died the little farm was unpaid for, and the wife found herself without any visible means of support, with a family of several to care for. Instead of being discouraged with what many would have called her hard lot, instead of rebelling against the circumstances in which she found herself, she faced the matter bravely, firmly believing that there were ways by which she could manage, though she could not see them clearly at the time. She took up her burden where she found it, and went bravely forward. For several years she has been taking care of summer boarders who come to that part of the country, getting up regularly, she told me, at from half-past three to four o'clock in the morning, and working until ten o'clock each night. In the winter time, when this means of revenue is cut off, she has gone out to do nursing in the country round about. In this way the little farm is now almost paid for; her children have been kept in school, and they are now able to aid her to a greater or less extent. Through it all she has entertained no fears nor forebodings; she has shown no rebellion of any kind. She has not kicked against the circumstances which brought about the conditions in which she found herself, but she has put herself into harmony with the law that would bring her into another set of conditions. And through it all, she told me, she has been continually grateful that she has been able to work, and that whatever her own circumstances have been, she has never yet failed to find some one whose circumstances were still a little worse than hers, and for whom it was possible for her to render some little service.

Most heartily she appreciates the fact, and most grateful is she for it, that the little home is now almost paid for, and soon no more of her earnings will have to go out in that channel. The dear little home, she said, would be all the more precious to her by virtue of the fact that it was finally hers through her own efforts. The strength and nobility of character that have come to her during these years, the sweetness of disposition, the sympathy and care for others, her faith in the final triumph of all that is honest and true and pure and good, are qualities that thousands and hundreds of thousands of women, yes, of both men and women, who are apparently in better circumstances in life, can justly envy. And should the little farm home be taken away tomorrow, she has gained something that a farm of a thousand acres could not buy. By going about her work in the way she has gone about it the burden of it all has been lightened, and her work has been made truly enjoyable.

Let us take a moment to see how these same conditions would have been met by a person of less wisdom, one not so far-sighted as this dear, good woman has been. For a time possibly her spirit would have been crushed. Fears and forebodings of all kinds would probably have taken hold of her, and she would have felt that nothing that she could do would be of any avail. Or she might have rebelled against the agencies, against the law which brought about the conditions in which she found herself, and she might have become embittered against the world, and gradually also against the various people with whom she came in contact. Or again, she might have thought that her efforts would be unable to meet the circumstances, and that it was the duty of someone to lift her out of her difficulties. In this way no progress at all would have been made towards the accomplishment of the desired results, and continually she would have felt more keenly the circumstances in which she found herself, because there was nothing else to occupy her mind. In this way the little farm would not have become hers, she would not have been able to do anything for others, and her nature would have become embittered against everything and everybody.

True it is, then, not, "What are the conditions in one's life?" but, "How does he meet the conditions that he finds there?" This will determine all. And if at any time we are apt to think that our own lot is about the hardest there is, and if we are able at any time to persuade ourselves that we can find no one whose lot is just a little harder than ours, let us then study for a little while the character Pompilia, in Browning's poem and after studying it, thank God that the conditions in our life are so favorable; and then set about with a trusting and intrepid spirit to actualize the conditions that we most desire.

Thought is at the bottom of all progress or retrogression, of all success or failure, of all that is desirable or undesirable in human life. The type of thought we entertain both creates and draws conditions that crystallize about it, conditions exactly the same in nature as is the thought that gives them form. Thoughts are forces, and each creates of its kind, whether we realize it or not. The great law of the drawing power of the mind, which says that like creates like, and that like attracts like, is continually working in every human life, for it is one of the great immutable laws of the universe. For one to take time to see clearly the things he would attain to, and then to hold that ideal steadily and continually before his mind, never allowing faith—his positive thought-forces—to give way to or to be neutralized by doubts and fears, and then to set about doing each day what his hands find to do, never complaining, but spending the time that he would otherwise spend in complaint in focusing his thought-forces upon the ideal that his mind has built, will sooner or later bring about the full materialization of that for which he sets out. There are those who, when they begin to grasp the fact that there is what we may term a "science of thought," who, when they begin to realize that through the instrumentality of our interior, spiritual, thought-forces we have the power of gradually molding the everyday conditions of life as we would have them, in their early enthusiasm are not able to see results as quickly as they expect and are apt to think, therefore, that after all there is not very much in that which has but newly come to their knowledge. They must remember, however, that in endeavoring to overcome an old habit or to grow a new habit, everything cannot be done all at once.

In the degree that we attempt to use the thought-forces do we continually become able to use them more effectively. Progress is slow at first, more rapid as we proceed. Power grows by using, or, in other words, using brings a continually increasing power. This is governed by law the same as are all things in our lives, and all things in the universe about us. Every act and advancement made by the musician is in full accordance with law. No one commencing the study of music can, for example, sit down to the piano and play the piece of a master at the first effort. He must not conclude, however, nor does he conclude, that the piece of the master cannot be played by him, or, for that matter, by anyone. He begins to practice the piece. The law of the mind that we have already noticed comes to his aid, whereby his mind follows the music more readily, more rapidly, and more surely each succeeding time, and there also comes into operation and to his aid the law underlying the action of the reflex nerve system of the body, which we have also noticed, whereby his fingers co-ordinate their movements with the movements of his mind more readily, more rapidly, and more accurately each succeeding time; until by and by the time comes when that which he stumbles through at first, that in which there is no harmony, nothing but discord, finally reveals itself as the music of the master, the music that thrills and moves masses of men and women. So it is in the use of the thought-forces. It is the reiteration, the constant reiteration of the thought that grows the power of continually stronger thought-focusing, and that finally brings manifestation.

There is character-building not only for the young but for the old as well. And what a difference there is in elderly people! How many grow old gracefully, and how many grow old in ways of quite a different nature. There is a sweetness and charm that combine for attractiveness in old age the same as there is something that cannot be described by these words. Some grow continually more dear to their friends and to the members of their immediate households, while others become possessed of the idea that their friends and the members of their households have less of a regard for them than they formerly had, and many times they are not far wrong. The one continually sees more in life to enjoy, the other sees continually less. The one becomes more dear and attractive to others, the other less so. And why is this? Through chance? By no means. Personally I do not believe there is any such thing as chance in the whole of human life, nor even in the world or the great universe in which we live. The one great law of cause and effect is absolute; and effect is always kindred to its own peculiar cause, although we may have at times to go back considerably farther than we are accustomed to in order to find the cause, the parent of this or that effect, or actualized, though not necessarily permanently actualized, condition.

Why, then, the vast difference in the two types of elderly people? The one keeps from worryings, and fearings, and frettings, and foundationless imaginings, while the other seems especially to cultivate these, to give himself or herself especially to them. And why is this? At a certain time in life, differing somewhat in different people, life-long mental states, habits, and characteristics begin to focus themselves and come to the surface, so to speak. Predominating thoughts and mental states begin to show themselves in actualized qualities and characteristics as never before, and no one is immune.

In the lane leading to the orchard is a tree. For years it has been growing only "natural fruit." Not long since it was grafted upon. The spring has come and gone. One-half of the tree was in bloom and the other half also. The blossoms on each part could not be distinguished by the casual observer. The blossoms have been followed by young fruit which hangs abundantly on the entire tree. There is but a slight difference in it now; but a few weeks later the difference in form, in size, in color, in flavor, in keeping qualities, will be so marked that no one can fail to tell them apart or have difficulty in choosing between them. The one will be a small, somewhat hard and gnarled, tart, yellowish-green apple, and will keep but a few weeks into the fall of the year. The other will be a large, delicately flavored apple, mellow, deep red in color, and will keep until the tree which bore it is in bloom again.

But why this incident from nature's garden? This. Up to a certain period in the fruit's growth, although the interior, forming qualities of the apples were slightly different from the beginning, there was but little to distinguish them. At a certain period in their growth, however, their differing interior qualities began to externalize themselves so rapidly and so markedly that the two fruits became of such a vastly different type that, as we have seen, no one could hesitate in choosing between them. And knowing once the soul, the forming, the determining qualities of each, we can thereafter tell beforehand with a certainty that is quite absolute what it, the externalized product of each portion of the tree, will be.

And it is quite the same in human life. If one would have a beautiful and attractive old age, he must begin it in youth and in middle life. If, however, he has neglected or failed in this, he can then wisely adapt himself to circumstances and give himself zealously to putting into operation all necessary counter-balancing forces and influences. Where there is life nothing is ever irretrievably lost, though the enjoyment of the higher good may be long delayed. But if one would have an especially beautiful and attractive old age he must begin it in early and in middle life, for there comes by and by a sort of "rounding-up" process when long-lived-in habits of thought begin to take unto themselves a strongly dominating power, and the thought habits of a lifetime begin to come to the surface.

Fear and worry, selfishness, a hard-fisted, grabbing, holding disposition, a carping, fault-finding, nagging tendency, a slavery of thought and action to the thinking or to the opinions of others, a lacking of consideration, thought, and sympathy for others, a lack of charity for the thoughts, the motives, and the acts of others, a lack of knowledge of the powerful and inevitable building qualities of thought, as well as a lack of faith in the eternal goodness and love and power of the Source of our being, all combine in time to make the old age of those in whom they find life, that barren, cheerless, unwelcome something, unattractive or even repellent to itself as well as to others, that we not infrequently find, while their opposites, on the contrary, combine, and seem to be helped on by heavenly agencies, to bring about that cheerful, hopeful, helpful, beautified, and hallowed old age that is so welcome and so attractive both to itself and to all with whom it comes in contact. Both types of thoughts, qualities, and dispositions, moreover, externalize themselves in the voice, in the peculiarly different ways in which they mark the face, in the stoop or lack of stoop in the form, as also in the healthy or unhealthy conditions of the mind and body, and their susceptibility to disorders and weaknesses of various kinds.

It is not a bad thing for each one early to get a little "philosophy" into his life. It will be of much aid as he advances in life; it will many times be a source of great comfort, as well as of strength, in trying times and in later life. We may even, though gently perhaps, make sport of the one who has his little philosophy, but unless we have something similar the time will come when the very lack of it will deride us. It may be at times, though not necessarily, that the one who has it is not always so successful in affairs when it comes to a purely money or business success, but it supplies many times a very real something in life that the one of money or business success only is starving for, though he doesn't know what the real lack is, and although he hasn't money enough in all the world to buy it did he know.

It is well to find our centre early, and if not early then late; but, late or early, the thing to do is to find it. While we are in life the one essential thing is to play our part bravely and well and to keep our active interest in all its varying phases, the same as it is well to be able to adapt ourselves always to changing conditions. It is by the winds of heaven blowing over it continually and keeping it in constant motion, or by its continual onward movement, that the water in pool or stream is kept sweet and clear, for otherwise it would become stagnant and covered with slime. If we are attractive or unattractive to ourselves and to others the cause lies in ourselves; this is true of all ages, and it is well for us, young or old, to recognize it. It is well, other things being equal, to adapt ourselves to those about us, but it is hardly fair for the old to think that all the adapting should be on the part of the young, with no kindred duty on their part. Many times old-age loses much of its attractiveness on account of a peculiar notion of this kind. The principle of reciprocity must hold in all ages in life, and whatever the age, if we fail to observe it, it results always sooner or later in our own undoing.

We are all in Life's great play—comedy and tragedy, smiles and tears, sunshine and shadow, summer and winter, and in time we take all parts. We must take our part, whatever it may be, at any given time, always bravely and with a keen appreciation of every opportunity, and a keen alertness at every turn as the play progresses. A good "entrance" and a good "exit" contribute strongly to the playing of a deservedly worthy role. We are not always able perhaps to choose just as we would the details of our entrance, but the manner of our playing and the manner of our exit we can all determine, and this no man, no power can deny us; this in every human life can be made indeed most glorious, however humble it may begin, or however humble it may remain or exalted it may become, according to conventional standards of judgment.

To me we are here for divine self-realization through experience. We progress in the degree that we manipulate wisely all things that enter into our lives, and that make the sum total of each one's life experience. Let us be brave and strong in the presence of each problem as it presents itself and make the best of all. Let us help the things we can help, and let us be not bothered or crippled by the things we cannot help. The great God of all is watching and manipulating these things most wisely and we need not fear or even have concern regarding them.

To live to our highest in all things that pertain to us, to lend a hand as best we can to all others for this same end, to aid in righting the wrongs that cross our path by means of pointing the wrongdoer to a better way, and thus aiding him in becoming a power for good, to remain in nature always sweet and simple and humble, and therefore strong, to open ourselves fully and to keep ourselves as fit channels for the Divine Power to work through us, to open ourselves, and to keep our faces always to the light, to love all things and to stand in awe or fear of nothing save our own wrong-doing, to recognize the good lying at the heart of all things, waiting for expression all in its own good way and time—this will make our part in life's great and as yet not fully understood play truly glorious, and we need then stand in fear of nothing, life nor death, for death is life. Or rather, it is the quick transition to life in another form; the putting off of the old coat and the putting on of a new; the falling away of the material body and the taking of the soul to itself a new and finer body, better adapted to its needs and surroundings in another world of experience and growth and still greater divine self-realization; a going out with all that it has gained of this nature in this world, but with no possessions material; a passing not from light to darkness, but from light to light; a taking up of life in another from just where we leave it off here; an experience not to be shunned or dreaded or feared, but to be welcomed when it comes in its own good way and time.

All life is from within out. This is something that cannot be reiterated too often. The springs of life are all from within. This being true, it would be well for us to give more time to the inner life than we are accustomed to give to it, especially in this Western world.

There is nothing that will bring us such abundant returns as to take a little time in the quiet each day of our lives. We need this to get the kinks out of our minds, and hence out of our lives. We need this to form better the higher ideals of life. We need this in order to see clearly in mind the things upon which we would concentrate and focus the thought-forces. We need this in order to make continually anew and to keep our conscious connection with the Infinite. We need this in order that the rush and hurry of our everyday life does not keep us away from the conscious realization of the fact that the spirit of Infinite life and power that is back of all, working in and through all, the life of all, is the life of our life, and the source of our power; and that outside of this we have no life and we have no power. To realize this fact fully, and to live in it consciously at all times, is to find the kingdom of God, which is essentially an inner kingdom, and can never be anything else. The kingdom of heaven is to be found only within, and this is done once for all, and in a manner in which it cannot otherwise be done, when we come into the conscious, living realization of the fact that in our real selves we are essentially one with the Divine life, and open ourselves continually so that this Divine life can speak to and manifest through us. In this way we come into the condition where we are continually walking with God. In this way the consciousness of God becomes a living reality in our lives; and in the degree in which it becomes a reality does it bring us into the realization of continually increasing wisdom, insight, and power. This consciousness of God in the soul of man is the essence, indeed, the sum and substance, of all religion. This identifies religion with every act and every moment of everyday life. That which does not identify itself with every moment of every day and with every act of life is religion in name only and not in reality. This consciousness of God in the soul of man is the one thing uniformly taught by all the prophets, by all the inspired ones, by all the seers and mystics in the world's history, whatever the time, wherever the country, whatever the religion, whatever minor differences we may find in their lives and teachings. In regard to this they all agree; indeed, this is the essence of their teaching, as it has also been the secret of their power and the secret of their lasting influence.

It is the attitude of the child that is necessary before we can enter into the kingdom of heaven. As it was said, "Except ye become as little children, ye cannot enter into the kingdom of heaven." For we then realize that of ourselves we can do nothing, but that it is only as we realize that it is the Divine life and power working within us, and it is only as we open ourselves that it may work through us, that we are or can do anything. It is thus that the simple life, which is essentially the life of the greatest enjoyment and the greatest attainment, is entered upon.

In the Orient the people as a class take far more time in the quiet, in the silence, than we take. Some of them carry this possibly to as great an extreme as we carry the opposite, with the result that they do not actualize and objectify in the outer life the things they dream in the inner life. We give so much time to the activities of the outer life that we do not take sufficient time in the quiet to form in the inner, spiritual, thought-life the ideals and the conditions that we would have actualized and manifested in the outer life. The result is that we take life in a kind of haphazard way, taking it as it comes, thinking not very much about it until, perhaps, pushed by some bitter experiences, instead of molding it, through the agency of the inner forces, exactly as we would have it. We need to strike the happy balance between the custom in this respect of the Eastern and Western worlds, and go to the extreme of neither the one nor the other. This alone will give the ideal life; and it is the ideal life only that is the thoroughly satisfactory life. In the Orient there are many who are day after day sitting in the quiet, meditating, contemplating, idealizing, with their eyes focused on their stomachs in spiritual revery, while through lack of outer activities, in their stomachs, they are actually starving. In this Western world, men and women, in the rush and activity of our accustomed life, are running hither and thither, with no centre, no foundation upon which to stand, nothing to which they can anchor their lives, because they do not take sufficient time to come into the realization of what the centre, of what the reality of their lives is.

If the Oriental would do his contemplating, and then get up and do his work, he would be in a better condition; he would be living a more normal and satisfactory life. If we in the Occident would take more time from the rush and activity of life for contemplation, for meditation, for idealization, for becoming acquainted with our real selves, and then go about our work manifesting the powers of our real selves, we would be far better off, because we would be living a more natural, a more normal life. To find one's centre, to become centred in the Infinite, is the first great essential of every satisfactory life; and then to go out, thinking, speaking, working, loving, living, from this centre.

In the highest character-building, such as we have been considering, there are those who feel they are handicapped by what we term heredity. In a sense they are right; in another sense they are totally wrong. It is along the same lines as the thought which many before us had inculcated in them through the couplet in the New England Primer: "In Adam's fall, we sinned all." Now, in the first place, it is rather hard to understand the justice of this if it is true. In the second place, it is rather hard to understand why it is true. And in the third place there is no truth in it at all. We are now dealing with the real essential self, and, however old Adam is, God is eternal. This means you; it means me; it means every human soul. When we fully realize this fact we see that heredity is a reed that is easily broken. The life of every one is in his own hands and he can make it in character, in attainment, in power, in divine self-realization, and hence in influence, exactly what he wills to make it. All things that he most fondly dreams of are his, or may become so if he is truly in earnest; and as he rises more and more to his ideal, and grows in the strength and influence of his character, he becomes an example and an inspiration to all with whom he comes in contact; so that through him the weak and faltering are encouraged and strengthened; so that those of low ideals and of a low type of life instinctively and inevitably have their ideals raised, and the ideals of no one can be raised without its showing forth in his outer life. As he advances in his grasp upon and understanding of the power and potency of the thought-forces, he finds that many times through the process of mental suggestion he can be of tremendous aid to one who is weak and struggling, by sending him now and then, and by continually holding him in, the highest thought, in the thought of the highest strength, wisdom and love. The power of "suggestion," mental suggestion, is one that has tremendous possibilities for good if we will but study into it carefully, understand it fully, and use it rightly.

The one who takes sufficient time in the quiet mentally to form his ideals, sufficient time to make and to keep continually his conscious connection with the Infinite, with the Divine life and forces, is the one who is best adapted to the strenuous life. He it is who can go out and deal, with sagacity and power, with whatever issues may arise in the affairs of everyday life. He it is who is building not for the years but for the centuries; not for time, but for the eternities. And he can go out knowing not whither he goes, knowing that the Divine life within him will never fail him, but will lead him on until he beholds the Father face to face.

He is building for the centuries because only that which is the highest, the truest, the noblest, and best will abide the test of the centuries. He is building for eternity because when the transition we call death takes place, life, character, self-mastery, divine self-realization—the only things that the soul when stripped of everything else takes with it—he has in abundance, in life, or when the time of the transition to another form of life comes, he is never afraid, never fearful, because he knows and realizes that behind him, within him, beyond him, is the Infinite wisdom and love; and in this he is eternally centred, and from it he can never be separated. With Whittier he sings:

> *I know not where His islands lift*
> *Their fronded palms in air;*
> *I only know I cannot drift*
> *Beyond His love and care*

THE GREATEST THING IN THE WORLD

And Other Addresses
HENRY DRUMMOND

Contents

Introductory   137

Love, the Greatest Thing in the World   139

Lessons from the Angelus   164

Pax Vobiscum   172

First! An Address to Boys   195

The Changed Life, the Greatest Need of the World   206

Dealing with Doubt   233

Introductory

I was staying with a party of friends in a country house during my visit to England in 1884. On Sunday evening as we sat around the fire, they asked me to read and expound some portion of Scripture. Being tired after the services of the day, I told them to ask Henry Drummond, who was one of the party. After some urging he drew a small Testament from his hip pocket, opened it at the 13th chapter of I Corinthians, and began to speak on the subject of Love.

It seemed to me that I had never heard anything so beautiful, and I determined not to rest until I brought Henry Drummond to Northfield to deliver that address. Since then I have requested the principals of my schools to have it read before the students every year. The one great need in our Christian life is love, more love to God and to each other. Would that we could all move into that Love chapter, and live there.

—D.L Moody

This volume contains, in addition to the address on Love, some other addresses which I trust will bring help and blessing to many.

Though I speak with the tongues of men and of angels, and have not love, I am become as sounding brass, or a tinkling cymbal. And though I have the gift of prophecy, and understand all mysteries, and all knowledge; and though I have all faith, so that I could remove mountains, and have not love, I am nothing. And though I bestow all my goods to feed the poor and though I gave my body to be burned, and have not love, it profiteth me nothing.

Love suffereth long, and is kind;
Love envieth not;
Love wanteth not itself, is not puffed up,
Doth no behave itself unseemly,
Seeketh not her own,
Is not easily provoked,
Thinketh no evil;
Rejoiceth not in iniquity, but rejoiceth in the truth;
Beareth all things, believeth all things, hopeth all things, endureth all things.

Love never faileth: but whether there be prophecies, they shall fail; whether there be tongues, they shall cease; whether there be knowledge, it shall vanish away. For we know in part, and we prophesy in part. But when that which is perfect is come, then that which is in part shall be done away. When I was a child, I spake as a child, I understood as a child, I thought as a child: but when I became a man, I put away childish things. For now we see through a glass, darkly; but then face to face: now I know in part; but then shall I know even as also I am known. And now abideth faith, hope, love, these three; but the greatest of these is love.

—*1 Corinthians 13*

Love: The Greatest Thing In the World

Every one has asked himself the great question of antiquity as of the modern world: What is the *summum bonum*—the supreme good? You have life before you. Once only you can live it. What is the noblest object of desire, the supreme gift to covet?

We have been accustomed to be told that the greatest thing in the religious world is Faith. That great word has been the key-note for centuries of the popular religion; and we have easily learned to look upon it as the greatest thing in the world. Well, we are wrong. If we have been told that, we may miss the mark. In the 13th chapter of I Corinthians, Paul takes us to CHRISTIANITY AT ITS SOURCE; and there we see, "The greatest of these is love."

It is not an oversight. Paul was speaking of faith just a moment before. He says, "If I have all faith, so that I can remove mountains, and have not love, I am nothing." So far from forgetting, he deliberately contrasts them, "Now abideth Faith, Hope, Love," and without a moment's hesitation the decision falls, "The greatest of these is Love."

And it is not prejudice. A man is apt to recommend to others his own strong point. Love was not Paul's strong point. The observing student can detect a beautiful tenderness growing and ripening all through his character as Paul gets old; but the hand that wrote, "The greatest of these is love," when we meet it first, is stained with blood.

Nor is this letter to the Corinthians peculiar in singling out love as the *summum bonum*. The masterpieces of Christianity are agreed about it. Peter says, "Above all things have fervent love among yourselves." *Above all things.* And John goes farther, "God is love."

You remember the profound remark which Paul makes elsewhere, "Love is the fulfilling of the law." Did you ever think what he meant by that? In those days men were working the passage to Heaven by keeping the Ten Commandments, and the hundred and ten other commandments which they had manufactured out of them. Christ came and said, "I will show you a more simple way. If you do one thing, you will do these hundred and ten things, without ever thinking about them. If you *love*, you will unconsciously fulfill the whole law."

You can readily see for yourselves how that must be so. Take any of the commandments. "Thou shalt have no other gods before Me." If a man love God, you will not require to tell him that. Love is the fulfilling of that law. "Take not His name in vain." Would he ever dream of taking His name in vain if he loved him? "Remember the Sabbath day to keep it holy." Would he not be too glad to have one day in seven to dedicate more exclusively to the object of his affection? Love would fulfill all these laws regarding God.

And so, if he loved man, you would never think of telling him to honor his father and mother. He could not do anything else. It would be preposterous to tell him not to kill. You could only insult him if you suggested that he should not steal—how could he steal from those he loved? It would be superfluous to beg him not to bear false witness against his neighbor. If he loved him it would be the last thing he would do. And you would never dream of urging him not to covet what his neighbors had. He would rather they possessed it than himself. In this way "Love is the fulfilling of the law." It is the rule for fulfilling all rules, the new commandment for keeping all the old commandments, Christ's one SECRET OF THE CHRISTIAN LIFE. Now Paul has learned that; and in this noble eulogy he has given us the most wonderful and original account extant of the *summum bonum*. We may divide it into three parts. In the beginning of the short chapter we have Love *contrasted*; in the heart of it, we have Love *analyzed*; toward the end, we have Love *defended* as the supreme gift.

I. THE CONTRAST.

Paul begins by contrasting Love with other things that men in those days thought much of. I shall not attempt to go over these things in detail. Their inferiority is already obvious.

He contrasts it with *eloquence*. And what a noble gift it is, the power of playing upon the souls and wills of men, and rousing them to lofty purposes and holy deeds! Paul says, "If I speak with the tongues of men and of angels, and have not love, I am become sounding brass, or a tinkling cymbal." We all know why. We have all felt the brazenness of words without emotion, the hollowness, the unaccountable unpersuasiveness, of eloquence behind which lies no Love.

He contrasts it with *prophecy*. He contrasts it with *mysteries*. He contrasts it with *faith*. He contrasts it with *charity*. Why is Love greater than faith? Because the end is greater than the means. And why is it greater than charity? Because the whole is greater than the part.

Love is greater than *faith*, because the end is greater than the means. What is the use of having faith? It is to connect the soul with God. And what is the object of connecting man with God? That he may become like God. But God is Love. Hence Faith, the means, is in order to Love, the end. Love, therefore, obviously is greater than faith. "If I have all faith, so as to remove mountains, but have not love, I am nothing."

It is greater than *charity*, again, because the whole is greater than a part. Charity is only a little bit of Love, one of the innumerable avenues of Love, and there may even be, and there is, a great deal of charity without Love. It is a very easy thing to toss a copper to a beggar on the street; it is generally an easier thing than not to do it. Yet Love is just as often in the withholding. We purchase relief from the sympathetic feelings roused by the spectacle of misery, at the copper's cost. It is too cheap—too cheap for us, and often too dear for the beggar. If we really loved him we would either do more for him, or less. Hence, "If I bestow all my goods to feed the poor, but have not love it profiteth me nothing."

Then Paul contrasts it with *sacrifice* and martyrdom: "If I give my body to be burned, but have not love, it profiteth me nothing." Missionaries can take nothing greater to the heathen world than the impress and reflection of the Love of God upon their own character. That is the universal language. It will take them years to speak in Chinese, or in the dialects of India. From the day they land, that language of Love, understood by all, will be pouring forth its unconscious eloquence.

It is the man who is the missionary, it is not his words. His character is his message. In the heart of Africa, among the great Lakes, I have come across black men and women who remembered the only white man they ever saw before—David Livingstone; and as you cross his footsteps in that dark continent, MEN'S FACES LIGHT UP as they speak of the kind doctor who passed there years ago. They could not understand him; but they felt the love that beat in his heart. They knew that it was love, although he spoke no word.

Take into your sphere of labor, where you also mean to lay down your life, that simple charm, and your lifework must succeed. You can take nothing greater, you need take nothing less. You may take every accomplishment; you may be braced for every sacrifice; but if you give your body to be burned, and have not Love, it will profit you and the cause of Christ *nothing*.

II. THE ANALYSIS.

After contrasting Love with these things, Paul, in three verses, very short, gives us an amazing analysis of what this supreme thing is.

I ask you to look at it. It is a compound thing, he tells us. It is like light. As you have seen a man of science take a beam of light and pass it through a crystal prism, as you have seen it come out on the other side of the prism broken up into its component colors—red, and blue, and yellow, and violet, and orange, and all the colors of the rainbow—so Paul passes this thing, Love, through the magnificent prism of his inspired intellect, and it comes out on the other side broken up into its elements.

In these few words we have what one might call THE SPECTRUM OF LOVE, the analysis of Love. Will you observe what its elements are? Will you notice that they have common names; that they are virtues which we hear about every day; that they are things which can be practised by every man in every place in life; and how, by a multitude of small things and ordinary virtues, the supreme thing, the *summum bonum*, is made up?

The Spectrum of Love has nine ingredients:

Patience	"Love suffereth long."
Kindness	"And is kind."
Generosity	"Love envieth not."
Humility	"Love vaunteth not itself, is not puffed up."
Courtesy	"Doth not behave itself unseemly."
Unselfishness	"Seeketh not its own."
Good temper	"Is not provoked."
Guilelessness	"Taketh not account of evil."
Sincerity	"Rejoiceth not in unrighteousness, but rejoiceth with the truth."

Patience; kindness; generosity; humility; courtesy; unselfishness; good temper; guilelessness; sincerity—these make up the supreme gift, the stature of the perfect man.

You will observe that all are in relation to men, in relation to life, in relation to the known to-day and the near to-morrow, and not to the unknown eternity. We hear much of love to God; Christ spoke much of love to man. We make a great deal of peace with heaven; Christ made much of peace on earth. Religion is not a strange or added thing, but the inspiration of the secular life, the breathing of an eternal spirit through this temporal world. The supreme thing, in short, is not a thing at all, but the giving of a further finish to the multitudinous words and acts which make up the sum of every common day.

Patience. This is the normal attitude of love; Love passive, Love waiting to begin; not in a hurry; calm; ready to do its work when the summons comes, but meantime wearing the ornament of a meek and quiet spirit. Love suffers long; beareth all things; believeth all things; hopeth all things. For Love understands, and therefore waits.

Kindness. Love active. Have you ever noticed how much of Christ's life was spent in doing kind things—in *merely* doing kind things? Run over it with that in view, and you will find that He spent a great proportion of His time simply in making people happy, in DOING GOOD TURNS to people. There is only one thing greater than happiness in the world, and that is holiness; and it is not in our keeping; but what God *has* put in our power is the happiness of those about us, and that is largely to be secured by our being kind to them.

"The greatest thing," says some one, "a man can do for his Heavenly Father is to be kind to some of His other children." I wonder why it is that we are not all kinder than we are? How much the world needs it! How easily it is done! How instantaneously it acts! How infallibly it is remembered! How superabundantly it pays itself back—for there is no debtor in the world so honorable, so superbly honorable, as Love. "Love never faileth." Love is success, Love is happiness, Love is life. "Love," I say with Browning, "is energy of life."

> *"For life, with all it yields of joy or woe*
> *And hope and fear,*
> *Is just our chance o' the prize of learning love,—*
> *How love might be, hath been indeed, and is."*

Where Love is, God is. He that dwelleth in Love dwelleth in God. God is Love. Therefore *love*. Without distinction, without calculation, without procrastination, love. Lavish it upon the poor, where it is very easy; especially upon the rich, who often need it most; most of all upon our equals, where it is very difficult, and for whom perhaps we each do least of all. There is a difference between *trying to please* and *giving pleasure*. Give pleasure. Lose no chance of giving pleasure; for that is the ceaseless and anonymous triumph of a truly loving spirit. "I shall pass through this world but once. Any good thing, therefore, that I can do, or any kindness that I can show to any human being, let me do it now. Let me not defer it or neglect it, for I shall not pass this way again."

Generosity. "Love envieth not." This is love in competition with others. Whenever you attempt a good work you will find other men doing the same kind of work, and probably doing it better. Envy them not. Envy is a feeling of ill-will to those who are in the same line as ourselves, a spirit of covetousness and detraction. How little Christian work even is a protection against un-Christian feeling! That most despicable of all the unworthy moods which cloud a Christian's soul assuredly waits for us on the threshold of every work, unless we are fortified with this grace of magnanimity. Only one thing truly need the Christian envy—the large, rich, generous soul which "envieth not."

And then, after having learned all that, you have to learn this further thing, *Humility*—to put a seal upon your lips and forget what you have done. After you have been kind, after Love has stolen forth into the world and done its beautiful work, go back into the shade again and say nothing about it. Love hides even from itself. Love waives even self-satisfaction. "Love vaunteth not itself, is not puffed up." Humility—love hiding.

The fifth ingredient is a somewhat strange one to find in this *summum bonum*: *Courtesy.* This is Love in society, Love in relation to etiquette. "Love does not behave itself unseemly."

Politeness has been defined as love in trifles. Courtesy is said to be love in little things. And the one secret of politeness is to love.

Love *cannot* behave itself unseemly. You can put the most untutored persons into the highest society, and if they have a reservoir of Love in their heart they will not behave themselves unseemly. They simply cannot do it. Carlisle said of Robert Burns that there was no truer gentleman in Europe than the ploughman-poet. It was because he loved everything—the mouse, and the daisy, and all the things, great and small, that God had made. So with this simple passport he could mingle with any society, and enter courts and palaces from his little cottage on the banks of the Ayr.

You know the meaning of the word "gentleman." It means a gentle man—a man who does things gently, with love. That is the whole art and mystery of it. The gentle man cannot in the nature of things do an ungentle, an ungentlemanly thing. The ungentle soul, the inconsiderate, unsympathetic nature, cannot do anything else. "Love doth not behave itself unseemly."

Unselfishness. "Love seeketh not her own." Observe: Seeketh not even that which is her own. In Britain the Englishman is devoted, and rightly, to his rights. But there come times when a man may exercise even THE HIGHER RIGHT of giving up his rights.

Yet Paul does not summon us to give up our rights. Love strikes much deeper. It would have us not seek them at all, ignore them, eliminate the personal element altogether from our calculations.

It is not hard to give up our rights. They are often eternal. The difficult thing is to give up *ourselves*. The more difficult thing still is not to seek things for ourselves at all. After we have sought them, bought them, won them, deserved them, we have taken the cream off them for ourselves already. Little cross then to give them up. But not to seek them, to look every man not on his own things, but on the things of others—that is the difficulty. "Seekest thou great things for thyself?" said the prophet; *"seek them not."* Why? Because there is no greatness in *things*. Things cannot be great. The only greatness is unselfish love. Even self-denial in itself is nothing, is almost a mistake. Only a great purpose or a mightier love can justify the waste.

It is more difficult, I have said, not to seek our own at all than, having sought it, to give it up. I must take that back. It is only true of a partly selfish heart. Nothing is a hardship to Love, and nothing is hard. I believe that Christ's "yoke" is easy. Christ's yoke is just His way of taking life. And I believe it is an easier way than any other. I believe it is a happier way than any other. The most obvious lesson in Christ's teaching is that there is no happiness in having and getting anything, but only in giving. I repeat, *there is no happiness in having or in getting, but only in giving.* Half the world is on the wrong scent in pursuit of happiness. They think it consists in having and getting, and in being served by others. It consists in giving, and in serving others. "He that would be great among you," said Christ, "let him serve." He that would be happy, let him remember that there is but one way—"it is more blessed, it is more happy, to give than to receive."

The next ingredient is a very remarkable one: *Good temper.* "Love is not provoked."

Nothing could be more striking than to find this here. We are inclined to look upon bad temper as a very harmless weakness. We speak of it as a mere infirmity of nature, a family failing, a matter of temperament, not a thing to take into very serious account in estimating a man's character. And yet here, right in the heart of this analysis of love, it finds a place; and the Bible again and again returns to condemn it as one of the most destructive elements in human nature.

The peculiarity of ill temper is that it is the vice of the virtuous. It is often the one blot on an otherwise noble character. You know men who are all but perfect, and women who would be entirely perfect, but for an easily ruffled, quick-tempered, or "touchy" disposition. This compatibility of ill temper with high moral character is one of the strangest and saddest problems of ethics. The truth is, there are two great classes of sins—sins of the *Body* and sins of the *Disposition*. The Prodigal Son may be taken as a type of the first, the Elder Brother of the second. Now, society has no doubt whatever as to which of these is the worse. Its brand falls, without a challenge, upon the Prodigal. But are we right? We have no balance to weigh one another's sins, and coarser and finer are but human words; but faults in the higher nature may be less venal than those in the lower, and to the eye of Him who is Love, a sin against Love may seem a hundred times more base. No form of vice, not worldliness, not greed of gold, not drunkenness itself, does more to un-Christianize society than evil temper. For embittering life, for breaking up communities, for destroying the most sacred relationships, for devastating homes, for withering up men and women, for taking the bloom of childhood, in short, FOR SHEER GRATUITOUS MISERY-PRODUCING POWER this influence stands alone.

Look at the Elder Brother—moral, hard-working, patient, dutiful—let him get all credit for his virtues—look at this man, this baby, sulking outside his own father's door. "He was angry," we read, "and would not go in." Look at the effect upon the father, upon the servants, upon the happiness of the guests. Judge of the effect upon the Prodigal—and how many prodigals are kept out of the Kingdom of God by the unlovely character of those who profess to be inside. Analyze, as a study in Temper, the thunder-cloud itself as it gathers upon the Elder Brother's brow. What is it made of? Jealousy, anger, pride, uncharity, cruelty, self-righteousness, touchiness, doggedness, sullenness—these are the ingredients of this dark and loveless soul. In varying proportions, also, these are the ingredients of all ill temper. Judge if such sins of the disposition are not worse to live in, and for others to live with, than the sins of the body. Did Christ indeed not answer the question Himself when He said, "I say unto you that the publicans and the harlots go into the Kingdom of Heaven before you"? There is really no place in heaven for a disposition like this. A man with such a mood could only make heaven miserable for all the people in it. Except, therefore, such a man be BORN AGAIN, he cannot, simply *cannot*, enter the kingdom of heaven.

You will see then why Temper is significant. It is not in what it is alone, but in what it reveals. This is why I speak of it with such unusual plainness. It is a test for love, a symptom, a revelation of an unloving nature at bottom. It is the intermittent fever which bespeaks unintermittent disease within; the occasional bubble escaping to the surface which betrays some rottenness underneath; a sample of the most hidden products of the soul dropped involuntarily when off one's guard; in a word, the lightning form of a hundred hideous and un-Christian sins. A want of patience, a want of kindness, a want of generosity, a want of courtesy, a want of unselfishness, are all instantaneously symbolized in one flash of Temper.

Hence it is not enough to deal with the Temper. We must go to the source, and change the inmost nature, and the angry humors will die away of themselves. Souls are made sweet not by taking the acid fluids out, but by putting something in—a great Love, a new Spirit, the Spirit of Christ. Christ, the Spirit of Christ, interpenetrating ours, sweetens, purifies, transforms all. This only can eradicate what is wrong, work a chemical change, renovate and regenerate, and rehabilitate the inner man. Will-power does not change men. Time does not change men. CHRIST DOES. Therefore, "Let that mind be in you which was also in Christ Jesus."

Some of us have not much time to lose. Remember, once more, that this is a matter of life or death. I cannot help speaking urgently, for myself, for yourselves. "Whoso shall offend one of these little ones, which believe in me, it were better for him that a millstone were hanged about his neck, and that he were drowned in the depth of the sea." That is to say, it is the deliberate verdict of the Lord Jesus that it is better not to live than not to love. *It is better not to live than not to love.*

Guilelessness and *Sincerity* may be dismissed almost without a word. Guilelessness is the grace for suspicious people. The possession of it is THE GREAT SECRET OF PERSONAL INFLUENCE. You will find, if you think for a moment, that the people who influence you are people who believe in you. In an atmosphere of suspicion men shrivel up; but in that atmosphere they expand, and find encouragement and educative fellowship.

It is a wonderful thing that here and there in this hard, uncharitable world there should still be left a few rare souls who think no evil. This is the great unworldliness. Love "thinketh no evil," imputes no motive, sees the bright side, puts the best construction on every action. What a delightful state of mind to live in! What a stimulus and benediction even to meet with it for a day! To be trusted is to be saved. And if we try to influence or elevate others, we shall soon see that success is in proportion to their belief of our belief in them. The respect of another is the first restoration of the self-respect a man has lost; our ideal of what he is becomes to him the hope and pattern of what he may become.

"Love rejoiceth not in unrighteousness, but rejoiceth with the truth." I have called this *Sincerity* from the words rendered in the Authorized Version by "rejoiceth in the truth." And, certainly, were this the real translation, nothing could be more just; for he who loves will love Truth not less than men. He will rejoice in the Truth—rejoice not in what he has been taught to believe; not in this church's doctrine or in that; not in this ism or in that ism; but "in *the Truth*." He will accept only what is real; he will strive to get at facts; he will search for *Truth* with a humble and unbiased mind, and cherish whatever he finds at any sacrifice. But the more literal translation of the Revised Version calls for just such a sacrifice for truth's sake here. For what Paul really meant is, as we there read, "Rejoiceth not in unrighteousness, but rejoiceth with the truth," a quality which probably no one English word—and certainly not *Sincerity*—adequately defines. It includes, perhaps more strictly, the self-restraint which refuses to make capital out of others' faults; the charity which delights not in exposing the weakness of others, but "covereth all things"; the sincerity of purpose which endeavors to see things as they are, and rejoices to find them better than suspicion feared or calumny denounced.

So much for the analysis of Love. Now the business of our lives is to have these things fitted into our characters. That is the supreme work to which we need to address ourselves in this world, to learn Love. Is life not full of opportunities for learning Love? Every man and woman every day has a thousand of them. The world is not a playground; it is a schoolroom. Life is not a holiday, but an education. And THE ONE ETERNAL LESSON for us all is *how better we can love.*

What makes a man a good cricketer? Practice. What makes a man a good artist, a good sculptor, a good musician? Practice. What makes a man a good linguist, a good stenographer? Practice. What makes a man a good man? Practice. Nothing else. There is nothing capricious about religion. We do not get the soul in different ways, under different laws, from those in which we get the body and the mind. If a man does not exercise his arm he develops no biceps muscle; and if a man does not exercise his soul, he acquires no muscle in his soul, no strength of character, no vigor of moral fibre, no beauty of spiritual growth. Love is not a thing of enthusiastic emotion. It is a rich, strong, manly, vigorous expression of the whole round Christian character—the Christlike nature in its fullest development. And the constituents of this great character are only to be built up by CEASELESS PRACTICE.

What was Christ doing in the carpenter's shop? Practising. Though perfect, we read that He *learned* obedience, and grew in wisdom and in favor with God. Do not quarrel, therefore, with your lot in life. Do not complain of its never-ceasing cares, its petty environment, the vexations you have to stand, the small and sordid souls you have to live and work with. Above all, do not resent temptation; do not be perplexed because it seems to thicken round you more and more, and ceases neither for effort nor for agony nor prayer. That is your practice. That is the practice which God appoints you; and it is having its work in making you patient, and humble, and generous, and unselfish, and kind, and courteous. Do not grudge the hand that is moulding the still too shapeless image within you. It is growing more beautiful, though you see it not; and every touch of temptation may add to its perfection. Therefore keep in the midst of life. Do not isolate yourself. Be among men and among things, and among troubles, and difficulties, and obstacles. You remember Goethe's words: "Talent develops itself in solitude; character in the stream of life." Talent develops itself in solitude—the talent of prayer, of faith, of meditation, of seeing the unseen; character grows in the stream of the world's life. That chiefly is where men are to learn love.

How? Now, how? To make it easier, I have named a few of the elements of love. But these are only elements. Love itself can never be defined. Light is a something more than the sum of its ingredients—a glowing, dazzling, tremulous ether. And love is something more than all its elements—a palpitating, quivering, sensitive, living thing. By synthesis of all the colors, men can make whiteness, they cannot make light. By synthesis of all the virtues, men can make virtue, they cannot make love. How then are we to have this transcendent living whole conveyed into our souls? We brace our wills to secure it. We try to copy those who have it. We lay down rules about it. We watch. We pray. But these things alone will not bring love into our nature. Love is an *effect*. And only as we fulfill the right condition can we have the effect produced. Shall I tell you what the *cause* is?

If you turn to the Revised Version of the First Epistle of John you find these words: "We love because He first loved us." "We love," not "We love *Him*." That is the way the old version has it, and it is quite wrong. "*We love*—because He first loved us." Look at that word "because." It is the *cause* of which I have spoken. "*Because* He first loved us," the effect follows that we love, we love Him, we love all men. We cannot help it. Because He loved us, we love, we love everybody. Our heart is slowly changed. Contemplate the love of Christ, and you will love. Stand before that mirror, reflect Christ's character, and you will be changed into the same image from tenderness to tenderness. There is no other way. You cannot love to order. You can only look at the lovely object, and fall in love with it, and grow into likeness to it. And so look at this Perfect Character, this Perfect Life. Look at THE GREAT SACRIFICE as He laid down Himself, all through life, and upon the Cross of Calvary; and you must love Him. And loving Him, you must become like Him. Love begets love. It is a process of induction. Put a piece of iron in the presence of an electrified body, and that piece of iron for a time becomes electrified. It is changed into a temporary magnet in the mere presence of a permanent magnet, and as long as you leave the two side by side, they are both magnets alike. Remain side by side with Him who loved us, and GAVE HIMSELF FOR US, and you, too, will become a permanent magnet, a permanently attractive force; and like Him you will draw all men unto you, like Him you will be drawn unto all men. That is the inevitable effect of Love. Any man who fulfills that cause must have that effect produced in him.

Try to give up the idea that religion comes to us by chance, or by mystery, or by caprice. It comes to us by natural law, or by supernatural law, for all law is Divine.

Edward Irving went to see a dying boy once, and when he entered the room he just put his hand on the sufferer's head, and said, "My boy, God loves you," and went away. The boy started from his bed, and called out to the people in the house, "God loves me! God loves me!" One word! It changed that boy. The sense that God loved him overpowered him, melted him down, and began the creating of a new heart in him. And that is how the love of God melts down the unlovely heart in man, and begets in him the new creature, who is patient and humble and gentle and unselfish. And there is no other way to get it. There is no mystery about it. We love others, we love everybody, we love our enemies, *because He first loved us.*

III. THE DEFENCE.

Now I have a closing sentence or two to add about Paul's reason for singling out love as the supreme possession.

It is a very remarkable reason. In a single word it is this: *it lasts.* "Love," urges Paul, "never faileth." Then he begins again one of his marvelous lists of the great things of the day, and exposes them one by one. He runs over the things that men thought were going to last, and shows that they are all fleeting, temporary, passing away.

"Whether there be *prophecies*, they shall be done away." It was the mother's ambition for her boy in those days that he should become a prophet. For hundreds of years God had never spoken by means of any prophet, and at that time the prophet was greater than the king. Men waited wistfully for another messenger to come, and hung upon his lips when he appeared, as upon the very voice of God. Paul says, "Whether there be prophecies, they shall fail." The Bible is full of prophecies. One by one they have "failed"; that is, having been fulfilled, their work is finished; they have nothing more to do now in the world except to feed a devout man's faith.

Then Paul talks about *tongues*. That was another thing that was greatly coveted. "Whether there be tongues, they shall cease." As we all know, many many centuries have passed since tongues have been known in this world. They have ceased. Take it in any sense you like. Take it, for illustration merely, as languages in general—a sense which was not in Paul's mind at all, and which though it cannot give us the specific lesson, will point the general truth. Consider the words in which these chapters were written—Greek. It has gone. Take the Latin—the other great tongue of those days. It ceased long ago. Look at the Indian language. It is ceasing. The language of Wales, of Ireland, of the Scottish Highlands is dying before our eyes. The most popular book in the English tongue at the present time, except the Bible, is one of Dickens' works, his *Pickwick Papers*. It is largely written in the language of London street-life; and experts assure us that in fifty years it will be unintelligible to the average English reader.

Then Paul goes farther, and with even greater boldness adds, "Whether there be *knowledge*, it shall be done away." The wisdom of the ancients, where is it? It is wholly gone. A schoolboy to-day knows more than Sir Isaac Newton knew; his knowledge has vanished away. You put yesterday's newspaper in the fire: its knowledge has vanished away. You buy the old editions of the great encyclopædias for a few cents: their knowledge has vanished away. Look how the coach has been superseded by the use of steam. Look how electricity has superseded that, and swept a hundred almost new inventions into oblivion. One of the greatest living authorities, Sir William Thompson, said in Scotland, at a meeting at which I was present, "The steam-engine is passing away." "Whether there be knowledge, it shall vanish away." At every workshop you will see, in the back yard, a heap of old iron, a few wheels, a few levers, a few cranks, broken and eaten with rust. Twenty years ago that was the pride of the city. Men flocked in from the country to see the great invention; now it is superseded, its day is done. And all the boasted science and philosophy of this day will soon be old.

In my time, in the university of Edinburgh, the greatest figure in the faculty was Sir James Simpson, the discoverer of chloroform.

Recently his successor and nephew, Professor Simpson, was asked by the librarian of the University to go to the library and pick out the books on his subject (midwifery) that were no longer needed. His reply to the librarian was this:

"Take every text-book that is more than ten years old and put it down in the cellar."

Sir James Simpson was a great authority only a few years ago: men came from all parts of the earth to consult him; and almost the whole teaching of that time is consigned by the science of to-day to oblivion. And in every branch of science it is the same. "Now we know in part. We see through a glass darkly." Knowledge does not last.

Can you tell me anything that is going to last? Many things Paul did not condescend to name. He did not mention money, fortune, fame; but he picked out the great things of his time, the things the best men thought had something in them, and brushed them peremptorily aside. Paul had no charge against these things in themselves. All he said about them was that they would not last. They were great things, but not supreme things. There were things beyond them. What we are stretches past what we do, beyond what we possess. Many things that men denounce as sins are not sins; but they are temporary. And that is a favorite argument of the New Testament. John says of the world, not that it is wrong, but simply that it "passeth away." There is a great deal in the world that is delightful and beautiful; there is a great deal in it that is great and engrossing; but IT WILL NOT LAST.

All that is in the world, the lust of the eye, the lust of the flesh, and the pride of life, are but for a little while. Love not the world therefore. Nothing that it contains is worth the life and consecration of an immortal soul. The immortal soul must give itself to something that is immortal. And the only immortal things are these: "Now abideth faith, hope, love, but the greatest of these is love."

Some think the time may come when two of these three things will also pass away—faith into sight, hope into fruition. Paul does not say so. We know but little now about the conditions of the life that is to come. But what is certain is that Love must last. God, the Eternal God, is Love. Covet, therefore, that everlasting gift, that one thing which it is certain is going to stand, that one coinage which will be current in the Universe when all the other coinages of all the nations of the world shall be useless and unhonored. You will give yourselves to many things, give yourself first to Love. Hold things in their proportion. *Hold things in their proportion.* Let at least the first great object of our lives be to achieve the character defended in these words, the character—and it is the character of Christ—which is built round Love.

I have said this thing is eternal. Did you ever notice how continually John associates love and faith with eternal life? I was not told when I was a boy that "God so loved the world that He gave His only-begotten Son, that whosoever believeth in Him should have everlasting life." What I was told, I remember, was, that God so loved the world that, if I trusted in Him, I was to have a thing called peace, or I was to have rest, or I was to have joy, or I was to have safety. But I had to find out for myself that whosoever trusteth in Him—that is, whosoever loveth Him, for trust is only the avenue to Love—hath EVERLASTING LIFE. The Gospel offers a man a life. Never offer a man a thimbleful of Gospel. Do not offer them merely joy, or merely peace, or merely rest, or merely safety; tell them how Christ came to give men a more abundant life than they have, a life abundant in love, and therefore abundant in salvation for themselves, and large in enterprise for the alleviation and redemption of the world. Then only can the Gospel take hold of the whole of a man, body, soul and spirit, and give to each part of his nature its exercise and reward. Many of the current Gospels are addressed only to a part of man's nature. They offer peace, not life; faith, not Love; justification, not regeneration. And men slip back again from such religion because it has never really held them. Their nature was not all in it. It offered no deeper and gladder life-current than the life that was lived before. Surely it stands to reason that only a fuller love can compete with the love of the world.

To love abundantly is to live abundantly, and to love forever is to live forever. Hence, eternal life is inextricably bound up with love. We want to live forever for the same reason that we want to live to-morrow. Why do we want to live to-morrow? Is it because there is some one who loves you, and whom you want to see to-morrow, and be with, and love back? There is no other reason why we should live on than that we love and are beloved. It is when a man has no one to love him that he commits suicide. So long as he has friends, those who love him and whom he loves, he will live, because to live is to love. Be it but the love of a dog, it will keep him in life; but let that go, he has no contact with life, no reason to live. He dies by his own hand.

Eternal life also is to know God, and God is love. This is Christ's own definition. Ponder it. "This is life eternal, that they might know Thee the only true God, and Jesus Christ whom Thou hast sent." Love must be eternal. It is what God is. On the last analysis, then, love is life. Love never faileth, and life never faileth, so long as there is love. That is the philosophy of what Paul is showing us; the reason why in the nature of things Love should be the supreme thing—because it is going to last; because in the nature of things it is an Eternal Life. It is a thing that we are living now, not that we get when we die; that we shall have a poor chance of getting when we die unless we are living now. NO WORSE FATE can befall a man in this world than to live and grow old alone, unloving and unloved. To be lost is to live in an unregenerate condition, loveless and unloved; and to be saved is to love; and he that dwelleth in love dwelleth already in God. For God is Love.

Now I have all but finished. How many of you will join me in reading this chapter once a week for the next three months? A man did that once and it changed his whole life. Will you do it? It is for the greatest thing in the world. You might begin by reading it every day, especially the verses which describe the perfect character. "Love suffereth long, and is kind; love envieth not; love vaunteth not itself." Get these ingredients into your life. Then everything that you do is eternal. It is worth doing. It is worth giving time to. No man can become a saint in his sleep; and to fulfill the condition required demands a certain amount of prayer and meditation and time, just as improvement in any direction, bodily or mental, requires preparation and care. Address yourselves to that one thing; at any cost have this transcendent character exchanged for yours.

You will find as you look back upon your life that the moments that stand out, the moments when you have really lived, are the moments when you have done things in a spirit of love. As memory scans the past, above and beyond all the transitory pleasures of life, there leap forward those supreme hours when you have been enabled to do unnoticed kindnesses to those round about you, things too trifling to speak about, but which you feel have entered into your eternal life. I have seen almost all the beautiful things God has made; I have enjoyed almost every pleasure that He has planned for man; and yet as I look back I see standing out above all the life that has gone four or five short experiences, when the love of God reflected itself in some poor imitation, some small act of love of mine, and these seem to be the things which alone of all one's life abide. Everything else in all our lives is transitory. Every other good is visionary. But the acts of love which no man knows about, or can ever know about—they never fail.

In the Book of Matthew, where the Judgment Day is depicted for us in the imagery of One seated upon a throne and dividing the sheep from the goats, the test of a man then is not, "How have I believed?" but "How have I loved?" The test of religion, the final test of religion, is not religiousness, but Love. I say the final test of religion at that great Day is not religiousness, but Love; not what I have done, not what I have believed, not what I have achieved, but how I have discharged the common charities of life. Sins of commission in that awful indictment are not even referred to. By what we have not done, *by sins of omission*, we are judged. It could not be otherwise. For the withholding of love is the negation of the spirit of Christ, the proof that we never knew Him, that for us He lived in vain. It means that He suggested nothing in all our thoughts, that He inspired nothing in all our lives, that we were not once near enough to Him, to be seized with the spell of His compassion for the world. It means that—

> *"I lived for myself, I thought for myself,*
> *For myself, and none beside—*
> *Just as if Jesus had never lived,*
> *As if He had never died."*

Thank God the Christianity of today is coming nearer the world's need. Live to help that on. Thank God men know better, by a hair's breadth, what religion is, what God is, who Christ is, where Christ is. Who is Christ? He who fed the hungry, clothed the naked, visited the sick. And where is Christ? Where?—"Whoso shall receive a little child in My name receiveth Me." And who are Christ's? "Every one that loveth is born of God."

Lessons from the Angelus

God often speaks to men's souls through music; He also speaks to us through art. Millet's famous painting entitled "The Angelus" is an illuminated text, upon which I am going to say a few words to you to-night.

There are three things in this picture—a potato field, a country lad and a country girl standing in the middle of it, and on the far horizon the spire of a village church. That is all there is to it—no great scenery and no picturesque people. In Roman Catholic countries at the evening hour the church bell rings out to remind the people to pray. Some go into the church, while those that are in the fields bow their heads for a few moments in silent prayer.

That picture contains the three great elements which go to make up a perfectly rounded Christian life. It is not enough to have the "root of the matter" in us, but that we must be whole and entire, lacking nothing. The Angelus may bring to us suggestions as to what constitutes a complete life.

I.

The first element in a symmetrical life is *work*.

Three-fourths of our time is probably spent in work. Of course the meaning of it is that our work should be just as religious as our worship, and unless we can work for the glory of God three-fourths of life remains unsanctified.

The proof that work is religious is that most of Christ's life was spent in work. During a large part of the first thirty years of His life He worked with the hammer and the plane, making ploughs and yokes and household furniture. Christ's public ministry occupied only about two and a half years of His earthly life; the great bulk of His time was simply spent in doing common everyday tasks, and ever since then work has had a new meaning.

When Christ came into the world He was revealed to three deputations who went to meet and worship Him. First came the shepherds, or working class; second, the wise men, or student class; and third, the two old people in the temple, Simeon and Anna; that is to say, Christ is revealed to men at their work, He is revealed to men at their books, and He is revealed to men at their worship. It was the old people who found Christ at their worship, and as we grow older we will spend more time exclusively in worship than we are able to do now. In the mean time we must combine our worship with our work, and we may expect to find Christ at our books and in our common task.

Why should God have provided that so many hours of every day should be occupied with work? It is because WORK MAKES MEN.

A university is not merely a place for making scholars, it is a place for making Christians. A farm is not a place for growing corn, it is a place for growing character, and a man has no character except that which is developed by his life and thought. God's Spirit does the building through the acts which a man performs from day to day. A student who cons out every word in his Latin and Greek instead of consulting a translation finds that honesty is translated into his character. If he works out his mathematical problems thoroughly, he not only becomes a mathematician, but becomes a thorough man. It is by constant and conscientious attention to daily duties that thoroughness and conscientiousness and honorableness are imbedded in our beings. Character is THE MUSIC OF THE SOUL, and is developed by exercise. Active use of the power entrusted to us is one of the chief means which God employs for producing the Christian graces. Hence the religion of a student demands that he be true to his work, and that he let his Christianity be shown to his fellow students and to his professors by the integrity and the conscientiousness of his academic life. A man who is not faithful in that which is least will not be faithful in that which is great. I have known men who struggled unsuccessfully for years to pass their examinations who, when they became Christians, found a new motive for work and thus were able to succeed where previously they had failed. A man's Christianity comes out as much in his work as in his worship.

Our work is not only to be done thoroughly, but it is to be done honestly. A man is not only to be honorable in his academic relations, but he must be honest with himself and in his attitude toward the truth. Students are not entitled to dodge difficulties, they must go down to the foundation principles. Perhaps the truths which are dear to us go down deeper even than we think, and we will get more out of them if we dig down for the nuggets than we will if we only pick up those that are on the surface. Other theories may perhaps be found to have false bases; if so, we ought to know it. It is well to take our soundings in every direction to see if there is deep water; if there are shoals we ought to find out where they are. Therefore, when we come to difficulties, let us not jump lightly over them, but let us be honest as seekers after truth.

It may not be necessary for people in general to sift the doctrines of Christianity for themselves, but a student is a man whose business it is to think, to exercise the intellect which God has given him in finding out the truth. Faith is never opposed to reason, though it is sometimes supposed by Bible teachers that it is; but you will find it is not. Faith is opposed to sight, but not to reason, though it is not limited to reason. In employing his intellect in the search for truth a student is drawing nearer to the Christ who said, "I am the way, the truth and the life." We talk a great deal about Christ as the way and Christ as the life, but there is a side of Christ especially for the student: "I am the truth," and every student ought to be a truth-lover and a truth-seeker for Christ's sake.

II.

Another element in life, which of course is first in importance, is *God*.

The Angelus is perhaps the most religious picture painted this century. You cannot look at it and see that young man standing in the field with his hat off, and the girl opposite him with her hands clasped and her head bowed on her breast, without feeling a sense of God.

Do we carry about with us the thought of God wherever we go? If not, we have missed the greatest part of life. Do we have a conviction of God's abiding presence wherever we are? There is nothing more needed in this generation than a larger and more Scriptural idea of God. A great American writer has told us that when he was a boy the conception of God which he got from books and sermons was that of a wise and very strict lawyer. I remember well the awful conception of God which I had when a boy. I was given an illustrated edition of Watts' hymns, in which God was represented as a great piercing eye in the midst of a great black thunder cloud. The idea which that picture gave to my young imagination was that of God as a great detective, playing the spy upon my actions, as the hymn says: "Writing now the story of what little children do."

That was a very mistaken and harmful idea which it has taken me years to obliterate. We think of God as "up there," or as one who made the world six thousand years ago and then retired. We must learn that He is not confined either to time or space. God is not to be thought of as merely back there in time, or up there in space. If not, where is He? "The word is nigh thee, even in thy mouth." The Kingdom of God is within you, and God Himself is among men. When are we to exchange the terrible, far-away, absentee God of our childhood for the everywhere present God of the Bible? Too many of the old Christian writers seem to have conceived of God as not much more than the greatest man—a kind of divine emperor. He is infinitely more; He is a spirit, as Jesus said to the woman at the well, and in Him we live and move and have our being. Let us think of God as Immanuel—God with us—an ever-present, omnipresent, eternal One. Long, long ago, God made matter, then He made the flowers and trees and animals, then He made man. Did He stop? Is God dead? If He lives and acts what is He doing? He is MAKING MEN BETTER. He it is that "worketh in you." The buds of our nature are not all out yet; the sap to make them comes from the God who made us, from the indwelling Christ. Our bodies are the temples of the Holy Ghost, and we must bear this in mind, because the sense of God is kept up, not by logic, but by experience.

Until she was seven years of age the life of Helen Keller, the Boston girl who was deaf and dumb and blind, was an absolute blank; nothing could go into that mind because the ears and eyes were closed to the outer world. Then by that great process which has been discovered, by which the blind see, and the deaf hear, and the mute speak, that girl's soul became opened, and they began to put in little bits of knowledge, and bit by bit they began to educate her. They reserved her religious instruction for Phillips Brooks. After some years, when she was twelve years old, they took her to him and he began to talk to her through the young lady who had been the means of opening her senses, and who could communicate with her by the exceedingly delicate process of touch. He began to tell her about God and what He had done, and how He loved men, and what He is to us. The child listened very intelligently, and finally said:

"Mr. Brooks, I knew all that before, but I didn't know His name."

How often we have felt something within us impelling us to do something which we would not have conceived of by ourselves, or enabling us to do something which we could not have done alone. "It is God which worketh in you." This great simple fact EXPLAINS MANY OF THE MYSTERIES OF LIFE, and takes away the fear which we would otherwise have in meeting the difficulties which lie before us.

Two Americans who were crossing the Atlantic met on Sunday night to sing hymns in the cabin. As they sang the hymn, "Jesus, Lover of my Soul," one of the Americans heard an exceedingly rich and beautiful voice behind him. He looked around, and although he did not know the face he thought that he recognized the voice.

So when the music ceased he turned around and asked the man if he had not been in the Civil war. The man replied that he had been a Confederate soldier. "Were you at such a place on such a night?" asked the first. "Yes," he said, "and a curious thing happened that night; this hymn recalled it to my mind. I was on sentry duty on the edge of a wood. It was a dark night and very cold, and I was a little frightened because the enemy were supposed to be very near at hand. I felt very homesick and miserable, and about midnight, when everything was very still, I was beginning to feel very weary and thought that I would comfort myself by praying and singing a hymn. I remember singing this hymn,

'All my trust on Thee is stayed,
All my help from Thee I bring,
Cover my defenceless head
With the shadow of Thy wing.'

After I had sung those words a strange peace came down upon me, and through the long night I remember having felt no more fear."

"Now," said the other man, "listen to my story. I was a Union soldier, and was in the wood that night with a party of scouts. I saw you standing up, although I didn't see your face, and my men had their rifles focused upon you waiting the word to fire, but when you sang out,

'Cover my defenceless head
With the shadow of Thy wing,'

I said, 'Boys, put down your rifles, we will go home.' I couldn't kill you after that."

God was working in each of them, in His own way carrying out His will. God keeps his people and guides them and without Him life is but a living death.

III.

The third element in life about which I wish to speak is *love*.

In this picture we notice the delicate sense of companionship, brought out by the young man and the young woman. It matters not whether they are brother and sister, or lover and loved; there you have the idea of friendship, the final ingredient in our life, after the two I have named. If the man or the woman had been standing in that field alone it would have been incomplete.

Love is the divine element in life, because "God is love." "He that loveth is born of God," therefore, as some one has said, let us "keep our friendships in repair." Let us cultivate the spirit of friendship, and let the love of Christ develop it into a great love, not only for our friends, but for all humanity. Wherever you go and whatever you do, your work will be a failure unless you have this element in your life.

These three things go far toward forming a well-rounded life. Some of us may not have these ingredients in their right proportion, but if you are lacking in one or the other of them, then pray for it and work for it that your life may be rounded and complete as God intended it should be.

Pax Vobiscum*

I once heard a sermon by a distinguished preacher upon "Rest." It was full of beautiful thoughts; but when I came to ask myself, "How does he say I can get Rest?" there was no answer. The sermon was sincerely meant to be practical, yet it contained no experience that seemed to me to be tangible, nor any advice that I could grasp—any advice, that is to say, which could help me to find the thing itself as I went about the world.

Yet this omission of what is, after all, the only important problem, was not the fault of the preacher. The whole popular religion is in the twilight here. And when pressed for really working specifics for the experiences with which it deals, it falters, and seems to lose itself in mist.

The want of connection between the great words of religion and every-day life has bewildered and discouraged all of us. Christianity possesses the noblest words in the language; its literature overflows with terms expressive of the greatest and happiest moods

---

* Copyright, James Pott & Co. Used by permission.

which can fill the soul of man. Rest, Joy, Peace, Faith, Love, Light—these words occur with such persistency in hymns and prayers that an observer might think they formed the staple of Christian experience. But on coming to close quarters with the actual life of most of us, how surely would he be disenchanted. I do not think we ourselves are aware how much our religious life is MADE UP OF PHRASES; how much of what we call Christian Experience is only a dialect of the Churches, a mere religious phraseology with almost nothing behind it in what we really feel and know.

To some of us, indeed, the Christian experiences seem further away than when we took the first steps in the Christian life. That life has not opened out as we had hoped. We do not regret our religion, but we are disappointed with it. There are times, perhaps, when wandering notes from a diviner music stray into our spirits; but these experiences come at few and fitful moments. We have no sense of possession in them. When they visit us, it is a surprise. When they leave us, it is without explanation. When we wish their return, we do not know how to secure it.

All which means a religion without solid base, and a poor and flickering life. It means a great bankruptcy in those experiences which give Christianity its personal solace and make it attractive to the world, and a great uncertainty as to any remedy. It is as if we knew everything about health—except the way to get it.

I am quite sure that the difficulty does not lie in the fact that men are not in earnest. This is simply not the fact. All around us Christians are wearing themselves out in trying to be better. The amount of spiritual longing in the world—in the hearts of unnumbered thousands of men and women in whom we should never suspect it; among the wise and thoughtful, among the young and gay, who seldom assuage and never betray their thirst—this is one of the most wonderful and touching facts of life. It is not more heat that is needed, but more light; not more force, but a wiser direction to be given to very real energies already there.

The usual advice when one asks for counsel on these questions is, "Pray." But this advice is far from adequate. I shall qualify the statement presently; but let me urge it here, with what you will perhaps call daring emphasis, that to pray for these things is not the way to get them. No one will get them without praying; but that men do not get them by praying is the simple fact. We have all prayed, and sincerely prayed, for such experiences as I have named; prayed, believing that that was the way to get them. And yet have we got them? The test is experience. I dare not limit prayer; still less the grace of God. If you have got them in this way, it is well. I am speaking to those, be they few or many, who have not got them; to ordinary men in ordinary circumstances. But if we have not got them, it by no means follows that prayer is useless. The correct conclusion is only that it is useless, or inadequate rather, for this particular purpose. To make prayer the sole resort, the universal panacea for every spiritual ill, is as radical a mistake as to prescribe only one medicine for every bodily trouble. The physician who does the last is a quack; the spiritual adviser who does the first is GROSSLY IGNORANT OF HIS PROFESSION. To do nothing but pray is a wrong done to prayer itself, and can only end in disaster. It is as if one tried to live only with the lungs, as if one assimilated only air and neglected solid food. The lungs are a first essential; the air is a first essential; but the body has many members, given for different purposes, secreting different things, and each has a method of nutrition as special to itself as its own activity. While prayer, then, is the characteristic sublimity of the Christian life, it is by no means the only one. And those who make it the sole alternative, and apply it to purposes for which it was never meant, are really doing the greatest harm to prayer itself. To couple the word "inadequate" with this mighty word is not to dethrone prayer, but to exalt it. WHAT DETHRONES PRAYER is unanswered prayer. When men pray for things which do not come that way—pray with sincere belief that prayer, unaided and alone, will compass what they ask—then, not getting what they ask, they often give up prayer.

This is the natural history of much atheism, not only an atheism of atheists, but a more terrible atheism of Christians, an unconscious atheism, whose roots have struck far into many souls whose last breath would be spent in denying it. So, I repeat, it is a mistaken Christianity which allow men to cherish a blind belief in the omnipotence of prayer. Prayer, certainly, when the appropriate conditions are fulfilled, is omnipotent, but not blind prayer. Blind prayer is a superstition. Prayer, in its true sense, contains the sane recognition that while man prays in faith, *God acts by law*. What that means in the immediate connection we shall see presently.

What, then, is the remedy? It is impossible to doubt that there is a remedy, and it is equally impossible to believe that it is a secret. The idea that some few men, by happy chance or happier temperament, have been given the secret—as if there were some sort of knack or trick of it—is wholly incredible and wrong. Religion must be for all, and the way into its loftiest heights must be by a gateway through which the peoples of the world may pass.

I shall have to lead up to this gateway by a very familiar path. But as this path is strangely unfrequented where it passes into the religious sphere, I must ask your forbearance for dwelling for a moment upon the commonest of commonplaces.

I. EFFECTS REQUIRE CAUSES.

Nothing that happens in the world happens by chance. God is a God of order. Everything is arranged upon definite principles, and never at random. The world, even the religious world, is governed by law. Character is governed by law. Happiness is governed by law. The Christian experiences are governed by law. Men, forgetting this, expect Rest, Joy, Peace, Faith to drop into their souls from the air like snow or rain. But in point of fact they do not do so; and if they did, they would no less have their origin in previous activities and be controlled by natural laws. Rain and snow do drop from the air, but not without a long previous history. They are the mature effects of former causes. Equally so are Rest and Peace and Joy. They, too, have each a previous history. Storms and winds and calms are not accidents, but brought about by antecedent circumstances. Rest and Peace are but calms in man's inward nature, and arise through causes as definite and as inevitable.

Realize it thoroughly; it is a methodical, not an accidental world. If a housewife turns out a good cake, it is the result of a sound receipt, carefully applied. She cannot mix the assigned ingredients and fire them for the appropriate time without producing the result. It is not she who has made the cake; it is nature. She brings related things together; sets causes at work; these causes bring about the result. She is not a creator, but an intermediary. She does not expect random causes to produce specific effects—random ingredients would only produce random cakes. So it is in the making of Christian experiences. Certain lines are followed; certain effects are the result. These effects cannot but be the result. But the result can never take place without the previous cause. To expect results without antecedents is to expect cakes without ingredients. That impossibility is precisely the almost universal expectation.

Now what I mainly wish to do is to help you firmly to grasp this simple principle of Cause and Effect in the spiritual world. And instead of applying the principle generally to each of the Christian experiences in turn, I shall examine its application to one in some little detail. The one I shall select is Rest. And I think any one who follows the application in this single instance will be able to apply it for himself to all the others.

Take such a sentence as this: African explorers are subject to fevers which cause restlessness and delirium.

Note the expression, "cause restlessness." *Restlessness has a cause.* Clearly, then, any one who wished to get rid of restlessness would proceed at once to deal with the cause. If that were not removed, a doctor might prescribe a hundred things, and all might be taken in turn, without producing the least effect. Things are so arranged in the original planning of the world that certain effects must follow certain causes, and certain causes must be abolished before certain effects can be removed. Certain parts of Africa are inseparably linked with the physical experience called fever; this fever is in turn infallibly linked with a mental experience called restlessness and delirium. To abolish the mental experience the radical method would be to abolish the physical experience, and the way of abolishing the physical experience would be to abolish Africa, or to cease to go there.

Now this holds good for all other forms of Restlessness. Every other form and kind of Restlessness in the world has a definite cause, and the particular kind of Restlessness can only be removed by removing the allotted cause.

All this is also true of Rest. Restlessness has a cause: must not *Rest* have a cause? Necessarily. If it were a chance world we would not expect this; but, being a methodical world, it cannot be otherwise. Rest, physical rest, moral rest, spiritual rest, every kind of rest has a cause, as certainly as restlessness. Now causes are discriminating. There is one kind of cause for every particular effect and no other, and if one particular effect is desired, the corresponding cause must be set in motion. It is no use proposing finely devised schemes, or going through general pious exercises in the hope that somehow Rest will come. The Christian life is not casual, but causal. All nature is a standing protest against the absurdity of expecting to secure spiritual effects, or any effects, without the employment of appropriate causes. The Great Teacher dealt what ought to have been the final blow to this infinite irrelevancy by a single question, "Do men gather grapes of thorns or figs of thistles?"

Why, then, did the Great Teacher not educate His followers fully? Why did He not tell us, for example, how such a thing as Rest might be obtained? The answer is that *He did*. But plainly, explicitly, in so many words? Yes, plainly, explicitly, in so many words. He assigned Rest to its cause, in words with which each of us has been familiar from his earliest childhood.

He begins, you remember—for you at once know the passage I refer to—almost as if Rest could be had without any cause; "Come unto me," He says, "and I will *give* you Rest."

Rest, apparently, was a favor to be bestowed; men had but to come to Him; He would give it to every applicant. But the next sentence takes that all back. The qualification, indeed, is added instantaneously. For what the first sentence seemed to give was next thing to an impossibility. For how, in a literal sense, can Rest be *given*? One could no more give away Rest than he could give away Laughter. We speak of "causing" laughter, which we can do; but we can not give it away. When we speak of "giving" pain, we know perfectly well we can not give pain away. And when we aim at "giving" pleasure, all that we do is to arrange a set of circumstances in such a way as that these shall cause pleasure. Of course there is a sense, and a very wonderful sense, in which a Great Personality breathes upon all who come within its influence an abiding peace and trust. Men can be to other men as the shadow of a great rock in a weary land; much more Christ; much more Christ as Perfect Man; much more still as Savior of the world. But it is not this of which I speak. When Christ said He would give men Rest, He meant simply that He would put them in the way of it. By no act of conveyance would or could He make over His own Rest to them. He could give them HIS RECEIPT for it. That was all. But He would not make it for them. For one thing it was not in His plan to make it for them; for another thing, men were not so planned that it could be made for them; and for yet another thing, it was a thousand times better that they should make it for themselves.

That this is the meaning becomes obvious from the wording of the second sentence: "Learn of me, and ye shall *find* Rest." Rest, (that is to say), is not a thing that can be *given*, but a thing to be *acquired*. It comes not by an act, but by a process. It is not to be found in a happy hour, as one finds a treasure; but slowly, as one finds knowledge. It could indeed be no more found in a moment than could knowledge. A soil has to be prepared for it. Like a fine fruit, it will grow in one climate, and not in another; at one altitude, and not at another. Like all growth it will have an orderly development and mature by slow degrees.

The nature of this slow process Christ clearly defines when He says we are to achieve Rest by *learning*. "Learn of me," He says, "and ye shall find rest to your souls."

Now consider the extraordinary ORIGINALITY OF THIS UTTERANCE.

How novel the connection between these two words "Learn" and "Rest." How few of us have ever associated them—ever thought that Rest was a thing to be learned; ever laid ourselves out for it as we would to learn a language; ever practised it as we would practice the violin? Does it not show how entirely new Christ's teaching still is to the world, that so old and threadbare an aphorism should still be so little known? The last thing most of us would have thought of would have been to associate *Rest* with *Work*.

What must one work at? What is that which if duly learned will find the soul of man in Rest? Christ answers without the least hesitation. He specifies two things—Meekness and Lowliness. "Learn of me," He says, "for I am *meek* and *lowly* in heart."

Now these two things are not chosen at random. To these accomplishments, in a special way, Rest is attached. Learn these, in short, and you have already found Rest. These as they stand are direct causes of Rest; will produce it at once; cannot but produce it at once. And if you think for a single moment, you will see how this is necessarily so, for causes are never arbitrary, and the connection between antecedent and consequent here and everywhere lies deep in the nature of things.

What is the connection, then? I answer by a further question. WHAT ARE THE CHIEF CAUSES OF UNREST? If you know yourself, you will answer—Pride; Selfishness, Ambition. As you look back upon the past years of your life, is it not true that its unhappiness has chiefly come from the succession of personal mortifications and almost trivial disappointments which the intercourse of life has brought you? Great trials come at lengthened intervals, and we rise to breast them; but it is the petty friction of our every-day life with one another, the jar of business or of work, the discord of the domestic circle, the collapse of our ambition, the crossing of our will or the taking down of our conceit, which make inward peace impossible. Wounded vanity, then, disappointed hopes, unsatisfied selfishness—these are the old, vulgar, universal SOURCES OF MAN'S UNREST.

Now it is obvious why Christ pointed out as the two chief objects for attainment the exact opposites of these. To meekness and lowliness these things simply do not exist. They cure unrest by making it impossible. These remedies do not trifle with surface symptoms; they strike at once at removing causes. The ceaseless chagrin of a self-centered life can be removed at once by learning meekness and lowliness of heart. He who learns them is forever proof against it. He lives henceforth a charmed life. Christianity is a fine inoculation, a transfusion of healthy blood into an anæmic or poisoned soul. No fever can attack a perfectly sound body; no fever of unrest can disturb a soul which has breathed the air or learned the ways of Christ.

Men sigh for the wings of a dove that they may fly away and be at Rest. But flying away will not help us. "The Kingdom of God is *within you*." We aspire to the top to look for Rest; it lies at the bottom. Water rests only when it gets to the lowest place. So do men. Hence, *be lowly*. The man who has no opinion of himself at all can never be hurt if others do not acknowledge him. Hence, *be meek*. He who is without expectation cannot fret if nothing comes to him. It is self-evident that these things are so. The lowly man and the meek man are really above all other men, above all other things.

They dominate the world because they do not care for it. The miser does not possess gold, gold possesses him. But the meek possess it. "The meek," said Christ, "inherit the earth." They do not buy it; they do not conquer it; but they inherit it.

There are people who go about the world looking out for slights, and they are necessarily miserable, for they find them at every turn—especially the imaginary ones. One has the same pity for such men as for the very poor. They are the morally illiterate. They have had no real education, for they have never learned HOW TO LIVE. Few men know how to live. We grow up at random carrying into mature life the merely animal methods and motives which we had as little children. And it does not occur to us that all this must be changed; that much of it must be reversed; that life is the finest of the Fine Arts; that it has to be learned with lifelong patience, and that the years of our pilgrimage are all too short to master it triumphantly.

Yet this is what Christianity is for—to teach men THE ART OF LIFE. And its whole curriculum lies in one word—"Learn of me." Unlike most education, this is almost purely personal; it is not to be had from books, or lectures or creeds or doctrines. It is a study from the life. Christ never said much in mere words about the Christian graces. He lived them, He was them. Yet we do not merely copy Him. We learn His art by living with Him, like the old apprentices with their masters.

Now we understand it all? Christ's invitation to the weary and heavy-laden is a call to begin life over again upon a new principle—upon His own principle. "Watch my way of doing things," He says; "Follow me. Take life as I take it. Be meek and lowly, and you will find Rest."

I do not say, remember, that the Christian life to every man, or to any man, can be a bed of roses. No educational process can be this. And perhaps if some men knew how much was involved in the simple "learn" of Christ, they would not enter His school with so irresponsible a heart. For there is not only much to learn, but MUCH TO UNLEARN. Many men never go to this school at all till their disposition is already half ruined and character has taken on its fatal set. To learn arithmetic is difficult at fifty—much more to learn Christianity. To learn simply what it is to be meek and lowly, in the case of one who has had no lessons in that in childhood, may cost him half of what he values most on earth. Do we realize, for instance, that the way of teaching humility is generally by *humiliation*? There is probably no other school for it. When a man enters himself as a pupil in such a school it means a very great thing. There is much Rest there, but there is also much Work.

I should be wrong, even though my theme is the brighter side, to ignore the cross and minimize the cost. Only it gives to the cross a more definite meaning, and a rarer value, to connect it thus directly and casually with the growth of the inner life. Our platitudes on the "benefits of affliction" are usually about as vague as our theories of Christian Experience. "Somehow" we believe affliction does us good. But it is not a question of "Somehow." The result is definite, calculable, necessary. It is under the strictest law of cause and effect. The first effect of losing one's fortune, for instance, is humiliation; and the effect of humiliation, as we have just seen, is to make one humble; and the effect of being humble is to produce Rest. It is a roundabout way, apparently, of producing Rest; but Nature generally works by circular processes; and it is not certain that there is any other way of becoming humble, or of finding Rest. If a man could make himself humble to order, it might simplify matters; but we do not find that this happens. Hence we must all go through the mill. Hence death, death to the lower self, is the nearest gate and the quickest road to life.

Yet this is only half the truth. Christ's life outwardly was one of the most troubled lives that was ever lived: tempest and tumult, tumult and tempest, the waves breaking over it all the time till the worn body was laid in the grave. But the inner life was a sea of glass. The great calm was always there. At any moment you might have gone to Him and found Rest. Even when the blood-hounds were dogging Him in the streets of Jerusalem, He turned to His disciples and offered them, as a last legacy, "My peace." Nothing ever for a moment broke the serenity of Christ's life on earth. Misfortune could not reach Him; He had no fortune. Food, raiment, money—fountain-heads of half the world's weariness—He simply did not care for; they played no part in His life; He "took no thought" for them. It was impossible to affect Him by lowering His reputation. He had already made Himself of no reputation. He was dumb before insult. When he was reviled, He reviled not again. In fact, there was NOTHING THAT THE WORLD COULD DO TO HIM that could ruffle the surface of His spirit.

Such living, as mere living, is altogether unique. It is only when we see what it was in Him that we can know what the word Rest means. It lies not in emotions, or in the absence of emotions. It is not a hallowed feeling that comes over us in church. It is not something that the preacher has in his voice. It is not in nature, or in poetry, or in music—though in all these there is soothing. It is the mind at leisure from itself. It is the perfect poise of the soul; the absolute adjustment of the inward man to the stress of all outward things; the preparedness against every emergency; the stability of assured convictions; the eternal calm of an invulnerable faith; the repose of a heart set deep in God. It is the mood of the man who says, with Browning, "God's in His Heaven, all's well with the world."

Two painters each painted a picture to illustrate his conception of rest. The first chose for his scene a still, lone lake among the far-off mountains. The second threw on his canvas a thundering waterfall, with a fragile birch-tree bending over the foam; at the fork of a branch, almost wet with the cataract's spray, a robin sat on its nest. The first was only *Stagnation*; the last was *Rest*. For in Rest there are always two elements—tranquillity and energy; silence and turbulence; creation and destruction; fearlessness and fearfulness. This it was in Christ.

It is quite plain from all this that whatever else He claimed to be or to do, He at least KNEW HOW TO LIVE. All this is the perfection of living, of living in the mere sense of passing through the world in the best way. Hence His anxiety to communicate His idea of life to others. He came, He said, to give men life, true life, a more abundant life than they were living; "the life," as the fine phase in the Revised Version has it, "that is life indeed." This is what He Himself possessed, and it was this which He offers to mankind. And hence His direct appeal for all to come to Him who had not made much of life, who were weary and heavy-laden. These He would teach His secret. They, also, should know "the life that is life indeed."

II. WHAT YOKES ARE FOR.

There is still one doubt to clear up. After the statement, "Learn of Me," Christ throws in the disconcerting qualification:

"*Take my yoke* upon you, and learn of Me."

Why, if all this be true, does He call it a *yoke*? Why, while professing to give Rest, does He with the next breath whisper "*burden*"? Is the Christian life, after all, what its enemies take it for—an additional weight to the already great woe of life, some extra punctiliousness about duty, some painful devotion to observances, some heavy restriction and trammeling of all that is joyous and free in the world? Is life not hard and sorrowful enough without being fettered with yet another yoke?

It is astounding how so glaring a misunderstanding of this plain sentence should ever have passed into currency. Did you ever stop to ask what a yoke is really for? Is it to be a burden to the animal which wears it? It is just the opposite. It is to make its burden light. Attached to the oxen in any other way than by a yoke, the plough would be intolerable. Worked by means of a yoke, it is light. A yoke is not an instrument of torture; it is AN INSTRUMENT OF MERCY.

It is not a malicious contrivance for making work hard; it is a gentle device to make hard labor light. It is not meant to give pain, but to save pain. And yet men speak of the yoke of Christ as if it were slavery, and look upon those who wear it as objects of compassion. For generations we have had homilies on "The Yoke of Christ"—some delighting in portraying its narrow exactions; some seeking in these exactions the marks of its divinity; others apologizing for it, and toning it down; still others assuring us that, although it be very bad, it is not to be compared with the positive blessings of Christianity. How many, especially among the young, has this one mistaken phrase driven forever away from the kingdom of God? Instead of making Christ attractive, it makes Him out a taskmaster, narrowing life by petty restrictions, calling for self-denial where none is necessary, making misery a virtue under the plea that it is the yoke of Christ, and happiness criminal because it now and then evades it. According to this conception, Christians are at best the victims of a depressing fate; their life is a penance; and their hope for the next world purchased by a slow martyrdom in this.

The mistake has arisen from taking the word "yoke" here in the same sense as in the expressions "under the yoke," or "wear the yoke in his youth." But in Christ's illustration it is not the *jugum* of the Roman soldier, but the simple "harness" or "ox-collar" of the Eastern peasant. It is the literal wooden yoke which He, with His own hands in the carpenter shop, had probably often made. He knew the difference between a smooth yoke and a rough one, a bad fit and a good fit; the difference also it made to the patient animal which had to wear it. The rough yoke galled, and the burden was heavy; the smooth yoke caused no pain, and the load was lightly drawn. The badly fitted harness was a misery; the well-fitted collar was "easy."

And what was the "burden"? It was not some special burden laid upon the Christian, some unique infliction that they alone must bear. It was what all men bear. It was simply life, human life itself, the general burden of life which all must carry with them from the cradle to the grave. Christ saw that men took life painfully. To some it was a weariness, to others a failure, to many a tragedy, to all a struggle and a pain. How to carry this burden of life had been the whole world's problem. It is still the whole world's problem. And here is Christ's solution: "Carry it as I do. Take life as I take it. Look at it from My point of view. Interpret it upon My principles. Take My yoke and learn of Me, and you will find it easy. For My yoke is easy, works easily, sits right upon the shoulders, and *therefore* My burden is light."

There is no suggestion here that religion will absolve any man from bearing burdens. That would be to absolve him from living, since it is life itself that is the burden. What Christianity does propose is to make it tolerable.

CHRIST'S YOKE is simply His secret for the alleviation of human life, His prescription for the best and happiest method of living. Men harness themselves to the work and stress of the world in clumsy and unnatural ways. The harness they put on is antiquated. A rough, ill-fitted collar at the best, they make its strain and friction past enduring, by placing it where the neck is most sensitive; and by mere continuous irritation this sensitiveness increases until the whole nature is quick and sore.

This is the origin, among other things, of a disease called "touchiness"—a disease which, in spite of its innocent name, is one of the gravest sources of restlessness in the world. Touchiness, when it becomes chronic, is a morbid condition of the inward disposition. It is self-love inflamed to the acute point; conceit, *with a hair-trigger.* The cure is to shift the yoke to some other place; to let men and things touch us through some new and perhaps as yet unused part of our nature; to become meek and lowly in heart while the old sensitiveness is becoming numb from want of use.

It is the beautiful work of Christianity everywhere to adjust the burden of life to those who bear it, and them to it. It has a perfectly miraculous gift of healing. Without doing any violence to human nature it sets it right with life, harmonizing it with all surrounding things, and restoring those who are jaded with the fatigue and dust of the world to a new grace of living. In the mere matter of altering the perspective of life and changing the proportions of things, its function in lightening the care of man is altogether its own.

The weight of a load depends upon the attraction of the earth. Suppose the attraction of the earth were removed? A ton on some other planet, where the attraction of gravity is less, does not weigh half a ton. Now Christianity removes the attraction of the earth; and this is one way in which it diminishes man's burden. It makes them citizens of another world. What was a ton yesterday is not half a ton today. So without changing one's circumstances, merely by offering a wider horizon and a different standard, it alters the whole aspect of the world.

Christianity as Christ taught is the truest philosophy of life ever spoken. But let us be quite sure when we speak of Christianity that we mean Christ's Christianity. Other versions are either caricatures, or exaggerations, or misunderstandings, or shortsighted and surface readings. For the most part their attainment is hopeless and the results wretched. But I care not who the person is, or through what vale of tears he has passed, or is about to pass, there is a new life for him along this path.

III. HOW FRUITS GROW.

Were Rest my subject, there are other things I should wish to say about it, and other kinds of Rest of which I should like to speak. But that is not my subject. My theme is that the Christian experiences are not the work of magic, but come under the law of Cause and Effect. I have chosen Rest only as a single illustration of the working of that principle. If there were time I might next run over all the Christian experiences in turn, and show the same wide law applies to each; but I think it may serve the better purpose if I leave this further exercise to yourselves. I know no Bible study that you will find more full of fruit, or which will take you nearer to the ways of God, or make the Christian life itself more solid or more sure. I shall add only a single other illustration of what I mean, before I close.

Where does Joy come from? I knew a Sunday scholar whose conception of Joy was that it was a thing made in lumps and kept somewhere in Heaven, and that when people prayed for it, pieces were somehow let down and fitted into their souls. I am not sure that views as gross and material are not often held by people who ought to be wiser. In reality, Joy is as much a matter of Cause and Effect as pain. No one can get Joy by merely asking for it. It is one of the ripest fruits of the Christian life, and, like all fruits, must be grown. There is a very clever trick in India called the mango trick. A seed is put in the ground and covered up, and after diverse incantations a full-blown mango-bush appears within five minutes. I never met any one who knew how the thing was done, but I never met any one who believed it to be anything else than a conjuring trick. The world is pretty unanimous now in its belief in the orderliness of Nature. Men may not know how fruits grow, but they do know that they cannot grow in an hour. Some lives have not even a stalk on which fruits could hang, even if they did grow in an hour. Some have never planted one sound seed of Joy in all their lives; and others who may have planted a germ or two have lived so little in sunshine that they never could come to maturity.

Whence, then, is joy? Christ put His teaching upon this subject into one of the most exquisite of His parables. I should in any instance have appealed to His teaching here, as in the case of Rest, for I do not wish you to think I am speaking words of my own. But it so happens that He has dealt with it in words of unusual fullness.

I need not recall the whole illustration. It is the parable of the Vine. Did you ever think why Christ spoke that parable? He did not merely throw it into space as a fine illustration of general truths. It was not simply a statement of the mystical union, and the doctrine of an indwelling Christ. It was that; but it was more. After He had said it, He did what was not an unusual thing when He was teaching His greatest lessons—He turned to the disciples and said He would tell them why He had spoken it. It was to tell them HOW TO GET JOY.

"These things have I spoken unto you," He said, "that My Joy might remain in you, and that your Joy might be full." It was a purposed and deliberate communication of His SECRET OF HAPPINESS.

Go back over these verses, then, and you will find the Causes of this Effect, the spring, and the only spring, out of which true Happiness comes. I am not going to analyze them in detail. I ask you to enter into the words for yourselves.

Remember, in the first place, that the Vine was the Eastern symbol of Joy. It was its fruit that made glad the heart of man. Yet, however innocent that gladness—for the expressed juice of the grape was the common drink at every peasant's board—the gladness was only a gross and passing thing. This was not true happiness, and the vine of the Palestine vineyards was not the true vine. "*Christ* was the *true* Vine." Here, then, is the ultimate source of Joy. Through whatever media it reaches us, all true Joy and Gladness find their source in Christ.

By this, of course, is not meant that the actual Joy experienced is transferred from Christ's nature, or is something passed on from Him to us. What is passed on is His method of getting it. There is, indeed, a sense in which we can share another's joy or another's sorrow. But that is another matter. Christ is the source of Joy to men in the sense in which He is the source of Rest. His people share His life, and therefore share its consequences, and one of these is Joy. His method of living is one that in the nature of things produces Joy. When He spoke of His Joy remaining with us He meant in part that the causes which produced it should continue to act. His followers, (that is to say), by *repeating* His life would experience its accompaniments. His Joy, His kind of Joy, would remain with them.

The medium through which this Joy comes is next explained: "He that abideth in Me, the same bringeth forth much fruit." Fruit first, Joy next; the one the cause or medium of the other. Fruit-bearing is the necessary antecedent; Joy both the necessary consequent and the necessary accompaniment. It lay partly in the bearing fruit, partly in the fellowship which made that possible. Partly, that is to say, Joy lay in mere constant living in Christ's presence, with all that that implied of peace, of shelter, and of love; partly in the influence of that Life upon mind and character and will; and partly in the inspiration to live and work for others, with all that that brought of self-riddance and joy in others' gain. All these, in different ways and at different times, are SOURCES OF PURE HAPPINESS.

Even the simplest of them—to do good to other people—is an instant and infallible specific. There is no mystery about Happiness whatever. Put in the right ingredients and it must come out. He that abideth in Him will bring forth much fruit; and bringing forth much fruit is Happiness. The infallible receipt for Happiness, then, is to do good; and the infallible receipt for doing good is to abide in Christ. The surest proof that all this is a plain matter of Cause and Effect is that men may try every other conceivable way of finding happiness, and they will fail. Only the right cause in each case can produce the right effect.

Then the Christian experiences are our own making? In the same sense in which grapes are our own making and no more. All fruits *grow*—whether they grow in the soil or in the soul; whether they are the fruits of the wild grape or of the True Vine. No man can *make* things grow. He can *get them to grow* by arranging all the circumstances and fulfilling all the conditions. But the growing is done by God. Causes and effects are eternal arrangements, set in the constitution of the world; fixed beyond man's ordering. What man can do is to place himself in the midst of a chain of sequences. Thus he can get things to grow: thus he himself can grow. But the power is the Spirit of God.

What more need I add but this—test the method by experiment. Do not imagine that you have got these things because you know how to get them. As well try to feed upon a cookery book. But I think I can promise that if you try in this simple and natural way, you will not fail. Spend the time you have spent in sighing for fruits in fulfilling the conditions of their growth. The fruits will come, must come. We have hitherto paid immense attention to *effects*, to the mere experiences themselves; we have described them, extolled them, advised them, prayed for them—done everything but find out what *caused* them. Henceforth LET US DEAL WITH CAUSES.

"To be," says Lotze, "is to be in relations." About every other method of living the Christian life there is an uncertainty. About every other method of acquiring the Christian experiences there is a "perhaps." But in so far as this method is the way of nature, it cannot fail. Its guarantee is the laws of the universe—and these are "the Hands of the Living God." THE TRUE VINE. "I am the true vine, and my Father is the husbandman. Every branch in me that beareth not fruit he taketh away; and every branch that beareth fruit, he purgeth it, that it may bring forth more fruit. Now ye are clean through the word which I have spoken unto you. Abide in me, and I in you. As the branch cannot bear fruit of itself, except it abide in the vine; no more can ye, except ye abide in me. I am the vine, ye are the branches: He that abideth in me, and I in him, the same bringeth forth much fruit: for without me ye can do nothing. If a man abide not in me, he is cast forth as a branch, and is withered; and men gather them, and cast them into the fire, and they are burned. If ye abide in me, and my word abide in you, ye shall ask what ye will, and it shall be done unto you. Herein is my Father glorified, that ye bear much fruit; so ye shall be my disciples. As the Father hath loved me, so have I loved you: continue ye in my love. If ye keep my commandments, ye shall abide in my love; even as I have kept my Father's commandments, and abide in his love. These things have I spoken unto you, that my joy might remain in you, and that your joy might be full."

"First!"
An Address to Boys

I have three heads to give you. The first is "Geography," the second is "Arithmetic," and the third is "Grammar."

I. Geography

First. Geography tells us where to find places.

Where is the Kingdom of God? It is said that when a Prussian officer was killed in the Franco-Prussian war, a map of France was very often found in his pocket. When we wish to occupy a country, we ought to know its geography. Now, *where* is the Kingdom of God? A boy over there says, "It is in heaven." No; it is not in heaven. Another boy says, "It is in the Bible." No; it is not in the Bible. Another boy says, "It must be in the Church," No; it is not in the Church. Heaven is only the capital of the Kingdom of God; the Bible is the guide-book to it; the Church is the weekly parade of those who belong to it. If you turn to the seventeenth chapter of Luke you will find out where the Kingdom of God really is: "The

Kingdom of God is within you"—within *you*. The Kingdom of God is *inside people*.

I remember once taking a walk by the river near where the Falls of Niagara are, and I noticed a remarkable figure walking along the river bank. I had been some time in America. I had seen black men, and red men, and yellow men, and white men; black men, the Negroes; red men, the Indians; yellow men, the Chinese; white men, the Americans. But this man looked quite different in his dress from anything I had ever seen. When he came a little closer, I saw he was wearing a kilt; when he came a little nearer still, I saw that he was dressed exactly like a Highland soldier. When he came quiet near, I said to him:

"What are you doing here?"

"Why should I not be here?" he replied; "don't you know this is British soil? When you cross the river you come into Canada."

This soldier was thousands of miles from England, and yet he was in the Kingdom of England. Wherever there is an English heart beating loyal to the Queen of Britain, there is England. Wherever there is a boy whose heart is loyal to the Kingdom of God, the Kingdom of God is within him.

What is the Kingdom of God? Every Kingdom has its exports, its products. Go down the river here and you will find ships coming in with cotton; you know they come from America. You will find ships with tea; you know they are from China. Ships with wool; you know they come from Australia. Ships with sugar; you know they come from Java.

What comes from the Kingdom of God? Again we must refer to our Guide-book. Turn to Romans, and we shall find what the Kingdom of God is. I will read it: "The Kingdom of God is righteousness, peace, joy"—three things. "The Kingdom of God is righteousness, peace, joy." Righteousness, of course, is just doing what is right. Any boy who does what is *right* has the Kingdom of God within him. Any boy who, instead of being quarrelsome, lives at peace with the other boys, has the Kingdom of God within him. Any boy whose heart is filled with joy because he does what is right, has the Kingdom of God within him. The Kingdom of God is not going to religious meetings, and hearing strange religious experiences; the Kingdom of God is doing what is right—living at peace with all men, being filled with joy in the Holy Ghost.

Boys, if you are going to be Christians, be Christians as boys, and not as your grandmothers. A grandmother has to be a Christian as a grandmother, and that is the right and the beautiful thing for her; but if you cannot read your Bible by the hour as your grandmother can, or delight in meetings as she can, don't think you are necessarily a bad boy. When you are your grandmother's age you will have your grandmother's kind of religion. Meantime, be a Christian as a boy. Live a boy's life. Do the straight thing; seek the kingdom of righteousness and honor and truth. Keep the peace with the boys about you, and be filled with the joy of being a loyal, and simple, and natural, and boy-like servant of Christ.

You can very easily tell a house, or a workshop, or an office where the Kingdom of God is *not*. The first thing you see in that place is that the "straight thing" is not always done. Customers do not get fair play. You are in danger of learning to cheat and to lie. Better a thousand times to starve than to stay in a place where you cannot do what is right.

Or, when you go into your workshop, you find everybody sulky, touchy, and ill-tempered, everybody at daggers-drawn with everybody else, some of the men not on speaking terms with some of the others, and the whole *feel* of the place miserable and unhappy. The

Kingdom of God is not there, for *it* is peace. It is the Kingdom of the Devil that is anger, and wrath and malice.

If you want to get the Kingdom of God into your workshop, or into your home, let the quarreling be stopped. Live in peace and harmony and brotherliness with everyone. For the Kingdom of God is a kingdom of brothers. It is a great Society, founded by Jesus Christ, of all the people who try to live like Him, and to make the world better and sweeter and happier. Wherever a boy is trying to do that, in the house or on the street, in the workshop or on the baseball field, there is the Kingdom of God. And every boy, however small or obscure or poor, who is seeking that, is a member of it. You see now, I hope, what the Kingdom is.

II. Arithmetic

I pass, therefore, to the second head; What was it? Arithmetic. Are there any arithmetic words in this text? "Added." What other arithmetic words? "First."

Now, don't you think you could not have anything better to seek "first" than the things I have named to do what is right, to live at peace, and be always making those about you happy? You see at once why Christ tells us to seek these things first—because they are THE BEST WORTH SEEKING.

Do you know anything better than these three things, anything happier, purer, nobler? If you do, seek them first. But if you do not, seek first the Kingdom of God. I do not tell you to be religious. You know that. I do not tell you to seek the Kingdom of God. I tell you to seek the Kingdom of God *first*. *First.* Not many people do that. They put a little religion into their life—once a week, perhaps. They might just as well let it alone. It is not worth seeking the Kingdom of God unless we seek it *first*.

Suppose you take the helm out of a ship and hang it over the bow, and send that ship to sea, will it ever reach the other side? Certainly not. It will drift about anyhow. Keep religion in its place, and it will take you straight through life and straight to your Father in heaven when life is over. But if you do not put it in its place, you may just as well have nothing to do with it. Religion out of its place in a human life is the most miserable thing in the world. There is nothing that requires so much to be kept in its place as religion, and its place is what? second? third? "First." Boys, *first* the Kingdom of God; make it so that it will be natural to you to think about that the very first thing.

There was a boy in Glasgow apprenticed to a gentleman who made telegraphs. (The gentleman told me this himself.) One day this boy was up on the top of a four-story house with a number of men fixing up a telegraph wire. The work was all but done. It was getting late, and the men said they were going away home, and the boy was to nip off the ends of the wire himself. Before going down they told him to be sure to go back to the workshop, when he was finished, with his master's tools.

"Do not leave any of them lying about, whatever you do," said the foreman.

The boy climbed up the pole and began to nip off the ends of the wire. It was a very cold winter night, and the dusk was gathering. He lost his hold and fell upon the slates, slid down, and then over and over to the ground below. A clothes-rope stretched across the "green" on to which he was just about to fall, caught him on the chest and broke his fall; but the shock was terrible, and he lay unconscious among some clothes upon the green.

An old woman came out; seeing her rope broken and the clothes all soiled, thought the boy was drunk, shook him, scolded him, and went for the policeman. The boy with the shaking came back to consciousness, rubbed his eyes, and got upon his feet. What do you think he did? He staggered, half-blind, up the stairs. He climbed the ladder. He got on to the roof of the house. He gathered up his tools, put them into his basket, took them down, and when he got to the ground again fainted dead away.

Just then the policeman came, saw there was something seriously wrong, and carried him away to the hospital, where he lay for some time. I am glad to say he got better.

What was his first thought at that terrible moment? His duty. He was not thinking of himself; he was thinking about his master. First, the Kingdom of God.

But there is another arithmetic word. What is it? "Added."

You know the difference between *addition* and *subtraction*. Now, that is A VERY IMPORTANT DIFFERENCE in religion, because—and it is a very strange thing—very few people know the difference when they begin to talk about religion. They often tell boys that if they seek the Kingdom of God, everything else is going to be *subtracted* from them. They tell them that they are going to become gloomy, miserable, and will lose everything that makes a boy's life worth living—that they will have to stop baseball and story-books, and become little old men, and spend all their time in going to meetings and in singing hymns.

Now, that is not true. Christ never said anything like that. Christ said we are to "Seek first the Kingdom of God," and EVERYTHING ELSE WORTH HAVING is to be *added* unto us. If there is anything I would like you to remember, it is these two arithmetic words—"first" and "added."

I do not mean by "added" that if you become religious you are all going to become *rich*. Here is a boy, who, in sweeping out the shop tomorrow, finds a quarter lying among the orange boxes. Well, nobody has missed it. He puts it in his pocket, and it begins to burn a hole there. By breakfast time he wishes that money were in his master's pocket. And by-and-by he goes to his master. He says (to *himself*, and not to his master), "I was at the Boys' Brigade yesterday, and I was told to seek *first* that which was right." Then he says to his master:

"Please, sir, here is a quarter that I found upon the floor."

The master puts it in the till. What has the boy got in his pocket? Nothing; *but he has got the Kingdom of God in his heart*. He has laid up treasure in heaven, which is of infinitely more worth than the quarter.

Now, that boy does not find a dollar on his way home. I have known that happen, but that is not what is meant by "adding." It does not mean that God is going to pay him in his own coin, for He pays in better coin.

Yet I remember once hearing of a boy who was paid in both ways. He was very, very poor. He lived in a foreign country, and his mother said to him one day that he must go into the great city and start in business, and she took his coat and cut it open and sewed between the lining and the coat forty golden dinars, which she had saved up for many years to start him in life. She told him to take care of robbers as he went across the desert; and as he was going out of the door she said:

"My boy, I have only two words for you—'Fear God, and never tell a lie.'"

The boy started off, and towards evening he saw glittering in the distance the minarets of the great city. But between the city and himself he saw a cloud of dust. It came nearer. Presently he saw that it was a band of robbers.

One of the robbers left the rest and rode toward him, and said:

"Boy, what have you got?"

The boy looked him in the face said:

"I have forty golden dinars sewed up in my coat."

The robber laughed and wheeled around his horse and went away back. He would not believe the boy.

Presently another robber came and he said:

"Boy, what have you got?"

"Forty golden dinars sewed up in my coat."

The robber said: "The boy is a fool," and wheeled his horse and rode away back.

By and by the robber captain came and he said:

"Boy, what have you got?"

"I have forty golden dinars sewed up in my coat."

The robber dismounted, and put his hand over the boy's breast, felt something round, counted one, two, three, four, five, till he counted out the forty golden coins. He looked the boy in the face and said:

"Why did you tell me that?

The boy said: "Because of God and my mother."

The robber leaned on his spear and thought and said:

"Wait a moment."

He mounted his horse, rode back to the rest of the robbers, and came back in about five minutes with his dress changed. This time he looked not like a robber, but like a merchant. He took the boy up on his horse and said:

"My boy, I have long wanted to do something for my God and for my mother, and I have this moment renounced my robber's life.

I am also a merchant. I have a large business house in the city. I want you to come and live with me, to teach me about your God; and you will be rich, and your mother some day will come and live with us."

And it all happened. By seeking first the Kingdom of God, all these things were added unto him.

Boys, banish forever from your minds the idea that religion is *subtraction*. It does not tell us to give things up, but rather gives us something so much better that they give themselves up. When you see a boy on the street whipping a top, you know, perhaps, that you could not make that boy happier than by giving him a top, a whip, and half an hour to whip it. But next birthday, when he looks back he says,

"What a goose I was last year to be delighted with a top. What I want now is a baseball bat."

Then when he becomes an old man, he does not care in the least for a baseball bat; he wants rest, and a snug fireside and a newspaper every day. He wonders how he could ever have taken up his thoughts with baseball bats and whipping-tops.

Now, when a boy becomes a Christian, he grows out of the evil things one by one—that is to say, if they are really evil—which he used to set his heart upon; (of course I do not mean baseball bats, for they are not evils); and so instead of telling people to give up things, we are safer to tell them to "seek first the Kingdom of God," and then they will get new things and better things, and THE OLD THINGS WILL DROP OFF of themselves. This is what is meant by the "new heart." It means that God puts into us new thoughts and new wishes, and we become quite different.

III. Grammar

Lastly, and very shortly. What was the third head? "Grammar." Right.

Now, I require a clever boy to answer the next question. What is the verb? "Seek." Very good: "seek." What mood is it in? "Imperative mood." What does that mean? "A command." What is the soldier's first lesson? "Obedience." Have you obeyed this command? Remember the imperative mood of these words, "*Seek* first the Kingdom of God."

This is the command of your King. It *must* be done. I have been trying to show you what a splendid thing it is; what a reasonable thing it is; what a happy thing it is; but beyond all these reasons, it is a thing that *must* be done, because we are *commanded* to do it by our Captain. Now, there is His command to seek *first* the Kingdom of God. Have you done it?

"Well," I know some boys will say, "we are going to have a good time, enjoy life, and then we are going to seek—*last*—the Kingdom of God."

Now, that is mean; it is nothing else than mean for a boy to take all the good gifts that God has given him, and then give him nothing back in return but HIS WASTED LIFE. God wants boys' *lives*, not only their souls. It is for active service that soldiers are drilled, and trained, and fed, and armed. That is why you and I are in the world at all—not to prepare to go out of it some day, but to serve God actively in it *now*. It is monstrous, and shameful, and cowardly to talk of seeking the Kingdom *last*. It is shirking duty, abandoning one's rightful post, playing into the enemy's hand by doing nothing to turn his flank. Every hour a Kingdom is coming in your heart, in your home, in the world near you, be it a Kingdom of Darkness or a Kingdom of Light. You are placed where you are, in a particular business, in a particular street, to help on there the Kingdom of God. You cannot do that when you are old and ready to die. By that time your companions will have fought their fight, and lost or won. If they lose, will you not be sorry that you did not help them? Will you not regret that only at the last you helped the Kingdom of God? Perhaps you will not be able to do it then. And then your life has been lost indeed.

Very few people have the opportunity to seek the Kingdom of God at the end. Christ, knowing all that, knowing that religion was a thing for our life, not merely for our death-bed, has laid this command upon us now: "Seek *first* the Kingdom of God."

I am going to leave you with this text itself. Every boy in the world should obey it.

Boys, before you go to work to-morrow, before you go to sleep to-night, resolve that, God helping you, you are going to seek *first* the Kingdom of God. Perhaps some boys here are deserters; they began once before to serve Christ, and they deserted. Come back again, come back again today! Others have never enlisted at all. Will you not do it now? You are old enough to decide. The grandest moment of a boy's life is that moment when he decides to "*Seek first the Kingdom of God.*"

The Changed Life: The Greatest Need of the World

God is all for quality; man is for quantity. The immediate need of the world at this moment is not more of us, but, if I may use the expression, a better brand of us. To secure ten men of an improved type would be better than if we had ten thousand more of the average Christians distributed all over the world. There is such a thing in the evangelistic sense as winning the whole world and losing our own soul. And the first consideration is our own life—our own spiritual relations to God—our own likeness to Christ. And I am anxious, briefly, to look at the right and the wrong way of becoming like Christ—of becoming better men: the right and the wrong way of sanctification.

Let me begin by naming, and in part discarding, some processes in vogue already for producing better lives. These processes are far from wrong; in their place they may even be essential. One ventures to disparage them only because they do not turn out the most perfect possible work.

1. The first imperfect method is to rely on RESOLUTION. In will power, in mere spasms of earnestness, there is no salvation. Strug-

gle, effort, even agony, have their place in Christianity, as we shall see; but this is not where they come in.

In mid-Atlantic the Etruria, in which I was sailing, suddenly stopped. Something had gone wrong with the engines. There were five hundred able-bodied men on board the ship. Do you think that if we had gathered together and pushed against the mast we could have pushed it on?

When one attempts to sanctify himself by effort, he is trying to make his boat go by pushing against the mast. He is like a drowning man trying to lift himself out of the water by pulling at the hair of his own head.

Christ held up this method almost to ridicule when He said, "Which of you by taking thought can add a cubit to his stature?" Put down that method forever as being futile.

The one redeeming feature of the self-sufficient method is this—that those who try it find out almost at once that it will not gain the goal.

2. Another experimenter says: "But that is not my method. I have seen the folly of a mere wild struggle in the dark. I work on a principle. My plan is not to waste power on random effort, but to concentrate on a single sin. By taking ONE AT A TIME and crucifying it steadily, I hope in the end to extirpate all."

To this, unfortunately, there are four objections: For one thing, life is too short; the name of sin is legion. For another thing, to deal with individual sins is to leave the rest of the nature for the time untouched. In the third place, a single combat with a special sin does not affect the root and spring of the disease. If you dam up a stream at one place, it will simply overflow higher up. If only one of the channels of sin be obstructed, experience points to an almost certain overflow through some other part of the nature.

Partial conversion is almost always accompanied by such moral leakage, for the pent-up energies accumulate to the bursting point, and the last state of that soul may be worse than the first. In the last place, religion does not consist in negatives, in stopping this sin and stopping that. The perfect character can never be produced with a pruning knife.

3. But a third protests: "So be it. I make no attempt to stop sins one by one. My method is just the opposite. I COPY THE VIRTUES one by one."

The difficulty about the copying method is that it is apt to be mechanical. One can always tell an engraving from a picture, an artificial flower from a real flower. To copy virtues one by one has somewhat the same effect as eradicating the vices one by one; the temporary result is an overbalanced and incongruous character. Some one defines a *prig* as "a creature that is over-fed for its size." One sometimes finds Christians of this species—over-fed on one side of their nature, but dismally thin and starved looking on the other. The result, for instance, of copying Humility, and adding it on to an otherwise worldly life, is simply grotesque. A rabid temperance advocate, for the same reason, is often the poorest of creatures, flourishing on a single virtue, and quite oblivious that his Temperance is making a worse man of him and not a better. These are examples of fine virtues spoiled by association with mean companions. Character is a unity, and all the virtues must advance together to make the perfect man.

This method of sanctification, nevertheless, is in the true direction. It is only in the details of execution that it fails.

4. A fourth method I need scarcely mention, for it is a variation on those already named. It is THE VERY YOUNG MAN'S

METHOD; and the pure earnestness of it makes it almost desecration to touch it. It is to keep a private note-book with columns for the days of the week, and a list of virtues, with spaces against each for marks. This, with many stern rules for preface, is stored away in a secret place, and from time to time, at nightfall, the soul is arraigned before it as before a private judgment bar.

This living by code was Franklin's method; and I suppose thousands more could tell how they had hung up in their bedrooms, or hid in locked-fast drawers, the rules which one solemn day they drew up to shape their lives.

This method is not erroneous, only somehow its success is poor. You bear me witness that it fails. And it fails generally for very matter-of-fact reasons—most likely because one day we forget the rules.

All these methods that have been named—the self-sufficient method, the self-crucifixion method, the mimetic method, and the diary method—are perfectly human, perfectly natural, perfectly ignorant, and as they stand perfectly inadequate. It is not argued, I repeat, that they must be abandoned. Their harm is rather that they distract attention from the true working method, and secure a fair result at the expense of the perfect one. What that perfect method is we shall now go on to ask.

I. THE FORMULA OF SANCTIFICATION.

A formula, a receipt for Sanctification—can one seriously speak of this mighty change as if the process were as definite as for the production of so many volts of electricity?

It is impossible to doubt it. Shall a mechanical experiment succeed infallibly, and the one vital experiment of humanity remain a chance? Is corn to grow by method, and character by caprice? If we cannot calculate to a certainty that the forces of religion will do their work, then is religion vain. And if we cannot express the law of these forces in simple words, then is Christianity not the world's religion, but the world's conundrum.

Where, then, shall one look for such a formula? Where one would look for any formula—among the text-books. And if we turn to the text-books of Christianity we shall find a formula for this problem as clear and precise as any in the mechanical sciences. If this simple rule, moreover, be but followed fearlessly, it will yield the result of a perfect character as surely as any result that is guaranteed by the laws of nature.

The finest expression of this rule in Scripture, or indeed in any literature, is probably one drawn up and condensed into a single verse by Paul. You will find it in a letter—the second to the Corinthians—written by him to some Christian people who, in a city which was a byword for depravity and licentiousness, were seeking the higher life. To see the point of the words we must take them from the immensely improved rendering of the Revised translation, for the older Version in this case greatly obscures the sense. They are these:

"We all, with unveiled face reflecting as a mirror the glory of the Lord, are transformed into the same image from glory to glory, even as from the Lord, the Spirit."

Now observe at the outset the entire contradiction of all our previous efforts, in the simple passive: *"We are transformed."*

We *are changed*, as the Old Version has it—we do not change ourselves. No man can change himself. Throughout the New Testament you will find that wherever these moral and spiritual transformations are described the verbs are in the passive. Presently it will be pointed out that there is a *rationale* in this; but meantime do not toss these words aside as if this passivity denied all human effort or ignored intelligible law. What is implied for the soul here is no more than is everywhere claimed for the body. In physiology the verbs describing the processes of growth are in the passive. Growth is not voluntary; it takes place, it happens, it is wrought upon matter. So here. "Ye must be born again"—we cannot born ourselves. "Be not conformed to this world, but *be ye transformed*"—we are subjects to transforming influence, we do not transform ourselves. Not more certain is it that it is something outside the thermometer that produces a change in the thermometer, than it is SOMETHING OUTSIDE THE SOUL OF MAN that produces a moral change upon him. That he must be susceptible to that change, that he must be a party to it, goes without saying; but that neither his aptitude nor his will can produce it, is equally certain.

Obvious as it ought to seem, this may be to some an almost startling revelation. The change we have been striving after is not to be produced by any more striving. It is to be wrought upon us by the moulding of hands beyond our own. As the branch ascends, and the bud bursts, and the fruit reddens under the co-operation of influences from the outside air, so man rises to the higher stature under invisible pressures from without. The radical defect of all our former methods of sanctification was the attempt to generate from within that which can only be wrought upon us from without. According to the first Law of Motion, every body continues in its state of rest, or of uniform motion in a straight line, except in so far as it may be compelled *by impressed forces* to change that state. This is also a first law of Christianity. Every man's character remains as it is, or continues in the direction in which it is going, until it is compelled *by impressed forces* to change that state. Our failure has been the failure to put ourselves in the way of the impressed forces. There is a clay, and there is a Potter; we have tried to get the clay to mould the clay.

Whence, then, these pressures, and where this Potter? The answer of the formula is—"By reflecting as a mirror the glory of the Lord we are changed." But this is not very clear. What is the "glory" of the Lord, and how can mortal man reflect it, and how can that act as an "impressed force" in moulding him to a nobler form? The word "glory"—the word which has to bear the weight of holding those "impressed forces"—is a stranger in current speech, and our first duty is to seek out its equivalent in working English. It suggests at first a radiance of some kind, something dazzling or glittering, some halo such as the old masters loved to paint round the head of their Ecce Homos. But that is paint, mere matter, the visible symbol of some unseen thing. What is that unseen thing? It is that of all unseen things the most radiant, the most beautiful, the most Divine, and that is *Character*. On earth, in Heaven, there is nothing so great, so glorious as this. The word has many meanings; in ethics it can have but one. Glory is character, and nothing less, and it can be nothing more. The earth is "full of the glory of the Lord," because it is full of His character. The "Beauty of the Lord" is character. "The effulgence of His Glory" is character. "The Glory of the Only Begotten" is character, the character which is "fullness of grace and truth." And when God told His people *His name*, He simply gave them His character, His character which was Himself: "And the Lord proclaimed the name of the Lord . . . the Lord, the Lord God, merciful and gracious, long-suffering and abundant in goodness and truth." Glory then is not something intangible, or ghostly, or transcendental. If it were this, how could Paul ask men to reflect it? Stripped of its physical enswathement it is Beauty, moral and spiritual Beauty, Beauty infinitely real, infinitely exalted, yet infinitely near and infinitely communicable.

With this explanation read over the sentence once more in paraphrase: We all reflecting as a mirror the character of Christ are transformed into the same Image from character to character—from a poor character to a better one, from a better one to a little better still, from that to one still more complete, until by slow degrees the Perfect Image is attained. Here THE SOLUTION OF THE PROBLEM OF SANCTIFICATION is compressed into a sentence: Reflect the character of Christ, and you will become like Christ. You will be changed, in spite of yourself and unknown to yourself, into the same image from character to character.

(1). All men are reflectors—that is THE FIRST LAW on which this formula is based. One of the aptest descriptions of a human being is that he is a mirror. As we sat at table to-night the world in which each of us lived and moved throughout this day was focused in the room. What we saw when we looked at one another was not one another, but one another's world. We were an arrangement of mirrors. The scenes we saw were all reproduced; the people we met walked to and fro; they spoke, they bowed, they passed us by, did everything over again as if it had been real. When we talked, we were but looking at our own mirror and describing what flitted across it; our listening was not hearing, but seeing—we but looked on our neighbor's mirror.

All human intercourse is a seeing of reflections. I meet a stranger in a railway carriage. The cadence of his first words tells me he is English and comes from Yorkshire. Without knowing it he has reflected his birthplace, his parents, and the long history of their race. Even physiologically he is a mirror. His second sentence records that he is a politician, and a faint inflection in the way he pronounces *The Times* reveals his party. In his next remarks I see reflected a whole world of experiences. The books he has read, the people he has met, the companions he keeps, the influences that have played upon him and made him the man he is—these are all registered there by a pen which lets nothing pass, and whose writing can NEVER BE BLOTTED OUT.

What I am reading in him meantime he also is reading in me; and before the journey is over we could half write each other's lives. Whether we like it or not, we live in glass houses. The mind, the memory, the soul, is simply a vast chamber panelled with looking-glass. And upon this miraculous arrangement and endowment depends the capacity of mortal souls to "reflect the character of the Lord."

(2). But this is not all. If all these varied reflections from our so-called secret life are patent to the world, how close the writing, complete the record within the soul itself! For the influences we meet are not simply held for a moment on the polished surface and thrown off again into space. Each is retained where first it fell, and stored up in the soul forever.

THIS LAW OF ASSIMILATION is the second, and by far the most impressive truth which underlies the formula of sanctification—the truth that men are not only mirrors, but that these mirrors, so far from being mere reflectors of the fleeting things they see, transfer into their own inmost substance, and hold in permanent preservation the things that they reflect.

No one knows how the soul can hold these things. No one knows how the miracle is done. No phenomenon in nature, no process in chemistry, no chapter in necromancy can ever help us to begin to understand this amazing operation. For, think of it, the past is not only *focused* there, in a man's soul, it *is* there. How could it be reflected from there if it were not there? All things that he has ever seen, known, felt, believed of the surrounding world are now within him, have become part of him, in part are him—he has been changed into their image. He may deny it, he may resent it, but they are there. They do not adhere to him, they are transfused through him. He cannot alter or rub them out. They are not in his memory, they are in *him*. His soul is as they have filled it, made it, left it. These things, these books, these events, these influences are his makers. In their hands are life and death, beauty and deformity. When once the image or likeness of any of these is fairly presented to the soul, no power on earth can hinder two things happening—it must be absorbed into the soul and forever reflected back again from character.

Upon these astounding yet perfectly obvious psychological facts, Paul bases his doctrine of sanctification. He sees that character is a thing built up by slow degrees, that it is hourly changing for better or for worse according to the images which flit across it. One step further and the whole length and breadth of the application of these ideas to the central problem of religion will stand before us.

II. THE ALCHEMY OF INFLUENCE.

If events change men, much more persons. No man can meet another on the street without making some mark upon him. We say we exchange words when we meet; what we exchange is souls. And when intercourse is very close and very frequent, so complete is this exchange that recognizable bits of the one soul begin to show in the other's nature, and the second is conscious of a similar and growing debt to the first.

Now, we become like those whom we habitually reflect. I could prove from science that applies even to the physical framework of animals—that they are influenced and organically changed by the environment in which they live.

This mysterious approximating of two souls, who has not witnessed? Who has not watched some old couple come down life's pilgrimage hand in hand, with such gentle trust and joy in one another that their very faces wore the self-same look? These were not two souls; it was a composite soul. It did not matter to which of the two you spoke, you would have said the same words to either. It was quite indifferent which replied, each would have said the same. Half a century's *reflecting* had told upon them; they were changed into the same image. It is the Law of Influence that *we become like those whom we habitually reflect*: these had become like because they habitually reflected. Through all the range of literature, of history, and biography this law presides. Men are all mosaics of other men. There was a savor of David about Jonathan, and a savor of Jonathan about David. Metempsychosis is a fact. George Eliot's message to the world was that men and women make men and women. The Family, the cradle of mankind, has no meaning apart from this. Society itself is nothing but a rallying point for these omnipotent forces to do their work. On the doctrine of Influence, in short, the whole vast pyramid of humanity is built.

But it was reserved for Paul to make the supreme application of the Law of Influence. It was a tremendous inference to make, but he never hesitated. He himself was a changed man; he knew exactly what had done it; IT WAS CHRIST.

On the Damascus road they met, and from that hour his life was absorbed in His. The effect could not but follow—on words, on deeds, on career, on creed. The "impressed forces" did their vital work. He became like Him Whom he habitually loved. "So we all," he writes, "reflecting as a mirror the glory of Christ, are changed into the same image."

Nothing could be more simple, more intelligible, more natural, more supernatural. It is an analogy from an every-day fact. Since we are what we are by the impacts of those who surround us, those who surround themselves with the highest will be those who change into the highest. There are some men and some women in whose company we are ALWAYS AT OUR BEST.

While with them we cannot think mean thoughts or speak ungenerous words. Their mere presence is elevation, purification, sanctity. All the best stops in our nature are drawn out by their intercourse, and we find a music in our souls that was never there before. Suppose even *that* influence prolonged through a month, a year, a lifetime, and what could not life become? Here, even on the common plane of life, talking our language, walking our streets, working side by side, are sanctifiers of souls; here, breathing through common clay, is Heaven; here, energies charged even through a temporal medium with the virtue of regeneration. If to live with men, diluted to the millionth degree with the virtue of the Highest, can exalt and purify the nature, what bounds can be set to the influence of Christ? To live with Socrates—with unveiled face—must have made one wise; with Aristides, just. Francis Assisi must have made one gentle; Savonarola, strong. But to have lived with Christ must have made one like Christ: that is to say, *A Christian*.

As a matter of fact, to live with Christ did produce this effect. It produced it in the case of Paul. And during Christ's lifetime the experiment was tried in an even more startling form. A few raw, unspiritual, uninspiring men, were admitted to the inner circle of His friendship. The change began at once. Day by day we can almost see the first disciple grow. First there steals over them the faintest possible adumbration of His character, and occasionally, very occasionally, they do a thing or say a thing that they could not have done or said had they not been living there. Slowly the spell of His Life deepens. Reach after reach of their nature is overtaken, thawed, subjugated, sanctified. Their manner softens, their words become more gentle, their conduct more unselfish. As swallows who have found a summer, as frozen buds the spring, their starved humanity bursts into a fuller life. They do not know how it is, but they are different men.

One day they find themselves like their Master, going about and doing good. To themselves it is unaccountable, but they cannot do otherwise. They were not told to do it, it came to them to do it. But the people who watch them know well how to account for it—"They have been," they whisper, "with Jesus." Already even, the mark and seal of His character is upon them—"They have been with Jesus." Unparalleled phenomenon, that these poor fishermen should remind other men of Christ! Stupendous victory and mystery of REGENERATION that mortal men should suggest *God* to the world!

There is something almost melting in the way His contemporaries, and John especially, speak of the influence of Christ. John lived himself in daily wonder at Him; he was overpowered, overawed, entranced, transfigured. To his mind it was impossible for any one to come under this influence and ever be the same again. "Whosoever abideth in Him sinneth not," he said. It was inconceivable that he should sin, as inconceivable as that ice should live in a burning sun, or darkness coexist with noon. If any one did sin, it was to John the simple proof that he could never have met Christ. "Whosoever sinneth," he exclaims, "hath not seen *Him*, neither known *Him*." Sin was abashed in this Presence. Its roots withered. Its sway and victory were forever at an end.

But these were His contemporaries. It was easy for *them* to be influenced by Him, for they were every day and all the day together. But how can we mirror that which we have never seen? How can all this stupendous result be produced by a Memory, by the scantiest of all Biographies, by One who lived and left this earth eighteen hundred years ago? How can modern men to-day make Christ, the absent Christ, their most constant companion still?

The answer is that FRIENDSHIP IS A SPIRITUAL THING. It is independent of Matter, or Space, or Time. That which I love in my friend is not that which I see. What influences me in my friend is not his body but his spirit. He influences me about as much in his absence as in his presence. It would have been an ineffable experience truly to have lived at that time—

> *"I think when I read the sweet story of old,*
> *How when Jesus was here among men,*
> *He took little children like lambs to His fold,*
> *I should like to have been with Him then.*
>
> *"I wish that His hand had been laid on my head,*
> *That His arms had been thrown around me,*
> *And that I had seen His kind look when he said,*
> *'Let the little ones come unto me.'"*

And yet, if Christ were to come into the world again, few of us probably would ever have a chance of seeing Him. Millions of her subjects in the little country of England have never seen their own Queen. And there would be millions of the subjects of Christ who could never get within speaking distance of Him if He were here. We remember He said: "It is expedient for you (not *for Me*) that I go away"; because by going away He could really be nearer to us than He would have been if He had stayed here. It would be geographically and physically impossible for most of us to be influenced by His person had He remained. And so our communion with Him is a spiritual companionship; but not different from most companionships, which, when you press them down to the roots, you will find to be essentially spiritual.

All friendship, all love, human and Divine, is purely spiritual. It was after He was risen that He influenced even the disciples most. Hence, in reflecting the character of Christ, it is no real obstacle that we may never have been in visible contact with Himself.

There lived once a young girl whose perfect grace of character was the wonder of those who knew her. She wore on her neck a gold locket which no one was ever allowed to open. One day, in a moment of unusual confidence, one of her companions was allowed to touch its spring and learn its secret. She saw written these words—"*Whom having not seen I love.*"

That was the secret of her beautiful life. She had been changed into the Same Image.

Now this is not imitation, but a much deeper thing. Mark this distinction, for the difference in the process, as well as in the result, may be as great as that between a photograph secured by the infallible pencil of the sun, and the rude outline from a school-boy's chalk. Imitation is mechanical, reflection organic. The one is occasional, the other habitual. In the one case, man comes to God and imitates him; in the other, God comes to man and imprints Himself upon him. It is quite true that there is an imitation of Christ which amounts to reflection. But Paul's term includes all that the other holds, and is open to no mistake.

What, then, is the practical lesson? It is obvious. "Make Christ your most constant companion"—this is what it practically means for us. Be more under His influence than under any other influence. Ten minutes spent in His society every day, ay, two minutes if it be face to face, and heart to heart, will make the whole day different. Every character has an inward spring,—let Christ be it. Every action has a key-note,—let Christ set it.

Yesterday you got a certain letter. You sat down and wrote a reply which almost scorched the paper. You picked the cruelest adjectives you knew and sent it forth, without a pang to do its ruthless work. You did that because your life was set in the wrong key. You began the day with the mirror placed at the wrong angle.

Tomorrow at day-break, turn it towards Him, and even to your enemy the fashion of your countenance will be changed. Whatever you then do, one thing you will find you could not do—you could not write that letter. Your first impulse may be the same, your judgment may be unchanged, but if you try it the ink will dry on your pen, and you will rise from your desk an unavenged, but a greater and more Christian man. Throughout the whole day your actions, down to the last detail, will do homage to that early vision.

Yesterday you thought mostly about yourself. Today the poor will meet you, and you will feed them. The helpless, the tempted, the sad, will throng about you, and each you will befriend. Where were all these people yesterday? Where they are today, but you did not see them. It is in reflected light that the poor are seen. But your soul today is NOT AT THE ORDINARY ANGLE. "Things which are not seen" are visible. For a few short hours you live the Eternal Life. The eternal life, the life of faith, is simply the life of a higher vision. Faith is an attitude—a mirror set at the right angle.

When tomorrow is over, and in the evening you review it, you will wonder how you did it. You will not be conscious that you strove for anything, or imitated anything, or crucified anything. You will be conscious of Christ; that He was with you, that without compulsion you were yet compelled; that without force, or noise, or proclamation, the revolution was accomplished. You do not congratulate yourself as one who has done a mighty deed, or achieved a personal success, or stored up a fund of "Christian experience" to ensure the same result again. What you are conscious of is "the glory of the Lord." And what the world is conscious of, if the result be a true one, is also "the glory of the Lord." In looking at a mirror one does not see the mirror, or think of it, but only of what it reflects. For a mirror never calls the attention to itself—except when there are flaws in it.

Let me say a word or two more about the effects which necessarily must follow from this contact, or fellowship, with Christ. I need not quote the texts upon the subject—the texts about abiding in Christ. "He that abideth in Him sinneth not." You cannot sin when you are standing in front of Christ. You simply cannot do it. Again: "If ye abide in Me, and My words abide in you, ye shall ask what ye will, and it shall be done unto you." Think of that! That is another inevitable consequence. And there is yet another: "He that abideth in Me, the same bringeth forth much fruit." Sinlessness—answered prayer—much fruit.

But in addition to these things, see how many of the highest Christian virtues and experiences necessarily flow from the assumption of that attitude toward Christ. For instance, the moment you assume that relation to Christ you begin to know what the *child-spirit* is. You stand before Christ, and He becomes your Teacher, and you instinctively become docile. Then you learn also to become *charitable* and *tolerant*; because you are learning of Him, and He is "meek and lowly in heart," and you catch that spirit. That is a bit of His character being reflected into yours. Instead of being critical and self-asserting, you become humble and have the mind of a little child.

I think, further, the only way of learning what *faith* is is to know Christ and be in His company. You hear sermons about the nine different kinds of faith—distinctions drawn between the right kind of faith and the wrong—and sermons telling you how to get faith. So far as I can see, there is ONLY ONE WAY in which faith is got, and it is the same in the religious world as it is in the world of men and women. I learn to trust you, my brother, just as I get to know you, and neither more nor less; and you get to trust me just as you get to know me. I do not trust you as a stranger, but as I come into contact with you, and watch you, and live with you, I find out that you are trustworthy, and I come to trust myself to you, and to lean upon you. But I do not do that to a stranger.

The way to trust Christ is to know Christ. You cannot help trusting Him then. You are changed. By knowing Him faith is begotten in you, as cause and effect. To trust Him without knowing Him as thousands do, is not faith, but credulity. I believe a great deal of prayer for faith is thrown away. What we should pray for is that we may be able to fulfill the condition, and when we have fulfilled the condition, the faith necessarily follows. The way, therefore, to increase our faith is to increase our intimacy with Christ. We trust Him more and more the better we know Him.

And then another immediate effect of this way of sanctifying the character is the tranquillity that it brings over the Christian life. How disturbed and distressed and anxious Christian people are about their growth in grace! Now, the moment you give that over into Christ's care—the moment you see that you are *being* changed—that anxiety passes away. You see that it must follow by an inevitable process and by a natural law if you fulfill the simple condition; so that peace is the reward of that life and fellowship with Christ.

Many other things follow. A man's usefulness depends to a large extent upon his fellowship with Christ. That is obvious. Only Christ can influence the world; but all that the world sees of Christ is what it sees of you and me. Christ said: "The world seeth Me no more, but ye see Me." You see Him, and standing in front of Him reflect Him, and the world sees the reflection. It cannot see Him. So that a Christian's usefulness depends solely upon that relationship.

Now, I have only pointed out a few of the things that follow from the standing before Christ—from the abiding in Christ. You will find, if you run over the texts about abiding in Christ, many other things will suggest themselves in the same relations. Almost everything in Christian experience and character follows, and follows necessarily, from standing before Christ and reflecting his character. But the supreme consummation is that we are changed into *the same image*, "even as by the Lord the Spirit." That is to say, that in some way, unknown to us, but possibly not more mysterious than the doctrine of personal influence, we are changed into the image of Christ.

This method cannot fail. I am not setting before you an opinion or a theory, but this is A CERTAINLY SUCCESSFUL MEANS of sanctification. "We all, with unveiled face, reflecting in a mirror the glory of Christ (the character of Christ) assuredly—without any miscarriage—without any possibility of miscarriage—are changed into the same image." It is an immense thing to be anchored in some great principle like that. Emerson says: "The hero is the man who is immovably centered." Get immovably centered in that doctrine of sanctification. Do not be carried away by the hundred and one theories of sanctification that are floating about in religious literature of the country at the present time; but go to the bottom of the thing for yourself, and see the *rationale* of it for yourself, and you will come to see that it is a matter of cause and effect, and that if you will fulfill the condition laid down by Christ, the effect must follow by a natural law.

What a prospect! To be changed into the same image. Think of that! That is what we are here for. That is what we are elected for. Not to be saved, in the common acceptation, but "whom He did foreknow He also did predestinate to be conformed to the image of His Son." Not merely to be saved, but *to be conformed to the image of His Son*. Conserve that principle. And as we must spend time in cultivating our earthly friendships if we are to have their blessings, so we must SPEND TIME in cultivating the fellowship and companionship of Christ. And there is nothing so much worth taking into our lives as a profounder sense of what is to be had by living in communion with Christ, and by getting nearer to Him. It will matter much if we take away with us some of the thoughts about theology, and some of the new light that has been shed upon the text of Scripture; it will matter infinitely more if our fellowship with the Lord Jesus become a little closer, and our theory of holy living a little more rational. And then as we go forth, men will take knowledge of us, that we have been with Jesus, and as we reflect Him upon them, they will begin to be changed into the same image.

It seems to me the preaching is of infinitely smaller account than the life which mirrors Christ. That is bound to tell; without speech or language—like the voices of the stars. It throws out its impressions on every side. The one simple thing we have to do is to be there—in the right relation; to go through life hand in hand with Him; to have Him in the room with us, and keeping us company wherever we go; to depend upon Him and lean upon Him, and so have His life reflected in the fullness of its beauty and perfection into ours.

III. THE FIRST EXPERIMENT.

Then you reduce religion to a common Friendship? A common Friendship—who talks of a *common* Friendship? There is no such thing in the world.

On earth no word is more sublime. Friendship is the nearest thing we know to what religion is. God is love. And to make religion akin to Friendship is simply to give it the highest expression conceivable by man. But if by demurring to "a common friendship" is meant a protest against the greatest and the holiest in religion being spoken of in intelligible terms, then I am afraid the objection is all too real. Men always look for a mystery when one talks of sanctification, some mystery apart from that which must ever be mysterious wherever Spirit works. It is thought some peculiar secret lies behind it, some occult experience which only the initiated know. Thousands of persons go to church every Sunday hoping to solve this mystery. At meetings, at conferences, many a time they have reached what they thought was the very brink of it, but somehow no further revelation came. Poring over religious books, how often were they not within a paragraph of it; the next page, the next sentence, would discover all, and they would be borne on a flowing tide forever. But nothing happened. The next sentence and the next page were read, and still it eluded them; and though the promise of its coming kept faithfully up to the end, the last chapter found them still pursuing.

Why did nothing happen? Because there was nothing to happen—nothing of the kind they were looking for. Why did it elude them? Because there was no "it." When shall we learn that the pursuit of holiness is simply THE PURSUIT OF CHRIST? When shall we substitute for the "it" of a fictitious aspiration, the approach to a Living Friend? Sanctity is in character and not in moods; Divinity in our own plain calm humanity, and in no mystic rapture of the soul.

And yet there are others who, for exactly a contrary reason, will find scant satisfaction here. Their complaint is not that a religion expressed in terms of Friendship is too homely, but that it is still too mystical. To "abide" in Christ, to "make Christ our most constant companion," is to them the purest mysticism. They want something absolutely tangible and absolutely direct. These are not the poetical souls who seek a sign, a mysticism in excess, but the prosaic natures whose want is mathematical definition in details. Yet it is perhaps not possible to reduce this problem to much more rigid elements. The beauty of Friendship is its infinity. One can never evacuate life of mysticism. Home is full of it, love is full of it, religion is full of it. Why stumble at that in the relation of man to Christ which is natural in the relation of man to man?

If any one cannot conceive or realize a mystical relation with Christ, perhaps all that can be done is to help him to step on to it by still plainer analogies from common life. How do I know Shakspere or Dante? By communing with their words and thoughts. Many men know Dante better than their own fathers. He influences them more. As a spiritual presence he is more near to them, as a spiritual force more real. Is there any reason why a greater than Shakspere or Dante, who also walked this earth, who left great words behind Him, who has greater works everywhere in the world now, should not also instruct, inspire and mould the characters of men? I do not limit Christ's influence to this: it is this, and it is more. But Christ, so far from resenting or discouraging this relation of Friendship, Himself proposed it. "Abide in me" was almost His last word to the world. And He partly met the difficulty of those who feel its intangibleness by adding the practical clause, "If ye abide in Me, *and My words abide in you.*"

Begin with His words. Words can scarcely ever be long impersonal. Christ himself was a Word, a word made Flesh. Make His words flesh; do them, live them, and you must live Christ. *"He that keepeth My Commandments,* he it is that loveth Me." Obey Him and you must love Him. Abide in Him, and you must obey Him. *Cultivate* His Friendship. Live after Christ, in His Spirit, as in His Presence, and it is difficult to think what more you can do. Take this at least as a first lesson, as introduction.

If you cannot at once and always feel the play of His life upon yours, watch for it also indirectly. "The whole earth is full of the character of the Lord." Christ is the Light of the world, and much of his Light is reflected from things in the world—even from clouds. Sunlight is stored in every leaf, from leaf through coal, and it comforts us thence when days are dark and we cannot see the sun. Christ shines through men, through books, through history, through nature, music, art. Look for Him there. "Every day one should either look at a beautiful picture, or hear beautiful music, or read a beautiful poem." The real danger of mysticism is not making it broad enough.

Do not think that nothing is happening because you do not see yourself grow, or hear the whir of the machinery. All great things grow noiselessly. You can see a mushroom grow, but never a child. Paul said for the comforting of all slowly perfecting souls that they grew "from character to character." "The inward man," he says elsewhere, "is renewed from day to day." All thorough work is slow; all true development by minute, slight and insensible metamorphoses. The higher the structure, moreover, the slower the progress. As the biologist runs his eye over the long Ascent of Life, he sees the lowest forms of animals develop in an hour; the next above these reach maturity in a day; those higher still take weeks or months to perfect; but the few at the top demand the long experiment of years. If a child and an ape are born on the same day, the last will be in full possession of its faculties and doing the active work of life before the child has left its cradle. Life is the cradle of eternity. As the man is to the animal in the slowness of his evolution, so is the spiritual man to the natural man. Foundations which have to bear the weight of an eternal life must be surely laid. Character is to wear forever; who will wonder or grudge that it cannot be developed in a day?

To await the growing of a soul, nevertheless, is an almost Divine act of faith. How pardonable, surely, the impatience of deformity with itself, of a consciously despicable character standing before Christ, wondering, yearning, hungering to be like that! Yet must one trust the process fearlessly and without misgiving. "The Lord the Spirit" will do His part. The tempting expedient is, in haste for abrupt or visible progress, to try some method less spiritual, or to defeat the end by watching for effects instead of keeping the eye on the Cause. A photograph prints from the negative only while exposed to the sun. While the artist is looking to see how it is getting on he simply stops the getting on. Whatever of wise supervision the soul may need, it is certain it can never be over-exposed, or that, being exposed, anything else in the world can improve the result or quicken it. The creation of a new heart, the renewing of a right spirit, is an omnipotent work of God. Leave it to the Creator. "He which hath begun a good work in you will perfect it unto that day."

No man, nevertheless, who feels the worth and solemnity of what is at stake will be careless as to his progress. To become LIKE CHRIST is the only thing in the world worth caring for, the thing before which every ambition of man is folly, and all lower achievement vain.

Those only who make this quest the supreme desire and passion of their lives can ever begin to hope to reach it. If, therefore, it has seemed up to this point as if all depended on passivity, let me now assert, with conviction more intense, that all depends on activity. A religion of effortless adoration may be a religion for an angel, but never for a man. Not in the contemplative, but in the active, lies true hope; not in rapture, but in reality, lies true life; not in the realm of ideals, but among tangible things, is man's sanctification wrought. Resolution, effort, pain, self-crucifixion, agony—all the things already dismissed as futile in themselves, must now be restored to office, and a tenfold responsibility laid upon them. For what is their office? Nothing less than to move the vast inertia of the soul, and place it, and keep it where the spiritual forces will act upon it. It is to rally the forces of the will, and keep the surface of the mirror bright and ever in position. It is to uncover the face which is to look at Christ, and draw down the veil when unhallowed sights are near.

You have, perhaps, gone with an astronomer to watch him photograph the spectrum of a star. As you enter the dark vault of the observatory you saw him begin by lighting a candle. To see the star with? No; but to adjust the instrument to see the star with. It was the star that was going to take the photograph; it was, also, the astronomer. For a long time he worked in the dimness, screwing tubes and polishing lenses and adjusting reflectors, and only after much labor the finely focused instrument was brought to bear. Then he blew out the light, and left the star to do its work upon the plate alone.

The day's task for the Christian is to bring his instrument to bear. Having done that he may blow out his candle. All the evidences of Christianity which have brought him there, all aids to Faith, all acts of worship, all the leverages of the Church, all Prayer and Meditation, all girding of the Will—these lesser processes, these candle-light activities for that supreme hour, may be set aside. But, remember, it is but for an hour. The wise man will be he who quickest lights his candle, the wisest he who never lets it out. Tomorrow, the next moment, he, a poor, darkened, blurred soul, may need it again to focus the Image better, to take a mote off the lens, to clear the mirror from a breath with which the world has dulled it.

No readjustment is ever required on behalf of the Star. That is one great fixed point in this shifting universe. But *the world moves*. And each day, each hour, demands a further motion and readjustment for the soul. A telescope in an observatory follows a star by clockwork, but the clockwork of the soul is called *the Will*. Hence, while the soul in passivity reflects the Image of the Lord, the Will in intense activity holds the mirror in position lest the drifting motion of the world bear it beyond the line of vision. To "follow

Christ" is largely to keep the soul in such position as will allow for the motion of the earth. And this calculated counteracting of the movements of the world, this holding of the mirror exactly opposite to the Mirrored, this steadying of the faculties unerringly through cloud and earthquake, fire and sword, is the stupendous co-operating labor of the Will. It is all man's work. It is all Christ's work. In practice it is both; in theory it is both. But the wise man will say in practice, "It depends upon myself."

In the Gallerie des Beaux Arts in Paris there stands a famous statue. It was the last work of a great genius, who, like many a genius, was very poor and lived in a garret, which served as a studio and sleeping-room alike. When the statue was all but finished, one midnight a sudden frost fell upon Paris. The sculptor lay awake in the fireless room and thought of the still moist clay, thought how the water would freeze in the pores and destroy in an hour the dream of his life. So the old man rose from his couch and heaped the bed-clothes reverently round his work. In the morning when the neighbors entered the room the sculptor was dead, but the statue was saved!

The Image of Christ that is forming within us—that is life's one charge. Let every project stand aside for that. The spirit of God who brooded upon the waters thousands of years ago, is busy now creating men, within these commonplace lives of ours, in the image of God. "Till Christ be formed," no man's work is finished, no religion crowned, no life has fulfilled its end. Is the infinite task begun? When, how, are we to be different? Time cannot change men. Death cannot change men. Christ can. Wherefore *put on Christ*.

Dealing with Doubt

There is a subject which I think workers amongst young men cannot afford to keep out of sight—I mean the subject of "Doubt." We are forced to face that subject. We have no choice. I would rather let it alone; but every day of my life I meet men who doubt, and I am quite sure that most Christian workers among men have innumerable interviews every year with men who raise skeptical difficulties about religion.

Now it becomes a matter of great practical importance that we should know how to deal wisely with these. Upon the whole, I think these are the best men in the country. I speak of my own country. I speak of the universities with which I am familiar, and I say that the men who are perplexed,—the men who come to you with serious and honest difficulties,—are the best men. They are men of intellectual honesty, and cannot allow themselves to be put to rest by words, or phrases, or traditions, or theologies, but who must get to the bottom of things for themselves. And if I am not mistaken, CHRIST WAS VERY FOND of these men. The outsiders always interested Him, and touched Him. The orthodox people—

the Pharisees—He was much less interested in. He went with publicans and sinners—with people who were in revolt against the respectability, intellectual and religious, of the day. And following Him, we are entitled to give sympathetic consideration to those whom He loved and took trouble with.

First, let me speak for a moment or two about THE ORIGIN OF DOUBT. In the first place, *we are born questioners*. Look at the wonderment of a little child in its eyes before it can speak. The child's great word when it begins to speak is, "Why?" Every child is full of every kind of question, about every kind of thing, that moves, and shines, and changes, in the little world in which it lives.

That is the incipient doubt in the nature of man. Respect doubt for its origin. It is an inevitable thing. It is not a thing to be crushed. It is a part of man as God made him. Heresy is truth in the making, and doubt is the prelude of knowledge.

Secondly: *The world is a Sphinx*. It is a vast riddle—an unfathomable mystery; and on every side there is temptation to questioning. In every leaf, in every cell of every leaf, there are a hundred problems. There are ten good years of a man's life in investigating what is in a leaf, and there are five good years more in investigating the things that are in the things that are in the leaf. God has planned the world to incite men to intellectual activity.

Thirdly: *The instrument with which we attempt to investigate truth is impaired*. Some say it fell, and the glass is broken. Some say prejudice, heredity, or sin, have spoiled its sight, and have blinded our eyes and deadened our ears. In any case the instruments with which we work upon truth, even in the strongest men, are feeble and inadequate to their tremendous task.

And in the fourth place, *all religious truths are doubtable*. There is no absolute truth for any one of them. Even that fundamental truth—the existence of a God—no man can prove by reason. The ordinary proof for the existence of God involves either an assumption, argument in a circle, or a contradiction. The impression of God is kept up by experience, not by logic. And hence, when the experimental religion of a man, of a community, or of a nation wanes, religion wanes—their idea of God grows indistinct, and that man, community or nation becomes infidel.

Bear in mind, then, that all religious truths are doubtable—even those which we hold most strongly.

What does this brief account of the origin of doubt teach us? It teaches us GREAT INTELLECTUAL HUMILITY.

It teaches us sympathy and toleration with all men who venture upon the ocean of truth to find out a path through it for themselves. Do you sometimes feel yourself thinking unkind things about your fellow-students who have intellectual difficulty? I know how hard it is always to feel sympathy and toleration for them; but we must address ourselves to that most carefully and most religiously. If my brother is shortsighted I must not abuse him or speak against him; I must pity him, and if possible try to improve his sight, or to make things that he is to look at so bright that he cannot help seeing. But never let us think evil of men who do not see as we do. From the bottom of our hearts let us pity them, and let us take them by the hand and spend time and thought over them, and try to lead them to the true light.

What has been THE CHURCH'S TREATMENT OF DOUBT in the past? It has been very simple. "There is a heretic. Burn him!" That is all. "There is a man who has gone off the road. Bring him back and torture him!"

We have got past that physically; have we got past it morally? What does the modern Church say to a man who is skeptical? Not

"Burn him!" but "Brand him!" "Brand him!"—call him a bad name. And in many countries at the present time, a man who is branded as a heretic is despised, tabooed and put out of religious society, much more than if he had gone wrong in morals. I think I am speaking within the facts when I say that a man who is unsound is looked upon in many communities with more suspicion and with more pious horror than a man who now and then gets drunk. "Burn him!" "Brand him!" "Excommunicate him!" That has been the Church's treatment of doubt, and that is perhaps to some extent the treatment which we ourselves are inclined to give to the men who cannot see the truths of Christianity as we see them.

Contrast CHRIST'S TREATMENT of doubt. I have spoken already of His strange partiality for the outsiders—for the scattered heretics up and down the country; of the care with which He loved to deal with them, and of the respect in which He held their intellectual difficulties. Christ never failed to distinguish between doubt and unbelief. Doubt is *"can't believe"*; unbelief is *"won't believe."* Doubt is honesty; unbelief is obstinacy. Doubt is looking for light; unbelief is content with darkness. Loving darkness rather than light—that is what Christ attacked, and attacked unsparingly. But for the intellectual questioning of Thomas, and Philip, and Nicodemus, and the many others who came to Him to have their great problems solved, He was respectful and generous and tolerant.

And how did He meet their doubts? The Church, as I have said, says, "Brand him!" Christ said, "Teach him." He destroyed by fulfilling. When Thomas came to Him and denied His very resurrection, and stood before Him waiting for the scathing words and lashing for his unbelief, they never came. They never came! Christ gave him facts—facts! No man can go around facts. Christ said,

"Behold My hands and My feet." The great god of science at the present time is a fact. It works with facts. Its cry is, "Give me facts. Found anything you like upon facts and we will believe it." The spirit of Christ was the scientific spirit. He founded His religion upon facts; and He asked all men to found their religion upon facts.

Now, get up the facts of Christianity, and take men to the facts. Theologies—and I am not speaking disrespectfully of theology; theology is as scientific a thing as any other science of facts—but theologies are HUMAN VERSIONS of Divine truths, and hence the varieties of the versions and the inconsistencies of them. I would allow a man to select whichever version of this truth he liked *afterwards*; but I would ask him to begin with no version, but go back to the facts and base his Christian life upon these.

That is the great lesson of the New Testament way of looking at doubt—of Christ's treatment of doubt. It is not "Brand him!"—but lovingly, wisely and tenderly to teach him. Faith is never opposed to reason in the New Testament; it is opposed to sight. You will find that a principle worth thinking over. *Faith is never opposed to reason in the New Testament, but to sight.*

With these principles in mind as to the origin of doubt, and as to Christ's treatment of it, how are we ourselves to deal with those who are in intellectual difficulty?

In the first place, I think *we must make all the concessions to them that we conscientiously can.*

When a doubter first encounters you, he pours out a deluge of abuse of churches, and ministers, and creeds, and Christians. Nine-tenths of what he says is probably true. Make concessions. Agree with him. It does him good to unburden himself of these things. He has been cherishing them for years—laying them up against Christians, against the Church, and against Christianity;

and now he is startled to find the first Christian with whom he has talked over the thing almost entirely agrees with him. We are, of course, not responsible for everything that is said in the name of Christianity; but a man does not give up medicine because there are quack doctors, and no man has a right to give up his Christianity because there are spurious or inconsistent Christians. Then, as I already said, creeds are human versions of Divine truths; and we do not ask a man to accept all the creeds, any more than we ask him to accept all the Christians. We ask him to accept Christ, and the facts about Christ and the words of Christ. You will find the battle is half won when you have endorsed the man's objections, and possibly added a great many more to the charges which he has against ourselves. These men are IN REVOLT against the kind of religion which we exhibit to the world—against the cant that is taught in the name of Christianity. And if the men that have never seen the real thing—if you could show them that, they would receive it as eagerly as you do. They are merely in revolt against the imperfections and inconsistencies of those who represent Christ to the world.

Second: *Beg them to set aside, by an act of will, all unsolved problems*: such as the problem of the origin of evil, the problem of the Trinity, the problem of the relation of human will and predestination, and so on—problems which have been investigated for thousands of years without result—ask them to set those problems aside as insoluble. In the meantime, just as a man who is studying mathematics may be asked to set aside the problem of squaring the circle, let him go on with what can be done, and what has been done, and leave out of sight the impossible.

You will find that will relieve the skeptic's mind of a great deal of UNNECESSARY CARGO that has been in his way.

Thirdly: *Talking about difficulties, as a rule, only aggravates them.*

Entire satisfaction to the intellect is unattainable about any of the greater problems, and if you try to get to the bottom of them by argument, there is no bottom there; and therefore you make the matter worse. But I would say what is known, and what can be honestly and philosophically and scientifically said about one or two of the difficulties that the doubter raises, just to show him that you can do it—to show him that you are not a fool—that you are not merely groping in the dark yourself, but you have found whatever basis is possible. But I would not go around all the doctrines. I would simply do that with one or two; because the moment you cut off one, a hundred other heads will grow in its place. It would be a pity if all these problems could be solved. The joy of the intellectual life would be largely gone. I would not rob a man of his problems, nor would I have another man rob me of my problems. They are the delight of life, and the whole intellectual world would be stale and unprofitable if we knew everything.

Fourthly—and this is the great point: *Turn away from the reason and go into the man's moral life.*

I don't mean, go into his moral life and see if the man is living in conscious sin, which is the great blinder of the eyes—I am speaking now of honest doubt; but open a new door into THE PRACTICAL SIDE OF MAN'S NATURE.

Entreat him not to postpone life and his life's usefulness until he has settled the problems of the universe. Tell him those problems will never all be settled; that his life will be done before he has begun to settle them; and ask him what he is doing with his life meantime. Charge him with wasting his life and his usefulness; and invite him to deal with the moral and practical difficulties of the world, and leave the intellectual difficulties as he goes along.

To spend time upon these is proving the less important before the more important; and, as the French say, "The good is the enemy of the best." It is a good thing to think; it is a better thing to work—it is a better thing to do good. And you have him there, you see. He can't get beyond that. You have to tell him, in fact, that there are two organs of knowledge: the one reason, the other obedience. And now tell him, as he has tried the first and found the little in it, just for a moment or two to join you in trying the second. And when he asks whom he is to obey, you tell him there is but One, and lead him to the great historical figure who calls all men to Him: the one perfect life—the one Savior of mankind—the one Light of the world. Ask him to begin to OBEY CHRIST; and, doing His will, he shall know of the doctrine whether it be of God.

That, I think, is about the only thing you can do with a man: to get him into practical contact with the needs of the world, and to let him lose his intellectual difficulties meantime. Don't ask him to give them up altogether. Tell him to solve them afterward one by one if he can, but meantime to give his life to Christ and his time to the kingdom of God. You fetch him completely around when you do that. You have taken him away from the false side of his nature, and to the practical and moral side of his nature; and for the first time in his life, perhaps, he puts things in their true place. He puts his nature in the relations in which it ought to be, and he then only begins to live. And by obedience he will soon become a learner and pupil for himself, and Christ will teach him things, and he will find whatever problems are solvable gradually solved as he goes along the path of practical duty.

Now, let me, in closing, give an instance of how to deal with specific points.

The question of miracles is thrown at my head every second day:

"What do you say to a man when he says to you, 'Why do you believe in miracles?'"

I say, "Because I have seen them."

He asks, "When?"

I say, "Yesterday."

"Where?"

"Down such-and-such a street I saw a man who was a drunkard redeemed by the power of an unseen Christ and saved from sin. That is a miracle."

The best apologetic for Christianity is a Christian. That is a fact which the man cannot get over. There are fifty other arguments for miracles, but none so good as that you have seen them. Perhaps you are one yourself. But take a man and show him a miracle with his own eyes. Then he will believe.

THE MAGIC STORY

FREDERICK VAN RENSSELAER DEY

Part One

I was sitting alone in the cafe, and had just reached for the sugar preparatory to putting it into my coffee. Outside, the weather was hideous. Snow and sleet came swirling down, and the wind howled frightfully. Every time the outer door opened, a draft of unwelcome air penetrated the uttermost corners of the room. Still, I was comfortable. The snow and sleet and wind conveyed nothing to me except an abstract thanksgiving that I was where it could not affect me. While I dreamed and sipped my coffee, the door opened and closed, and admitted—Sturtevant.

Sturtevant was an undeniable failure, but, withal, an artist of more than ordinary talent. He had, however, fallen into the rut traveled by ne'er-do-wells, and was out at the elbows as well as insolvent.

As I raised my eyes to Sturtevant's, I was conscious of mild surprise at the change in his appearance. Yet he was not dressed differently. He wore the same threadbare coat in which he always appeared, and the old brown hat was the same. And yet there was something new and strange in his appearance. As he swished his hat around to relieve it of the burden of snow deposited by the howling nor'wester, there was something new in the gesticulation. I could not remember when I had invited Sturtevant to dine with me, but involuntarily I beckoned to him. He nodded, and presently seated himself opposite to me. I asked him what he would have, and he, after scanning the bill of fare carelessly, ordered from it leisurely, and invited me to join him in coffee for two. I watched him in stupid wonder, but, as I had invited the obligation, I was prepared to pay for it, although I knew I hadn't sufficient cash to settle the bill. Meanwhile, I noted the brightness of his usual lackluster eyes, and the healthful, hopeful glow upon his cheek, with increasing amazement.

"Have you lost a rich uncle?" I asked.

"No," he replied, calmly, "but I have found my mascot."

"Brindle bull, or terrier?" I inquired.

"Currier," said Sturtevant, at length, pausing with his coffee cup half way to his lips, "I see that I have surprised you. It is not strange, for I am a surprise to myself. I am a new man, a different man,—and the alteration has taken place in the last few hours. You have seen me come into this place broke' many a time, when you have turned away, so that I would think you did not see me. I knew why you did that. It was not because you did not want to pay for a dinner, but because you did not have the money to do it. Is that your check? Let me have it. Thank you. I haven't any money with me to-night, but I,—well, this is my treat."

He called the waiter to him, and, with an inimitable flourish, signed his name on the backs of the two checks, and waved him away. After that he was silent a moment while he looked into my eyes, smiling at the astonishment which I in vain strove to conceal.

"Do you know an artist who possesses more talent than I?" he asked, presently. "No. Do you happen to know anything in the line of my profession that I could not accomplish, if I applied myself to it? No. You have been a reporter on the dailies for—how many?—seven or eight years. Do you remember when I ever had any credit until to-night? No. Was I refused just now? You have seen for yourself. To-morrow my new career begins. Within a month I shall have a bank account. Why? Because I have discovered the secret of success."

"Yes," he continued, when I did not reply, "my fortune is made. I have been reading a strange story, and, since reading it, I feel that my fortune is assured. It will make your fortune, too. All you have to do is to read it. You have no idea what it will do for you. Nothing is impossible after you know that story. It makes everything as plain as A, B, C. The very instant you grasp its true meaning, success is certain. This morning I was a hopeless, aimless bit of garbage in the metropolitan ash can; to-night I wouldn't change places with a millionaire. That sounds foolish, but it is true. The millionaire has spent his enthusiasm; mine Is all at hand."

"You amaze me," I said, wondering if he had been drinking absinthe. "Won't you tell me the story? I should like to hear it."

"Certainly. I mean to tell it to the whole world. It is really remarkable that it should have been written and should remain in print so long, with never a soul to appreciate it until now. This morning I was starving. I hadn't any credit, nor a place to get a meal. I was seriously meditating suicide. I had gone to three of the papers for which I had done work, and had been handed back all that I had submitted. I had to choose quickly between death by suicide and death slowly by starvation.

Then I found the story and read it. You can hardly imagine the transformation. Why, my dear boy, everything changed at once,—and there you are."

"But what is the story, Sturtevant?"

"Wait; let me finish. I took those same old drawings to other editors, and every one of them was accepted at once."

"Can the story do for others what it has done for you? For example, would it be of assistance to me?" I asked.

"Help you? why not? Listen and I will tell it to you, although, really, you should read it. Still, I will tell it as best I can. It is like this: you see, "The waiter interrupted us at that moment. He informed Sturtevant that he was wanted at the telephone, and, with a word of apology, the artist left the table. Five minutes later I saw him rush out into the sleet and wind and disappear. Within the recollection of the frequenters of that cafe, Sturtevant had never before been called out by telephone. That, of itself, was substantial proof of a change in his circumstances.

One night, on the street, I encountered Avery, a former college chum, then a reporter on one of the evening papers. It was about a month after my memorable interview with Sturtevant, which, by that time, was almost forgotten.

"Hello, old chap," he said; "how's the world using you? Still on space?"

"Yes," I replied, bitterly, "with prospects of being on the town. shordy. But you look as if things were coming your way. Tell me all about it."

"Things have been coming my way, for a fact, and it is all remarkable, when all is said. You know Sturtevant, don't you? It's all due to him. I was plumb down on my luck,—thinking of the morgue and all that,—looking for you, in fact, with the idea that you would lend me enough to pay my room rent, when I met Sturtevant.

He told me a story, and, really, old man, it is the most remarkable story you ever heard; it made a new man of me. Within twenty-four hours I was on my feet, and I've hardly known a care or a trouble since."

Avery's statement, uttered calmly, and with the air of one who had merely pronounced an axiom, recalled to my mind the conversation with Sturtevant in the cafe that stormy night, nearly a month before.

"It must be a remarkable story," I said, incredulously. "Sturtevant mentioned it to me once. I have not seen him since. Where is he now?"

"He has been making war sketches in Cuba, at two hundred a week; he's just returned. It is a fact that everybody that has heard that story has done well since. There are Cosgrove and Phillips,—friends of mine,—you don't know them. One's a real estate agent; the other a broker's clerk. Sturtevant told them the story, and they have experienced the same result that I have; and they are not the only ones, either."

"Do you know the story?" I asked. "Will you try its effect on me?"

"Certainly; with the greatest pleasure in the world. I would like to have it printed in big black type, and posted on the elevated stations throughout New York. It certainly would do a lot of good, and it's as simple as A, B, C; like living on a farm. Excuse me a minute, will you ? I see Danforth over there. Back in a minute, old chap."

He nodded and smiled,—and was gone. I saw him join the man whom he had designated as Danforth. My attention was distracted for a moment, and, when I looked again, both had disappeared.

If the truth be told, I was hungry. My pocket at that moment contained exactly five cents; just enough to pay my fare up-town, but insufficient also to stand the expense of filling my stomach. There was a "night owl" wagon in the neighborhood, where I had frequently "stood up" the purveyor of midnight dainties, and to him I applied. He was leaving the wagon as I was on the point of entering it, and I accosted him.

"I'm broke again," I said, with extreme cordiality. "You'll have to trust me once more. Some ham and eggs, I think, will do for the present."

He coughed, hesitated a moment, and then re-entered the wagon with me.

"Mr. Currier is good for anything he orders," he said to the man in charge; "one of my old customers. This is Mr. Bryan, Mr. Currier. He will take good care of you, and 'stand for' you, just the same as I would. The fact is, I have sold out. I've just turned over the outfit to Bryan. By the way, isn't Mr. Sturtevant a friend of yours?"

I nodded. I couldn't have spoken if I had tried.

"Well," continued the ex-"night owl" man, **he came here one night, about a month ago, and told me the most wonderful story I ever heard. I've just bought a place in Eighth Avenue, where I am going to run a regular restaurant— near Twenty-third Street. Come and see me." He was out of the wagon, and the sliding door had been banged shut before I could stop him; so I ate my ham and eggs in silence, and resolved that I would hear that story before I slept. In fact, I began to regard it with superstition. If it had made so many fortunes, surely it should be capable of making mine.

The certainty that the wonderful story—I began to regard it as magic,—was in the air, possessed me. As I started to walk homeward, fingering the solitary nickel in my pocket and contemplating the certainty of riding down town in the morning, I experienced the sensation of something stealthily pursuing me, as if Fate were treading along behind me, yet never overtaking, and I was conscious that I was possessed with or by the story. When I reached Union Square, I examined my address book for the home of Sturtevant. It was not recorded there. Then I remembered the cafe in University place, and, although the hour was late, it occurred to me that he might be there.

He was I In a far corner of the room, surrounded by a group of acquaintances, I saw him. He discovered me at the same instant, and motioned to me to join them at the table. There was no chance for the story, however. There were half a dozen around the table, and I was the farthest removed from Sturtevant. But I kept my eyes upon him, and bided my time, determined that, when he rose to depart, I would go with him. A silence, suggestive of respectful awe, had fallen upon the party when I took my seat. Every one seemed to be thinking, and the attention of all was fixed upon Sturtevant. The cause was apparent. He had been telling the story. I had entered the cafe just too late to hear it. On my right, when I took my seat, was a doctor; on my left a lawyer. Facing me on the other side was a novelist with whom I had some acquaintance. The others were artists and newspaper men.

"It's too bad, Mr. Currier," remarked the doctor; "you should have come a little sooner. Sturtevant has been telling us a story; it is quite wonderful, really. I say, Sturtevant, won't you tell that story again, for the benefit of Mr. Currier?"

"Why, yes. I believe that Currier has, somehow, failed to hear the magic story, although, as a matter of fact, I think he was the first one to whom I mentioned it at all. It was here, in this cafe, too,—at this very table. Do you remember what a wild night that was, Currier? Wasn't I called to the telephone, or something like that ? To be sure I I remember, now; interrupted just at the point when I was beginning the story. After that, I told it to three or four fellows, and it 'braced them up,' as it had me. It seems incredible that a mere story can have such a tonic effect upon the success of so many persons who are engaged in such widely different occupations, but that is what it has done. It is a kind of neverfailing remedy, like a cough mixture that is warranted to cure everything, from a cold in the head to galloping consumption. There was Parsons, for example. He is a broker, you know, and had been on the wrong side of the market for a month. He had utterly lost his grip, and was on the verge of failure. I happened to meet him at the time he was feeling the bluest, and, before we parted, something brought me around to the subject of the story, and I related it to him. It had the same effect upon him that it had on me, and has had upon everybody who has heard it, as far as I know. I think you will all agree with me, that it is not the story itself that performs the surgical operation on the minds of those who are familiar with it; it is the way it is told,—in print, I mean. The author has, somehow, produced a psychological effect which is indescribable. The reader is hypnotized. He receives a mental and moral tonic. Perhaps, doctor, you can give some scientific explanation of the influence exerted by the story. It is a sort of elixir manufactured out of words, eh?"

From that the company entered upon a general discussion of theories. Now and then slight references were made to the story itself, and they were just sufficient to tantalize me,—the only one present who had not heard it.

At length, I left my chair, and, passing around the table, seized Sturtevant by one arm, and succeeded in drawing him away from the party.

"If you have any consideration for an old friend who is rapidly being driven mad by the existence of that confounded story, which

Fate seems determined that I shall never hear, you will relate it to me now," I said, savagely.

Sturtevant stared at me in mild surprise.

"All right," he said. "The others will excuse me for a few moments, I think. Sit down here, and you shall have it. I found it pasted in an old scrapbook I purchased in Ann Street, for three cents; and there isn't a thing about it by which one can get any idea in what publication it originally appeared, or who wrote it. When I discovered it, I began casually to read it, and in a moment I was interested. Before I left it, I had read it through many times, so that I could repeat it almost word for word. It affected me strangely,—as if I had come in contact with some strong personality. There seems to be in the story a personal element that applies to every one who reads it. Well, after I had read it several times, I began to think it over. I couldn't stay in the house, so I seized my coat and hat and went out. I must have walked several miles, buoyantly, without realizing that I was the same man who, only a short time before, had been in the depths of despondency. That was the day I met you here,—you remember."

We were interrupted at that instant by a uniformed messenger, who handed Sturtevant a telegram. It was from his chief, and demanded his instant attendance at the office. The messenger had already been delayed an hour, and there was no help for it; he must go at once.

"Too bad!" said Sturtevant, rising and extending his hand. "Tell you what I'll do, old chap. I'm not likely to be gone any more than an hour or two. You take my key and wait for me in my room. In the escritoire near the window you will find an old scrapbook, bound in rawhide. It was manufactured, I have no doubt, by the author of the magic story. Wait for me in my room until I return."

With that he went out, and I lost no time in taking advantage of the permission he had given me.

I found the book without difficulty. It was a quaint, home-made affair, covered, as Sturtevant had said, with rawhide, and bound with leather thongs. The pages formed an odd combination of yellow paper, vellum and home-made parchment. I found the story, curiously printed on the last-named material. It was quaint and strange. Evidently, the printer had "set" it under the supervision of the writer. The phraseology was an unusual combination of seventeenth and eighteenth century mannerisms, and the interpolation of italics and capitals could have originated in no other brain than that of its author.

In reproducing the following story, the peculiarities of type, spelling, etc., are eliminated, but in other respects it remains unchanged.

Nothing worth while is attainable without effort. By the same token, a thoughtful reading of "The Magic Story" and a correct interpretation of its "lessons" are essential to a full appreciation of its inspirational value.

The author has woven into this story in a remarkably effective way the basic principles of a successful life, and it is safe to say that persistent application of these principles will accomplish almost, if not quite, all that is claimed for them in the development of a self-reliant, success-compelling spirit.

Enthusiastic readers of this unusual book, appreciating its inspiriting force, give it generous publicity, and as a result its sphere of influence is being constantly enlarged.

Part Two

In the Old Scrap Book

INASMUCH as I have evolved from my experience the one great secret of success for all worldly undertakings, I deem it wise, now that the number of my days is nearly counted, to give to the generations that are to follow me the benefit of whatsoever knowledge I possess. I do not apologize for the manner of my expression, nor for lack* of literary merit, the latter being, I wot, its own apology. Tools much heavier than the pen have been my portion, and, moreover, the weight of years has somewhat palsied hand and brain; nevertheless, the fact I can tell, and that I deem the meat within the nut. What mattereth it, in what manner the shell be broken, so that the meat be obtained and rendered useful? I doubt not that I shall use, in the telling, expressions that have clung to my memory since childhood; for, when men attain the number of my years, happenings of youth are like to be clearer to their perceptions than are events of recent date; nor doth it matter much how a thought is expressed, if it be wholesome and helpful, and findeth the understanding.

Much have I wearied my brain anent the question, how best to describe this recipe for success that I have discovered, and it seemeth advisable to give it as it came to me; that is, if I relate somewhat of the story of my life, the directions for agglomerating the substances, and supplying the seasoning for the accomplishment of the dish, will plainly be perceived. Happen they may; and that men may be born generations after I am dust, who will live to bless me for the words I write.

My father, then, was a seafaring man who, early in life, forsook his vocation, and settled on a plantation in the colony of Virginia, where, some years thereafter, I was born, which event took place in the year 1642; and that was over a hundred years ago. Better for my father had it been had he hearkened to the wise advice of my mother, that he remain in the calling of his education; but he would not have it so, and the good vessel he captained was bartered for the land I spoke of. Here beginneth the first lesson to be acquired:

Man should not be blinded to whatsoever merit exists in the opportunity which he hath in hand, remembering that a thousand promises for the future should weigh as naught against the possession of a single piece of silver.

When I had achieved ten years, my mother's soul took flight, and two years thereafter my worthy father followed her. I, being their only begotten, was left alone; howbeit, there were friends who, for a time, cared for me; that is to say, they offered me a home beneath their roof,—a thing which I took advantage of for the space of five months. From my father's estate there came to me naught; but, in the wisdom that came with increasing years, I convinced myself that his friend, under whose roof I lingered for some time, had defrauded him, and therefore me.

Of the time from the age of twelve and a half until I was three and twenty, I will make no recital here, since that time hath naught to do with this tale; but some time after, having in my possession the sum of sixteen guineas, ten, which I had saved from the fruits of my labor, I took ship to Boston town, where I began work first as a cooper, and thereafter as a ship's carpenter, although always after the craft was docked; for the sea was not amongst my desires.

Fortune will sometimes smile upon an intended victim because of pure perversity of temper. Such was one of my experiences. I prospered, and, at seven and twenty, owned the yard wherein, less than four years earlier, I had worked for hire. Fortune, howbeit, is a jade who must be coerced; she will not be coddled. Here beginneth the second lesson to be acquired:

Fortune is ever elusive, and can only be retained by force. Deal with her tenderly and she will forsake you for a stronger man. (In that, methinks, she is not unlike other women of my knowledge.) About this time, Disaster (which is one of the heralds of broken spirits and lost resolve), paid me a visit. Fire ravaged my yards, leaving nothing in its blackened paths but debts, which I had not the coin wherewith to defray. I labored with my acquaintances, seeking assistance for a new start, but the fire that had burned my competence seemed also to have consumed their sympathies. So it happened, within a short time, that not only had I lost all, but I was hopelessly indebted to others; and for that they cast me into prison. It is possible that I might have rallied from my losses but for this last indignity, which broke down my spirits so that I became utterly despondent. Upward of a year was I detained within the gaol; and, when I did come forth, it was not the same hopeful, happy man, content with his lot, and with confidence in the world and its people, who had entered there.

Life has many pathways, and of them by far the greater number lead downward. Some are precipitous, others are less abrupt; but ultimately, no matter at what inclination the angle may be fixed, they arrive at the same destination,—failure. And here beginneth the third lesson:

Failure exists only in the grave. Man, being alive, hath not yet failed; always he may turn about and ascend by the same path he descended by; and there may be one that is less abrupt (albeit longer of achievement), and more adaptable to his condition.
When I came forth from prison, I was penniless. In all the world I possessed naught beyond the poor garments which covered me, and a walking stick which the turnkey had permitted me to retain, since it was worthless. Being a skilled workman, howbeit, I speedily found employment at good wages; but, having eaten of the fruit of worldly advantage, dissatisfaction possessed me. I became morose and sullen; whereat, to cheer my spirits, and for the sake of forgetting the losses I had sustained, I passed my evenings at the tavern. Not that I drank overmuch of liquor, except on occasion (for I have ever been somewhat abstemious), but that I could laugh, and sing, and parry wit and badinage with my ne'er-do-well companions; and here might be included the fourth lesson :

Seek comrades among the industrious, for those who are idle will sap your energies from you.
It was my pleasure at that time to relate, upon slight provocation, the tale of my disasters, and to rail against the men whom I

deemed to have wronged me, because they had seen fit not to come to my aid. Moreover, I found childish delight in filching from my employer, each day, a few moments of the time for which he paid me. Such a thing is less honest than downright theft.

This habit continued and grew upon me until the day dawned which found me not only without employment, but also without character, which meant that I could not hope to find work with any other employer in Boston town.

It was then that I regarded myself a failure. I can liken my condition at that time for naught more similar than that of a man who, descending the steep side of a mountain, loses his foothold. The farther he slides, the faster he goes. I have also heard this condition described by the word Ishma elite, which I understand to be a man whose hand is against everybody, and who thinks that the hands of every other man are against him; and here beginneth the fifth lesson:

The Ishmaelite and the leper are the same, since both are abominations in the sight of man,—albeit they differ much, in that the former may be restored to perfect health. The former is entirely the result of imagination; the latter has poison in his blood.

I will not discourse at length upon the gradual degeneration of my energies. It is not meet ever to dwell much upon misfortunes (which saying is also worthy of remembrance) . It is enough if I add that the day came when I possessed naught wherewith to purchase food and raiment, and I found myself like unto a pauper, save at infrequent times when I could earn a few pence, or, mayhap, a shilling. Steady employment I could not secure, so I became emaciated in body, and naught but a skeleton in spirit.

My condition, then, was deplorable; not so much for the body, be it said, as for the mental part of me, which was sick unto death. In my imagination I deemed myself ostracised by the whole world, for I had sunk very low indeed; and here beginneth the sixth and final lesson to be acquired (which cannot be told in one sentence, nor in one paragraph, but must needs be adapted from the remainder of this tale).

Well do I remember my awakening, for it came in the night, when, in truth, I did awake from sleep. My bed was a pile of shavings in the rear of the cooper shop where once I had worked for hire; my roof was the pyramid of casks, underneath which I had established myself. The night was cold, and I was chilled, albeit, paradoxically, I had been dreaming of light and warmth and of the repletion of good things. You will say, when I relate the effect the vision had on me, that my mind was affected. So be it, for it is the hope that the minds of others might be likewise influenced which disposes me to undertake the labor of this writing. It was the dream which converted me to the belief—nay, to the knowledge,—that I was possessed of two identities; and it was my own better self that afforded me the assistance for which I had pleaded in vain from my acquaintances. I have heard this condition described by the word "double." Nevertheless, that word does not comprehend my meaning. A double can be naught more than a double, neither half being possessed of individuality. But I will not philosophize, since philosophy is naught but a suit of garments for the decoration of a dummy figure.

Moreover, it was not the dream itself which affected me; it was the impression made by it, and the influence that it exerted over me, which accomplished my enfranchisement. In a word, then, I encouraged my other identity. After toiling through a tempest of snow and wind, I peered into a window and saw that other being. He was rosy with health; before him, on the hearth, blazed a fire of logs; there was conscious power and force in his demeanor; he was physically and mentally muscular. I rapped timidly upon the door, and he bade me enter. There was a not unkindly smile of derision in his eyes as he motioned me to a chair by the fire; but he uttered no word of welcome; and, when I had warmed myself, I went forth again into the tempest, burdened with the shame which the contrast between us had forced upon me. It was then that I awoke; and here Cometh the strange part of my tale, for, when I did awake, I was not alone. There was a Presence with me; intangible to others, I discovered later, but real to me.

The Presence was in my likeness, yet was it strikingly unlike. The brow, not more lofty than my own, yet seemed more round and full; the eyes, clear, direct, and filled with purpose, glowed with enthusiasm and resolution; the lips, chin,—ay, the whole contour of face and figure was dominant and determined.

He was calm, steadfast, and self-reliant; I was cowering, filled with nervous trembling, and fearsome of intangible shadows. When the Presence turned away, I followed, and throughout the day I never lost sight of it, save when it disappeared for a time beyond some doorway where I dared not enter; at such places, I awaited its return with trepidation and awe, for I could not help wondering at the temerity of the Presence (so like myself, and yet so unlike), in daring to enter where my own feet feared to tread.

It seemed also, as if purposely I was led to the place and to the men where and before whom I most dreaded to appear; to offices where once I had transacted business; to men with whom I had financial dealings. Throughout the day I pursued the Presence, and at evening saw it disappear beyond the portals of a hostelry famous for its cheer and good living. I sought the pyramid of casks and shavings.

Not again in my dreams that night did I encounter the Better Self (for that is what I have named it), albeit, when, perchance, I awakened from slumber, it was near to me, ever wearing that calm smile of kindly derision which could not* be mistaken for pity, nor for condolence in any form. The contempt of it stung me sorely.

The second day was not unlike the first, being a repetition of its forerunner, and I was again doomed to wait outside during the visits which the Presence paid to places where I fain would have gone had I possessed the requisite courage. It is fear which deporteth a man's soul from his body and rendereth it a thing to be despised. Many a time I essayed to address it, but enunciation rattled in my throat, unintelligible; and the day closed like its predecessor.

This happened many days, one following another, until I ceased to count them; albeit, I discovered that constant association with the Presence was producing an effect upon me; and one night, when I awoke among the casks and discerned that he was present, I made bold to speak, albeit with marked timidity.

"Who are you?" I ventured to ask; and I was startled into an upright posture by the sound of my own voice; and the question seemed to give pleasure to my companion, so that I fancied there was less of derision in his smile when he responded.

"I am that I am," was the reply. "I am he who you have been; I am he who you may be again; wherefore do you hesitate ? I am he who you were, and whom you have cast out for other company. I am the man made in the image of God, who once possessed your body.

Once we dwelt within it together, not in harmony, for that can never be, nor yet in unity, for that is impossible, but as tenants in common who rarely fought for full possession. Then you were a puny thing, but you became selfish and exacting until I could no longer abide with you, wherefore I stepped out. There is a plus-entity and a minus-entity in every human body that is born into the world. Whichever one of these is favored by the flesh becomes dominant; then is the other inclined to abandon its habitation, temporarily or for all time. I am the plus-entity of yourself; you are the minus-entity. I own all things; you possess naught. That body which we both inhabited is mine, but it is unclean, and I will not dwell within it.

Cleanse It, and I will take possession.

"Why do you pursue me?" I next asked the Presence.

"You have pursued me, not I you. You can exist without me for a time, but your path leads downward, and the end is death. Now that you approach the end, you debate if it be not politic that you should cleanse your house and invite me to enter. Step aside, then, from the brain and the will; cleanse them of your presence; only on that condition will I ever occupy them again."

"The brain hath lost its power," I faltered. "The will is a weak thing, now; can you repair them?"

"Listen 1" said the Presence, and he towered over me while I cowered abjectly at his feet. "To the plus-entity of a man, all things are possible. The world belongs to him,—is his estate. He fears naught, dreads naught, stops at naught; he asks no privileges, but demands them; he dominates, and cannot cringe; his requests are orders; opposition flees at his approach; he levels mountains, fills in vales, and travels on an even plane where stumbling is unknown."

Thereafter, I slept again, and, when I awoke, I seemed to be in a different world. The sun was shining and I was conscious that birds twittered above my head. My body, yesterday trembling and uncertain, had become vigorous and filled with energy. I gazed upon the pyramid of casks in amazement that I had so long made use of it for an abiding place, and I was wonderingly conscious that I had passed my last night beneath its shelter.

The events of the night recurred to me, and I looked about me for the Presence. It was not visible. But anon I discovered, cowering in a far corner of my resting place, a puny, abject, shuddering figure, distorted of visage, deformed of shape, disheveled and unkempt of appearance. It tottered as it walked, for it approached me piteously; but I laughed aloud, mercilessly. Perchance I knew then that it was the minus-entity, and that the plus-entity was within me; albeit I did not then realize it. Moreover, I was in haste to get away; I had no time for philosophy. There was much for me to do,—much; strange it was that I had not thought of that yesterday. But yesterday was gone,—to-day was with me,—it had just begun.

As had once been my daily habit, I turned my steps in the direction of the tavern where formerly I had partaken of my meals. I nodded cheerily as I entered, and smiled in recognition of returned salutations. Men who had ignored me for months bowed graciously when I passed them on the thoroughfare. I went to the washroom, and from there to the breakfast table; afterwards, when I passed the taproom, I paused a moment and said to the landlord :

"I will occupy the same room that I formerly used, if, perchance, you have it at disposal. If not, another will do as well, until I can obtain it."

Then I went out and hurried with all haste to the cooperage. There was a huge wain in the yard, and men were loading it with casks for shipment. I asked no questions, but, seizing barrels, began hurling them to the men who worked atop of the load. When this was finished, I entered the shop. There was a vacant bench;

I recognized its disuse by the litter on its top. It was the same at which I had once worked. Stripping off my coat, I soon cleared it of impedimenta. In a moment more I was seated, with my foot on the vice-lever, shaving staves.

It was an hour later when the master workman entered the room, and he paused in surprise at sight of me; already there was a goodly pile of neatly shaven staves beside me, for in those days I was an excellent workman; there was none better, but, alas I now, age hath deprived me of my skill. I replied to his unasked question with the brief but comprehensive sentence: "I have returned to work, sir." He nodded his head and passed on, viewing the work of other men, albeit anon he glanced askance in my direction.

Here endeth the sixth and last lesson to be acquired, although there is more to be said, since from that moment I was a successful man, and ere long possessed another shipyard, and had acquired a full competence of worldly goods.

I pray you who read, heed well the following admonitions, since upon them depend the word "success" and all that it implies :

Whatsoever you desire of good is yours. You have but to stretch forth your hand and take it.

Learn that the consciousness of dominant power within you is the possession of all things attainable.

Have no fear of any sort or shape, for fear is an adjunct of the minus-entity.

If you have skill, apply it; the world must profit by it, and, therefore, you.

Make a daily and nightly companion of your plus-entity; if you heed its advice, you cannot go wrong.

Remember, philosophy is an argument; the world, which is your property, is an accumulation of facts.

Go, therefore, and do that which is within you to do; take no heed of gestures which would beckon you aside; ask of no man permission to perform.

The minus-entity requests favors; the plus-entity grants them. Fortune waits upon every footstep you take; seize her, bind her, hold her, for she is yours; she belongs to you.

Start out now, with these admonitions in your mind. Stretch out your hand, and grasp the plus, which, maybe, you have never made use of, save in grave emergencies. Life is an emergency most grave.

Your plus-entity is beside you now; cleanse your brain, and strengthen your will. It will take possession. It waits upon you.

Start tonight; start now upon this new journey.

Be always on your guard. Whichever entity controls you, the other hovers at your side; beware lest the evil enter, even for a moment.

My task is done. I have written the recipe for "success." If followed, it cannot fail. Wherein I may not be entirely comprehended, the plus-entity of whosoever reads will supply the deficiency; and upon that Better Self of mine, I place the burden of imparting to generations that are to come, the secret of this all-pervading good, the secret of being what you have it within you to be.

THE MAJESTY OF CALMNESS

Individual Problems and Possibilities...

WILLIAM GEORGE JORDAN

Contents

The Majesty of Calmness 271

Hurry, the Scourge of America 275

The Power of Personal Influence 280

The Dignity of Self-Reliance 285

Failure as a Success 291

Doing Our Best at All Times 297

The Royal Road to Happiness 304

The Majesty of Calmness

Calmness is the rarest quality in human life. It is the poise of a great nature, in harmony with itself and its ideals. It is the moral atmosphere of a life self-centred, self-reliant, and self-controlled. Calmness is singleness of purpose, absolute confidence, and conscious power,—ready to be focused in an instant to meet any crisis.

The Sphinx is not a true type of calmness,—petrifaction is not calmness; it is death, the silencing of all the energies; while no one lives his life more fully, more intensely and more consciously than the man who is calm.

The Fatalist is not calm. He is the coward slave of his environment, hopelessly surrendering to his present condition, recklessly indifferent to his future. He accepts his life as a rudderless ship, drifting on the ocean of time. He has no compass, no chart, no known port to which he is sailing. His self-confessed inferiority to all nature is shown in his existence of constant surrender. It is not,—calmness.

The man who is calm has his course in life clearly marked on his chart. His hand is ever on the helm. Storm, fog, night, tempest, danger, hidden reefs,—he is ever prepared and ready for them. He is made calm and serene by the realization that in these crises of his voyage he needs a clear mind and a cool head; that he has naught to do but to do each day the best he can by the light he has; that he will never flinch nor falter for a moment; that, though he may have to tack and leave his course for a time, he will never drift, he will get back into the true channel, he will keep ever headed toward his harbor. *When* he will reach it, *how* he will reach it, matters not to him. He rests in calmness, knowing he has done his best. If his best seem to be overthrown or overruled, then he must still bow his head,—in calmness. To no man is permitted to know the future of his life, the finality. God commits to man ever only new beginnings, new wisdom, and new days to use the best of his knowledge.

Calmness comes ever from within. It is the peace and restfulness of the depths of our nature. The fury of storm and of wind agitate only the surface of the sea; they can penetrate only two or three hundred feet,—below that is the calm, unruffled deep. To be ready for the great crises of life we must learn serenity in our daily living. Calmness is the crown of self-control.

When the worries and cares of the day fret you, and begin to wear upon you, and you chafe under the friction,—be calm. Stop, rest for a moment, and let calmness and peace assert themselves. If you let these irritating outside influences get the better of you, you are confessing your inferiority to them, by permitting them to dominate you. Study the disturbing elements, each by itself, bring all the will power of your nature to bear upon them, and you will find that they will, one by one, melt into nothingness, like vapors fading before the sun. The glow of calmness that will then pervade your mind, the tingling sensation of an inflow of new strength, may be to you the beginning of the revelation of the supreme calmness that is possible for you. Then, in some great hour of your life, when you stand face to face with some awful trial, when the structure of your ambition and life-work crumbles in a moment, you will be brave. You can then fold your arms calmly, look out undismayed and undaunted upon the ashes of your hope, upon the wreck of what you have faithfully built, and with brave heart and unfaltering voice you may say: "So let it be,—I will build again."

When the tongue of malice and slander, the persecution of inferiority, tempts you for just a moment to retaliate, when for an instant you forget yourself so far as to hunger for revenge,—be calm. When the grey heron is pursued by its enemy, the eagle, it does not run to escape; it remains calm, takes a dignified stand, and waits quietly, facing the enemy unmoved. With the terrific force with which the eagle makes its attack, the boasted king of birds is often impaled and run through on the quiet, lance-like bill of the heron. The means that man takes to kill another's character becomes suicide of his own.

No man in the world ever attempted to wrong another without being injured in return,—someway, somehow, sometime. The only weapon of offence that Nature seems to recognize is the boomerang. Nature keeps her books admirably; she puts down every item, she closes all accounts finally, but she does not always balance them at the end of the month. To the man who is calm, revenge is so far beneath him that he cannot reach it,—even by stooping. When injured, he does not retaliate; he wraps around him the royal robes of Calmness, and he goes quietly on his way.

When the hand of Death touches the one we hold dearest, paralyzes our energy, and eclipses the sun of our life, the calmness that has been accumulating in long years becomes in a moment our refuge, our reserve strength.

The most subtle of all temptations is the *seeming* success of the wicked. It requires moral courage to see, without flinching, material prosperity coming to men who are dishonest; to see politicians rise into prominence, power and wealth by trickery and corruption; to see virtue in rags and vice in velvets; to see ignorance at a premium, and knowledge at a discount. To the man who is really calm these puzzles of life do not appeal. He is living his life as best he can; he is not worrying about the problems of justice, whose solution must be left to Omniscience to solve.

When man has developed the spirit of Calmness until it becomes so absolutely part of him that his very presence radiates it, he has made great progress in life. Calmness cannot be acquired of itself and by itself; it must come as the culmination of a series of virtues. What the world needs and what individuals need is a higher standard of living, a great realizing sense of the privilege and dignity of life, a higher and nobler conception of individuality.

With this great sense of calmness permeating an individual, man becomes able to retire more into himself, away from the noise, the confusion and strife of the world, which come to his ears only as faint, far-off rumblings, or as the tumult of the life of a city heard only as a buzzing hum by the man in a balloon.

The man who is calm does not selfishly isolate himself from the world, for he is intensely interested in all that concerns the welfare of humanity. His calmness is but a Holy of Holies into which he can retire *from* the world to get strength to live *in* the world. He realizes that the full glory of individuality, the crowning of his self-control is,—the majesty of calmness.

Hurry, the Scourge of America

The first sermon in the world was preached at the Creation. It was a Divine protest against Hurry. It was a Divine object lesson of perfect law, perfect plan, perfect order, perfect method. Six days of work carefully planned, scheduled and completed were followed by,—rest. Whether we accept the story as literal or as figurative, as the account of successive days or of ages comprising millions of years, matters little if we but learn the lesson.

Nature is very un-American. Nature never hurries. Every phase of her working shows plan, calmness, reliability, and the absence of hurry. Hurry always implies lack of definite method, confusion, impatience of slow growth. The Tower of Babel, the world's first skyscraper, was a failure because of hurry. The workers mistook their arrogant ambition for inspiration. They had too many builders,—and no architect. They thought to make up the lack of a head by a superfluity of hands. This is a characteristic of Hurry. It seeks ever to make energy a substitute for a clearly defined plan,— the result is ever as hopeless as trying to transform a hobby-horse into a real steed by brisk riding.

Hurry is a counterfeit of haste. Haste has an ideal, a distinct aim to be realized by the quickest, direct methods. Haste has a single compass upon which it relies for direction and in harmony with which its course is determined. Hurry says: "I must move faster. I will get three compasses; I will have them different; I will be guided by all of them. One of them will probably be right." Hurry never realizes that slow, careful foundation work is the quickest in the end.

Hurry has ruined more Americans than has any other word in the vocabulary of life. It is the scourge of America; and is both a cause and a result of our high-pressure civilization. Hurry adroitly assumes so many masquerades of disguise that its identity is not always recognized.

Hurry always pays the highest price for everything, and, usually the goods are not delivered. In the race for wealth men often sacrifice time, energy, health, home, happiness and honor,—everything that money cannot buy, the very things that money can never bring back. Hurry is a phantom of paradoxes. Business men, in their desire to provide for the future happiness of their family, often sacrifice the present happiness of wife and children on the altar of Hurry. They forget that their place in the home should be something greater than being merely "the man that pays the bills;" they expect consideration and thoughtfulness that they are not giving.

We hear too much of a wife's duties to a husband and too little of the other side of the question. "The wife," they tell us, "should meet her husband with a smile and a kiss, should tactfully watch his moods and be ever sweetness and sunshine." Why this continual swinging of the censer of devotion to the man of business? Why should a woman have to look up with timid glance at the face of her husband, to "size up his mood"? Has not her day, too, been one of care, and responsibility, and watchfulness? Has not mother-love been working over perplexing problems and worries of home and of the training of the children that wifely love may make her seek to solve in secret? Is man, then, the weaker sex that he must be pampered and treated as tenderly as a boil trying to keep from contact with the world?

In their hurry to attain some ambition, to gratify the dream of a life, men often throw honor, truth, and generosity to the winds. Politicians dare to stand by and see a city poisoned with foul water until they "see where they come in" on a water-works appropriation. If it be necessary to poison an army,—that, too, is but an incident in the hurry for wealth.

This is the Age of the Hothouse. The element of natural growth is pushed to one side and the hothouse and the force-pump are substituted. Nature looks on tolerantly as she says: "So far you may go, but no farther, my foolish children."

The educational system of to-day is a monumental institution dedicated to Hurry. The children are forced to go through a series of studies that sweep the circle of all human wisdom. They are given everything that the ambitious ignorance of the age can force into their minds; they are taught everything but the essentials,—how to use their senses and how to think. Their minds become congested by a great mass of undigested facts, and still the cruel, barbarous forcing goes on. You watch it until it seems you cannot stand it a moment longer, and you instinctively put out your hand and say: "Stop! This modern slaughter of the Innocents must *not* go on!" Education smiles suavely, waves her hand complacently toward her thousands of knowledge-prisons over the country, and says: "Who are you that dares speak a word against our sacred, school system?" Education is in a hurry. Because she fails in fifteen years to do what half the time should accomplish by better methods, she should not be too boastful. Incompetence is not always a reason for pride. And they hurry the children into a hundred textbooks, then into ill-health, then into the colleges, then into a diploma, then into life,—with a dazed mind, untrained and unfitted for the real duties of living.

Hurry is the deathblow to calmness, to dignity, to poise. The old-time courtesy went out when the new-time hurry came in. Hurry is the father of dyspepsia. In the rush of our national life, the bolting of food has become a national vice. The words "Quick Lunches" might properly be placed on thousands of headstones in our cemeteries. Man forgets that he is the only animal that dines; the others merely feed. Why does he abrogate his right to dine and go to the end of the line with the mere feeders? His self-respecting stomach rebels, and expresses its indignation by indigestion. Then man has to go through life with a little bottle of pepsin tablets in his vest-pocket. He is but another victim to this craze for speed. Hurry means the breakdown of the nerves. It is the royal road to nervous prostration.

Everything that is great in life is the product of slow growth; the newer, and greater, and higher, and nobler the work, the slower is its growth, the surer is its lasting success. Mushrooms attain their full power in a night; oaks require decades. A fad lives its life in a few weeks; a philosophy lives through generations and centuries. If you are sure you are right, do not let the voice of the world, or of friends, or of family swerve you for a moment from your purpose. Accept slow growth if it must be slow, and know the results *must* come, as you would accept the long, lonely hours of the night,— with absolute assurance that the heavy-leaded moments *must* bring the morning.

Let us as individuals banish the word "Hurry" from our lives. Let us care for nothing so much that we would pay honor and self-respect as the price of hurrying it. Let us cultivate calmness, restfulness, poise, sweetness,—doing our best, bearing all things as bravely as we can; living our life undisturbed by the prosperity of the wicked or the malice of the envious. Let us not be impatient, chafing at delay, fretting over failure, wearying over results, and weakening under opposition. Let us ever turn our face toward the future with confidence and trust, with the calmness of a life in harmony with itself, true to its ideals, and slowly and constantly progressing toward their realization.

Let us see that cowardly word Hurry in all its most degenerating phases, let us see that it ever kills truth, loyalty, thoroughness; and let us determine that, day by day, we will seek more and more to substitute for it the calmness and repose of a true life, nobly lived.

The Power of Personal Influence

The only responsibility that a man cannot evade in this life is the one he thinks of least,—his personal influence. Man's conscious influence, when he is on dress-parade, when he is posing to impress those around him,—is woefully small. But his unconscious influence, the silent, subtle radiation of his personality, the effect of his words and acts, the trifles he never considers,—is tremendous. Every moment of life he is changing to a degree the life of the whole world. Every man has an atmosphere which is affecting every other. So silent and unconsciously is this influence working, that man may forget that it exists.

All the forces of Nature,—heat, light, electricity and gravitation,—are silent and invisible. We never *see* them; we only know that they exist by seeing the effects they produce. In all Nature the wonders of the "seen" are dwarfed into insignificance when compared with the majesty and glory of the "unseen." The great sun itself does not supply enough heat and light to sustain animal and vegetable life on the earth. We are dependent for nearly half of our light and heat upon the stars, and the greater part of this supply of life-giving energy comes from *invisible* stars, millions of miles from the earth. In a thousand ways Nature constantly seeks to lead men to a keener and deeper realization of the power and the wonder of the invisible.

Into the hands of every individual is given a marvellous power for good or for evil,—the silent, unconscious, unseen influence of his life. This is simply the constant radiation of what a man really *is*, not what he pretends to be. Every man, by his mere living, is radiating sympathy, or sorrow, or morbidness, or cynicism, or happiness, or hope, or any of a hundred other qualities. Life is a state of constant radiation and absorption; to exist is to radiate; to exist is to be the recipient of radiations.

There are men and women whose presence seems to radiate sunshine, cheer and optimism. You feel calmed and rested and restored in a moment to a new and stronger faith in humanity. There are others who focus in an instant all your latent distrust, morbidness and rebellion against life. Without knowing why, you chafe and fret in their presence. You lose your bearings on life and its problems. Your moral compass is disturbed and unsatisfactory. It is made untrue in an instant, as the magnetic needle of a ship is deflected when it passes near great mountains of iron ore.

There are men who float down the stream of life like icebergs,—cold, reserved, unapproachable and self-contained. In their presence you involuntarily draw your wraps closer around you, as you wonder who left the door open. These refrigerated human beings have a most depressing influence on all those who fall under the spell of their radiated chilliness. But there are other natures, warm, helpful, genial, who are like the Gulf Stream, following their own course, flowing undaunted and undismayed in the ocean of colder waters. Their presence brings warmth and life and the glow of sunshine, the joyous, stimulating breath of spring. There are men who are like malarious swamps,—poisonous, depressing and weakening by their very presence. They make heavy, oppressive and gloomy the atmosphere of their own homes; the sound of the children's play is stilled, the ripples of laughter are frozen by their presence. They go through life as if each day were a new big funeral, and they were always chief mourners. There are other men who seem like the ocean; they are constantly bracing, stimulating, giving new draughts of tonic life and strength by their very presence.

There are men who are insincere in heart, and that insincerity is radiated by their presence. They have a wondrous interest in your welfare,—when they need you. They put on a "property" smile so suddenly, when it serves their purpose, that it seems the smile must be connected with some electric button concealed in their clothes. Their voice has a simulated cordiality that long training may have made almost natural. But they never play their part absolutely true, the mask *will* slip down sometimes; their cleverness cannot teach their eyes the look of sterling honesty; they may deceive some people, but they cannot deceive all. There is a subtle power of revelation which makes us say: "Well, I cannot explain how it is, but I know that man is not honest."

Man cannot escape for one moment from this radiation of his character, this constantly weakening or strengthening of others. He cannot evade the responsibility by saying it is an unconscious influence. He can *select* the qualities that he will permit to be radiated. He can cultivate sweetness, calmness, trust, generosity, truth, justice, loyalty, nobility,—make them vitally active in his character,—and by these qualities he will constantly affect the world.

Discouragement often comes to honest souls trying to live the best they can, in the thought that they are doing so little good in the world. Trifles unnoted by us may be links in the chain of some great purpose. In 1797, William Godwin wrote The Inquirer, a collection of revolutionary essays on morals and politics. This book influenced Thomas Malthus to write his Essay on Population, published in 1798. Malthus' book suggested to Charles Darwin a point of view upon which he devoted many years of his life, resulting, in 1859, in the publication of The Origin of Species,—the most influential book of the nineteenth century, a book that has revolutionized all science. These were but three links of influence extending over sixty years. It might be possible to trace this genealogy of influence back from Godwin, through generation and generation, to the word or act of some shepherd in early Britain, watching his flock upon the hills, living his quiet life, and dying with the thought that he had done nothing to help the world.

Men and women have duties to others,—and duties to themselves. In justice to ourselves we should refuse to live in an atmosphere that keeps us from living our best. If the fault be in us, we should master it. If it be the personal influence of others that, like a noxious vapor, kills our best impulses, we should remove from that influence,—if we can *possibly* move without forsaking duties. If it be wrong to move, then we should take strong doses of moral quinine to counteract the malaria of influence. It is not what those around us *do* for us that counts,—it is what they *are* to us. We carry our house-plants from one window to another to give them the proper heat, light, air and moisture. Should we not be at least as careful of ourselves?

To make our influence felt we must live our faith, we must practice what we believe. A magnet does not attract iron, as iron. It must first convert the iron into another magnet before it can attract it. It is useless for a parent to try to teach gentleness to her children when she herself is cross and irritable. The child who is told to be truthful and who hears a parent lie cleverly to escape some little social unpleasantness is not going to cling very zealously to truth. The parent's words say "don't lie," the influence of the parent's life says "do lie." No man can ever isolate himself to evade this constant power of influence, as no single corpuscle can rebel and escape from the general course of the blood. No individual is so insignificant as to be without influence. The changes in our varying moods are all recorded in the delicate barometers of the lives of others. We should ever let our influence filter through human love and sympathy. We should not be merely an influence,—we should be an inspiration. By our very presence we should be a tower of strength to the hungering human souls around us.

The Dignity of Self-Reliance

Self-confidence, without self-reliance, is as useless as a cooking recipe,—without food. Self-confidence sees the possibilities of the individual; self-reliance realizes them. Self-confidence sees the angel in the unhewn block of marble; self-reliance carves it out for himself.

The man who is self-reliant says ever: "No one can realize my possibilities for me, but me; no one can make me good or evil but myself." He works out his own salvation,—financially, socially, mentally, physically, and morally. Life is an individual problem that man must solve for himself. Nature accepts no vicarious sacrifice, no vicarious service. Nature never recognizes a proxy vote. She has nothing to do with middle-men,—she deals only with the individual. Nature is constantly seeking to show man that he is his own best friend, or his own worst enemy. Nature gives man the option on which he will be to himself.

All the athletic exercises in the world are of no value to the individual unless he compel those bars and dumb-bells to yield to him, in strength and muscle, the power for which he, himself, pays in time and effort. He can never develop his muscles by sending his valet to a gymnasium.

The medicine-chests of the world are powerless, in all the united efforts, to help the individual until he reach out and take for himself what is needed for his individual weakness.

All the religions of the world are but speculations in morals, mere theories of salvation, until the individual realize that he must save himself by relying on the law of truth, as he sees it, and living his life in harmony with it, as fully as he can. But religion is not a Pullman car, with soft-cushioned seats, where he has but to pay for his ticket,—and some one else does all the rest. In religion, as in all other great things, he is ever thrown back on his self-reliance. He should accept all helps, but,—he must live his own life. He should not feel that he is a mere passenger; he is the engineer, and the train is his life. We must rely on ourselves, live our own lives, or we merely drift through existence,—losing all that is best, all that is greatest, all that is divine.

All that others can do for us is to give us opportunity. We must ever be prepared for the opportunity when it comes, and to go after it and find it when it does not come, or that opportunity is to us,— nothing. Life is but a succession of opportunities. They are for good or evil,—as we make them.

Many of the alchemists of old felt that they lacked but one element; if they could obtain that one, they believed they could transmute the baser metals into pure gold. It is so in character. There are individuals with rare mental gifts, and delicate spiritual discernment who fail utterly in life because they lack the one element,—self-reliance. This would unite all their energies, and focus them into strength and power.

The man who is not self-reliant is weak, hesitating and doubting in all he does. He fears to take a decisive step, because he dreads failure, because he is waiting for some one to advise him or because he dare not act in accordance with his own best judgment. In his cowardice and his conceit he sees all his non-success due to others. He is "not appreciated," "not recognized," he is "kept down." He feels that in some subtle way "society is conspiring against him." He grows almost vain as he thinks that no one has had such poverty, such sorrow, such affliction, such failure as have come to him.

The man who is self-reliant seeks ever to discover and conquer the weakness within him that keeps him from the attainment of what he holds dearest; he seeks within himself the power to battle against all outside influences. He realizes that all the greatest men in history, in every phase of human effort, have been those who have had to fight against the odds of sickness, suffering, sorrow. To him, defeat is no more than passing through a tunnel is to a traveller,—he knows he must emerge again into the sunlight.

The nation that is strongest is the one that is most self-reliant, the one that contains within its boundaries all that its people need. If, with its ports all blockaded it has not within itself the necessities of life and the elements of its continual progress then,—it is weak, held by the enemy, and it is but a question of time till it must surrender. Its independence is in proportion to its self-reliance, to its power to sustain itself from within. What is true of nations is true of individuals. The history of nations is but the biography of individuals magnified, intensified, multiplied, and projected on the screen of the past. History is the biography of a nation; biography is the history of an individual. So it must be that the individual who is most strong in any trial, sorrow or need is he who can live from his inherent strength, who needs no scaffolding of commonplace sympathy to uphold him. He must ever be self-reliant.

The wealth and prosperity of ancient Rome, relying on her slaves to do the real work of the nation, proved the nation's downfall. The constant dependence on the captives of war to do the thousand details of life for them, killed self-reliance in the nation and in the individual. Then, through weakened self-reliance and the increased opportunity for idle, luxurious ease that came with it, Rome, a nation of fighters, became,—a nation of men more effeminate than women. As we depend on others to do those things we should do for ourselves, our self-reliance weakens and our powers and our control of them becomes continuously less.

Man to be great must be self-reliant. Though he may not be so in all things, he must be self-reliant in the one in which he would be great. This self-reliance is not the self-sufficiency of conceit. It is daring to stand alone. Be an oak, not a vine. Be ready to give support, but do not crave it; do not be dependent on it. To develop your true self-reliance, you must see from the very beginning that life is a battle you must fight for yourself,—you must be your own soldier. You cannot buy a substitute, you cannot win a reprieve, you can never be placed on the retired list. The retired list of life is,—death. The world is busy with its own cares, sorrows and joys, and pays little heed to you. There is but one great password to success,—self-reliance.

If you would learn to converse, put yourself into positions where you *must* speak. If you would conquer your morbidness, mingle with the bright people around you, no matter how difficult it may be. If you desire the power that some one else possesses, do not envy his strength, and dissipate your energy by weakly wishing his force were yours. Emulate the process by which it became his, depend on your self-reliance, pay the price for it, and equal power may be yours. The individual must look upon himself as an investment, of untold possibilities if rightly developed,—a mine whose resources can never be known but by going down into it and bringing out what is hidden.

Man can develop his self-reliance by seeking constantly to surpass himself. We try too much to surpass others. If we seek ever to surpass ourselves, we are moving on a uniform line of progress, that gives a harmonious unifying to our growth in all its parts. Daniel Morrell, at one time President of the Cambria Rail Works, that employed 7,000 men and made a rail famed throughout the world, was asked the secret of the great success of the works. "We have no secret," he said, "but this,—we always try to beat our last batch of rails." Competition is good, but it has its danger side. There is a tendency to sacrifice real worth to mere appearance, to have seeming rather than reality. But the true competition is the competition of the individual with himself,—his present seeking to excel his past. This means real growth from within. Self-reliance develops it, and it develops self-reliance. Let the individual feel thus as to his own progress and possibilities, and he can almost create his life as he will. Let him never fall down in despair at dangers and sorrows at a distance; they may be harmless, like Bunyan's stone lions, when he nears them.

The man who is self-reliant does not live in the shadow of some one else's greatness; he thinks for himself, depends on himself, and acts for himself. In throwing the individual thus back upon himself it is not shutting his eyes to the stimulus and light and new life that come with the warm pressure of the hand, the kindly word and the sincere expressions of true friendship. But true friendship is rare; its great value is in a crisis,—like a lifeboat. Many a boasted friend has proved a leaking, worthless "lifeboat" when the storm of adversity might make him useful. In these great crises of life, man is strong only as he is strong from within, and the more he depends on himself the stronger will he become, and the more able will he be to help others in the hour of their need. His very life will be a constant help and a strength to others, as he becomes to them a living lesson of the dignity of self-reliance.

Failure as a Success

It ofttimes requires heroic courage to face fruitless effort, to take up the broken strands of a life-work, to look bravely toward the future, and proceed undaunted on our way. But what, to our eyes, may seem hopeless failure is often but the dawning of a greater success. It may contain in its débris the foundation material of a mighty purpose, or the revelation of new and higher possibilities.

Some years ago, it was proposed to send logs from Canada to New York, by a new method. The ingenious plan of Mr. Joggins was to bind great logs together by cables and iron girders and to tow the cargo as a raft. When the novel craft neared New York and success seemed assured, a terrible storm arose. In the fury of the tempest, the iron bands snapped like icicles and the angry waters scattered the logs far and wide. The chief of the Hydrographic Department at Washington heard of the failure of the experiment, and at once sent word to shipmasters the world over, urging them to watch carefully for these logs which he described; and to note the precise location of each in latitude and longitude and the time the observation was made.

Hundreds of captains, sailing over the waters of the earth, noted the logs, in the Atlantic Ocean, in the Mediterranean, in the South Seas—for into all waters did these venturesome ones travel. Hundreds of reports were made, covering a period of weeks and months. These observations were then carefully collated, systematized and tabulated, and discoveries were made as to the course of ocean currents that otherwise would have been impossible. The loss of the Joggins raft was not a real failure, for it led to one of the great discoveries in modern marine geography and navigation.

In our superior knowledge we are disposed to speak in a patronizing tone of the follies of the alchemists of old. But their failure to transmute the baser metals into gold resulted in the birth of chemistry. They did not succeed in what they attempted, but they brought into vogue the natural processes of sublimation, filtration, distillation, and crystallization; they invented the alembic, the retort, the sand-bath, the water-bath and other valuable instruments. To them is due the discovery of antimony, sulphuric ether and phosphorus, the cupellation of gold and silver, the determining of the properties of saltpetre and its use in gunpowder, and the discovery of the distillation of essential oils. This was the success of failure, a wondrous process of Nature for the highest growth,—a mighty lesson of comfort, strength, and encouragement if man would only realize and accept it.

Many of our failures sweep us to greater heights of success, than we ever hoped for in our wildest dreams. Life is a successive unfolding of success from failure. In discovering America Columbus failed absolutely. His ingenious reasoning and experiment led him to believe that by sailing westward he would reach India. Every redman in America carries in his name "Indian," the perpetuation of the memory of the failure of Columbus. The Genoese navigator did not reach India; the cargo of "souvenirs" he took back to Spain to show to Ferdinand and Isabella as proofs of his success, really attested his failure. But the discovery of America was a greater success than was any finding of a "back-door" to India.

When David Livingstone had supplemented his theological education by a medical course, he was ready to enter the missionary field. For over three years he had studied tirelessly, with all energies concentrated on one aim,—to spread the gospel in China. The hour came when he was ready to start out with noble enthusiasm for his chosen work, to consecrate himself and his life to his unselfish ambition. Then word came from China that the "opium war" would make it folly to attempt to enter the country. Disappointment and failure did not long daunt him; he offered himself as missionary to Africa,—and he was accepted. His glorious failure to reach China opened a whole continent to light and truth. His study proved an ideal preparation for his labors as physician, explorer, teacher and evangel in the wilds of Africa.

Business reverses and the failure of his partner threw upon the broad shoulders and the still broader honor and honesty of Sir Walter Scott a burden of responsibility that forced him to write. The failure spurred him to almost super-human effort. The masterpieces of Scotch historic fiction that have thrilled, entertained and uplifted millions of his fellow-men are a glorious monument on the field of a seeming failure.

When Millet, the painter of the "Angelus" worked on his almost divine canvas, in which the very air seems pulsing with the regenerating essence of spiritual reverence, he was painting against time, he was antidoting sorrow, he was racing against death. His brush strokes, put on in the early morning hours before going to his menial duties as a railway porter, in the dusk like that perpetuated on his canvas,—meant strength, food and medicine for the dying wife he adored. The art failure that cast him into the depths of poverty unified with marvellous intensity all the finer elements of his nature. This rare spiritual unity, this purging of all the dross of triviality as he passed through the furnace of poverty, trial, and sorrow gave eloquence to his brush and enabled him to paint as never before,—as no prosperity would have made possible.

Failure is often the turning-point, the pivot of circumstance that swings us to higher levels. It may not be financial success, it may not be fame; it may be new draughts of spiritual, moral or mental inspiration that will change us for all the later years of our life. Life is not really what comes to us, but what we get from it.

Whether man has had wealth or poverty, failure or success, counts for little when it is past. There is but one question for him to answer, to face boldly and honestly as an individual alone with his conscience and his destiny:

"How will I let that poverty or wealth affect me? If that trial or deprivation has left me better, truer, nobler, then,—poverty has been riches, failure has been a success. If wealth has come to me and has made me vain, arrogant, contemptuous, uncharitable, cynical, closing from me all the tenderness of life, all the channels of higher development, of possible good to my fellow-man, making me the mere custodian of a money-bag, then,—wealth has lied to me, it has been failure, not success; it has not been riches, it has been dark, treacherous poverty that stole from me even Myself." All things become for us then what we take from them.

Failure is one of God's educators. It is experience leading man to higher things; it is the revelation of a way, a path hitherto unknown to us. The best men in the world, those who have made the greatest real successes look back with serene happiness on their failures. The turning of the face of Time shows all things in a wondrously illuminated and satisfying perspective.

Many a man is thankful to-day that some petty success for which he once struggled, melted into thin air as his hand sought to clutch it. Failure is often the rock-bottom foundation of real success. If man, in a few instances of his life can say, "Those failures were the best things in the world that could have happened to me," should he not face new failures with undaunted courage and trust that the miraculous ministry of Nature may transform these new stumbling-blocks into new stepping-stones?

Our highest hopes, are often destroyed to prepare us for better things. The failure of the caterpillar is the birth of the butterfly; the passing of the bud is the becoming of the rose; the death or destruction of the seed is the prelude to its resurrection as wheat. It is at night, in the darkest hours, those preceding dawn, that plants grow best, that they most increase in size. May this not be one of Nature's gentle showings to man of the times when he grows best, of the darkness of failure that is evolving into the sunlight of success. Let us fear only the failure of not living the right as we see it, leaving the results to the guardianship of the Infinite.

If we think of any supreme moment of our lives, any great success, any one who is dear to us, and then consider how we reached that moment, that success, that friend, we will be surprised and strengthened by the revelation. As we trace each one, back, step by step, through the genealogy of circumstances, we will see how logical has been the course of our joy and success, from sorrow and failure, and that what gives us most happiness to-day is inextricably connected with what once caused us sorrow. Many of the rivers of our greatest prosperity and growth have had their source and their trickling increase into volume among the dark, gloomy recesses of our failure.

There is no honest and true work, carried along with constant and sincere purpose that ever really fails. If it sometime seem to be wasted effort, it will prove to us a new lesson of "how" to walk; the secret of our failures will prove to us the inspiration of possible successes. Man living with the highest aims, ever as best he can, in continuous harmony with them, is a success, no matter what statistics of failure a near-sighted and half-blind world of critics and commentators may lay at his door.

High ideals, noble efforts will make seeming failures but trifles, they need not dishearten us; they should prove sources of new strength. The rocky way may prove safer than the slippery path of smoothness. Birds cannot fly best with the wind but against it; ships do not progress in calm, when the sails flap idly against the unstrained masts.

The alchemy of Nature, superior to that of the Paracelsians, constantly transmutes the baser metals of failure into the later pure gold of higher success, if the mind of the worker be kept true, constant and untiring in the service, and he have that sublime courage that defies fate to its worst while he does his best.

Doing Our Best
at All Times

Life is a wondrously complex problem for the individual, until, some day, in a moment of illumination, he awakens to the great realization that he can make it simple,—never quite simple, but always simpler. There are a thousand mysteries of right and wrong that have baffled the wise men of the ages. There are depths in the great fundamental questions of the human race that no plummet of philosophy has ever sounded. There are wild cries of honest hunger for truth that seek to pierce the silence beyond the grave, but to them ever echo back,—only a repetition of their unanswered cries.

To us all, comes, at times, the great note of questioning despair that darkens our horizon and paralyzes our effort: "If there really be a God, if eternal justice really rule the world," we say, "why should life be as it is? Why do some men starve while others feast; why does virtue often languish in the shadow while vice triumphs in the sunshine; why does failure so often dog the footsteps of honest effort, while the success that comes from trickery and dishonor is greeted with the world's applause? How is it that the loving father of one family is taken by death, while the worthless incumbrance of another is spared? Why is there so much unnecessary pain, sorrowing and suffering in the world—why, indeed, should there be any?"

Neither philosophy nor religion can give any final satisfactory answer that is capable of logical demonstration, of absolute proof. There is ever, even after the best explanations, a residuum of the unexplained. We must then fall back in the eternal arms of faith, and be wise enough to say, "I will not be disconcerted by these problems of life, I will not permit them to plunge me into doubt, and to cloud my life with vagueness and uncertainty. Man arrogates much to himself when he demands from the Infinite the full solution of all His mysteries. I will found my life on the impregnable rock of a simple fundamental truth: 'This glorious creation with its millions of wondrous phenomena pulsing ever in harmony with eternal law must have a Creator, that Creator must be omniscient and omnipotent. But that Creator Himself cannot, in justice, demand of any creature more than the best that that individual can give.' I will do each day, in every moment, the best I can by the light I have; I will ever seek more light, more perfect illumination of truth, and ever live as best I can in harmony with the truth as I see it. If failure come I will meet it bravely; if my pathway then lie in the shadow of trial, sorrow and suffering, I shall have the restful peace and the calm strength of one who has done his best, who can look back upon the past with no pang of regret, and who has heroic courage in facing the results, whatever they be, knowing that he could not make them different."

Upon this life-plan, this foundation, man may erect any superstructure of religion or philosophy that he conscientiously can erect; he should add to his equipment for living every shred of strength and inspiration, moral, mental or spiritual that is in his power to secure. This simple working faith is opposed to no creed, is a substitute for none; it is but a primary belief, a citadel, a refuge where the individual can retire for strength when the battle of life grows hard.

A mere theory of life, that remains but a theory, is about as useful to a man, as a gilt-edged menu is to a starving sailor on a raft in mid-ocean. It is irritating but not stimulating. No rule for higher living will help a man in the slightest, until he reach out and appropriate it for himself, until he make it practical in his daily life, until that seed of theory in his mind blossom into a thousand flowers of thought and word and act.

If a man honestly seeks to live his best at all times, that determination is visible in every moment of his living, no trifle in his life can be too insignificant to reflect his principle of living. The sun illuminates and beautifies a fallen leaf by the roadside as impartially as a towering mountain peak in the Alps. Every drop of water in the ocean is an epitome of the chemistry of the whole ocean; every drop is subject to precisely the same laws as dominate the united infinity of billions of drops that make that miracle of Nature, men call the Sea. No matter how humble the calling of the individual, how uninteresting and dull the round of his duties, he should do his best. He should dignify what he is doing by the mind he puts into it, he should vitalize what little he has of power or energy or ability or opportunity, in order to prepare himself to be equal to higher privileges when they come. This will never lead man to that weak content that is satisfied with whatever falls to his lot. It will rather fill his mind with that divine discontent that cheerfully accepts the best,—merely as a temporary substitute for something better.

The man who is seeking ever to do his best is the man who is keen, active, wide-awake, and aggressive. He is ever watchful of himself in trifles; his standard is not "What will the world say?" but "Is it worthy of me?"

Edwin Booth, one of the greatest actors on the American stage, would never permit himself to assume an ungraceful attitude, even in his hours of privacy. In this simple thing, he ever lived his best. On the stage every move was one of unconscious grace. Those of his company who were conscious of their motions were the awkward ones, who were seeking in public to undo or to conceal the carelessness of the gestures and motions of their private life. The man who is slipshod and thoughtless in his daily speech, whose vocabulary is a collection of anæmic commonplaces, whose repetitions of phrases and extravagance of interjections act but as feeble disguises to his lack of ideas, will never be brilliant on an occasion when he longs to outshine the stars. Living at one's best is constant preparation for instant use. It can never make one over-precise, self-conscious, affected, or priggish. Education, in its highest sense, is *conscious* training of mind or body to act *unconsciously*. It is conscious formation of mental habits, not mere acquisition of information.

One of the many ways in which the individual unwisely eclipses himself, is in his worship of the fetich of luck. He feels that all others are lucky, and that whatever he attempts, fails. He does not realize the untiring energy, the unremitting concentration, the heroic courage, the sublime patience that is the secret of some men's success. Their "luck" was that they had prepared themselves to be equal to their opportunity when it came and were awake to recognize it and receive it. His own opportunity came and departed unnoted, it would not waken him from his dreams of some untold wealth that would fall into his lap. So he grows discouraged and envies those whom he should emulate, and he bandages his arm and chloroforms his energies, and performs his duties in a perfunctory way, or he passes through life, just ever "sampling" lines of activity.

The honest, faithful struggler should always realize that failure is but an episode in a true man's life,—never the whole story. It is never easy to meet, and no philosophy can make it so, but the steadfast courage to master conditions, instead of complaining of them, will help him on his way; it will ever enable him to get the best out of what he has. He never knows the long series of vanquished failures that give solidity to some one else's success; he does not realize the price that some rich man, the innocent football of political malcontents and demagogues, has heroically paid for wealth and position.

The man who has a pessimist's doubt of all things; who demands a certified guarantee of his future; who ever fears his work will not be recognized or appreciated; or that after all, it is really not worth while, will never live his best. He is dulling his capacity for real progress by his hypnotic course of excuses for inactivity, instead of a strong tonic of reasons for action.

One of the most weakening elements in the individual make-up is the surrender to the oncoming of years. Man's self-confidence dims and dies in the fear of age. "This new thought," he says of some suggestion tending to higher development, "is good; it is what we need. I am glad to have it for my children; I would have been happy to have had some such help when I was at school, but it is too late for me. I am a man advanced in years."

This is but blind closing of life to wondrous possibilities. The knell of lost opportunity is never tolled in this life. It is never too late to recognize truth and to live by it. It requires only greater effort, closer attention, deeper consecration; but the impossible does not exist for the man who is self-confident and is willing to pay the price in time and struggle for his success or development. Later in life, the assessments are heavier in progress, as in life insurance, but that matters not to that mighty self-confidence that *will* not grow old while knowledge can keep it young.

Socrates, when his hair whitened with the snow of age, learned to play on instruments of music. Cato, at fourscore, began his study of Greek, and the same age saw Plutarch beginning, with the enthusiasm of a boy, his first lessons in Latin. The Character of Man, Theophrastus' greatest work, was begun on his ninetieth birthday. Chaucer's Canterbury Tales was the work of the poet's declining years. Ronsard, the father of French poetry, whose sonnets even translation cannot destroy, did not develop his poetic faculty until nearly fifty. Benjamin Franklin at this age had just taken his really first steps of importance in philosophic pursuits. Arnauld, the theologian and sage, translated Josephus in his eightieth year. Winckelmann, one of the most famous writers on classic antiquities, was the son of a shoemaker, and lived in obscurity and ignorance until the prime of life. Hobbes, the English philosopher, published his version of the Odyssey in his eighty-seventh year, and his Iliad one year later. Chevreul, the great French scientist, whose untiring labors in the realm of color have so enriched the world, was busy, keen and active when Death called him, at the age of 103.

These men did not fear age; these few names from the great muster-roll of the famous ones who defied the years, should be voices of hope and heartening to every individual whose courage and confidence is weak. The path of truth, higher living, truer development in every phase of life, is never shut from the individual—until he closes it himself. Let man feel this, believe it and make this faith a real and living factor in his life and there are no limits to his progress. He has but to live his best at all times, and rest calm and untroubled no matter what results come to his efforts. The constant looking backward to what might have been, instead of forward to what may be, is a great weakener of self-confidence. This worry for the old past, this wasted energy, for that which no power in the world can restore, ever lessens the individual's faith in himself, weakens his efforts to develop himself for the future to the perfection of his possibilities.

Nature in her beautiful love and tenderness, says to man, weakened and worn and weary with the struggle, "Do in the best way you can the trifle that is under your hand at this moment; do it in the best spirit of preparation for the future your thought suggests; bring all the light of knowledge from all the past to aid you. Do this and you have done your best. The past is forever closed to you. It is closed forever to you. No worry, no struggle, no suffering, no agony of despair can alter it. It is as much beyond your power as if it were a million years of eternity behind you. Turn all that past, with its sad hours, weakness and sin, its wasted opportunities as light; in confidence and hope, upon the future. Turn it all in fuller truth and light so as to make each trifle of this present a new past it will be joy to look back to; each trifle a grander, nobler, and more perfect preparation for the future. The present and the future you can make from it, is yours; the past has gone back, with all its messages, all its history, all its records to the God who loaned you the golden moments to use in obedience to His law."

The Royal Road to Happiness

During my whole life I have not had twenty-four hours of happiness." So said Prince Bismarck, one of the greatest statesmen of the nineteenth century. Eighty-three years of wealth, fame, honors, power, influence, prosperity and triumph,—years when he held an empire in his fingers,—but not one day of happiness!

Happiness is the greatest paradox in Nature. It can grow in any soil, live under any conditions. It defies environment. It comes from within; it is the revelation of the depths of the inner life as light and heat proclaim the sun from which they radiate. Happiness consists not of having, but of being; not of possessing, but of enjoying. It is the warm glow of a heart at peace with itself. A martyr at the stake may have happiness that a king on his throne might envy. Man is the creator of his own happiness; it is the aroma of a life lived in harmony with high ideals. For what a man *has*, he may be dependent on others; what he *is*, rests with him alone. What he *ob*tains in life is but acquisition; what he *at*tains, is growth. Happiness is the soul's joy in the possession of the intangible. Absolute, perfect, continuous happiness in life, is impossible for the human. It would mean the consummation of attainments, the individual consciousness of a perfectly fulfilled destiny. Happiness is paradoxic because it may coexist with trial, sorrow and poverty. It is the gladness of the heart,—rising superior to all conditions.

Happiness has a number of under-studies,—gratification, satisfaction, content, and pleasure,—clever imitators that simulate its appearance rather than emulate its method. Gratification is a harmony between our desires and our possessions. It is ever incomplete, it is the thankful acceptance of part. It is a mental pleasure in the quality of what one receives, an unsatisfiedness as to the quantity. It may be an element in happiness, but, in itself,—it is not happiness.

Satisfaction is perfect identity of our desires and our possessions. It exists only so long as this perfect union and unity can be preserved. But every realized ideal gives birth to new ideals, every step in advance reveals large domains of the unattained; every feeding stimulates new appetites,—then the desires and possessions are no longer identical, no longer equal; new cravings call forth new activities, the equipoise is destroyed, and dissatisfaction reënters. Man might possess everything tangible in the world and yet not be happy, for happiness is the satisfying of the soul, not of the mind or the body. Dissatisfaction, in its highest sense, is the keynote of all advance, the evidence of new aspirations, the guarantee of the progressive revelation of new possibilities.

Content is a greatly overrated virtue. It is a kind of diluted despair; it is the feeling with which we continue to accept substitutes, without striving for the realities. Content makes the trained individual swallow vinegar and try to smack his lips as if it were wine. Content enables one to warm his hands at the fire of a past joy that exists only in memory. Content is a mental and moral chloroform that deadens the activities of the individual to rise to higher planes of life and growth. Man should never be contented with anything less than the best efforts of his nature can possibly secure for him. Content makes the world more comfortable for the individual, but it is the death-knell of progress. Man should be content with each step of progress merely as a station, discontented with it as a destination; contented with it as a step; discontented with it as a finality. There are times when a man should be content with what he *has*, but never with what he *is*.

But content is not happiness; neither is pleasure. Pleasure is temporary, happiness is continuous; pleasure is a note, happiness is a symphony; pleasure may exist when conscience utters protests; happiness,—never. Pleasure may have its dregs and its lees; but none can be found in the cup of happiness.

Man is the only animal that can be really happy. To the rest of the creation belong only weak imitations of the understudies. Happiness represents a peaceful attunement of a life with a standard of living. It can never be made by the individual, by himself, for himself. It is one of the incidental by-products of an unselfish life. No man can make his own happiness the one object of his life and attain it, any more than he can jump on the far end of his shadow. If you would hit the bull's-eye of happiness on the target of life, aim above it. Place other things higher than your own happiness and it will surely come to you. You can buy pleasure, you can acquire content, you can become satisfied,—but Nature never put real happiness on the bargain-counter. It is the undetachable accompaniment of true living. It is calm and peaceful; it never lives in an atmosphere of worry or of hopeless struggle.

The basis of happiness is the love of something outside self. Search every instance of happiness in the world, and you will find, when all the incidental features are eliminated, there is always the constant, unchangeable element of love,—love of parent for child; love of man and woman for each other; love of humanity in some form, or a great life work into which the individual throws all his energies.

Happiness is the voice of optimism, of faith, of simple, steadfast love. No cynic or pessimist can be really happy. A cynic is a man who is morally near-sighted,—and brags about it. He sees the evil in his own heart, and thinks he sees the world. He lets a mote in his eye eclipse the sun. An incurable cynic is an individual who should long for death,—for life cannot bring him happiness, death might. The keynote of Bismarck's lack of happiness was his profound distrust of human nature.

There is a royal road to happiness; it lies in Consecration, Concentration, Conquest and Conscience.

Consecration is dedicating the individual life to the service of others, to some noble mission, to realizing some unselfish ideal. Life is not something to be lived *through*; it is something to be lived *up to*. It is a privilege, not a penal servitude of so many decades on earth. Consecration places the object of life above the mere acquisition of money, as a finality. The man who is unselfish, kind, loving, tender, helpful, ready to lighten the burden of those around him, to hearten the struggling ones, to forget himself sometimes in remembering others,—is on the right road to happiness. Consecration is ever active, bold and aggressive, fearing naught but possible disloyalty to high ideals.

Concentration makes the individual life simpler and deeper. It cuts away the shams and pretences of modern living and limits life to its truest essentials. Worry, fear, useless regret,—all the great wastes that sap mental, moral or physical energy must be sacrificed, or the individual needlessly destroys half the possibilities of living. A great purpose in life, something that unifies the strands and threads of each day's thinking, something that takes the sting from the petty trials, sorrows, sufferings and blunders of life, is a great aid to Concentration. Soldiers in battle may forget their wounds, or even be unconscious of them, in the inspiration of battling for what they believe is right. Concentration dignifies an humble life; it makes a great life,—sublime. In morals it is a shortcut to simplicity. It leads to right for right's sake, without thought of policy or of reward. It brings calm and rest to the individual,—a serenity that is but the sunlight of happiness.

Conquest is the overcoming of an evil habit, the rising superior to opposition and attack, the spiritual exaltation that comes from resisting the invasion of the grovelling material side of life. Sometimes when you are worn and weak with the struggle; when it seems that justice is a dream, that honesty and loyalty and truth count for nothing, that the devil is the only good paymaster; when hope grows dim and flickers, then is the time when you must tower in the great sublime faith that Right must prevail, then must you throttle these imps of doubt and despair, you must master yourself to master the world around you. This is Conquest; this is what counts. Even a log can float with the current, it takes a man to fight sturdily against an opposing tide that would sweep his craft out of its course. When the jealousies, the petty intrigues and the meannesses and the misunderstandings in life assail you,—rise above them. Be like a lighthouse that illumines and beautifies the snarling, swashing waves of the storm that threaten it, that seek to undermine it and seek to wash over it. This is Conquest. When the chance to win fame, wealth, success or the attainment of your heart's desire, by sacrifice of honor or principle, comes to you and it does not affect you long enough even to seem a temptation, you have been the victor. That too is Conquest. And Conquest is part of the royal road to Happiness.

Conscience, as the mentor, the guide and compass of every act, leads ever to Happiness. When the individual can stay alone with his conscience and get its approval, without using force or specious logic, then he begins to know what real Happiness is. But the individual must be careful that he is not appealing to a conscience perverted or deadened by the wrongdoing and subsequent deafness of its owner. The man who is honestly seeking to live his life in Consecration, Concentration and Conquest, living from day to day as best he can, by the light he has, may rely explicitly on his Conscience. He can shut his ears to "what the world says" and find in the approval of his own conscience the highest earthly tribune,— the voice of the Infinite communing with the Individual.

Unhappiness is the hunger to get; Happiness is the hunger to give. True happiness must ever have the tinge of sorrow outlived, the sense of pain softened by the mellowing years, the chastening of loss that in the wondrous mystery of time transmutes our suffering into love and sympathy with others.

If the individual should set out for a single day to give Happiness, to make life happier, brighter and sweeter, not for himself, but for others, he would find a wondrous revelation of what Happiness really is. The greatest of the world's heroes could not by any series of acts of heroism do as much real good as any individual living his whole life in seeking, from day to day, to make others happy.

Each day there should be fresh resolution, new strength, and renewed enthusiasm. "Just for Today" might be the daily motto of thousands of societies throughout the country, composed of members bound together to make the world better through constant simple acts of kindness, constant deeds of sweetness and love. And Happiness would come to them, in its highest and best form, not because they would seek to *absorb* it, but,—because they seek to *radiate* it.

THE SCIENCE OF GETTING RICH

WALLACE D. WATTLES

Contents

Preface   317

chapter one
The Right To Be Rich   319

chapter two
There is A Science of Getting Rich   323

chapter three
Is Opportunity Monopolized?   327

chapter four
The First Principle in
The Science of Getting Rich   331

chapter five
Increasing Life   337

chapter six
How Riches Come to You   343

chapter seven
Gratitude   348

chapter eight
Thinking in the Certain Way   352

chapter nine
How to Use the Will   357

chapter ten
Further Use of the Will   362

chapter eleven
Acting in the Certain Way   367

chapter twelve
Efficient Action   373

chapter thirteen
Getting into the Right Business   378

chapter fourteen
The Impression of Increase   383

chapter fifteen
The Advancing Man 388

chapter sixteen
Some Cautions, and Concluding Observations 393

chapter seventeen
Summary of the Science of Getting Rich 398

Preface

This book is pragmatical, not philosophical; a practical manual, not a treatise upon theories. It is intended for the men and women whose most pressing need is for money; who wish to get rich first, and philosophize afterward. It is for those who have, so far, found neither the time, the means, nor the opportunity to go deeply into the study of metaphysics, but who want results and who are willing to take the conclusions of science as a basis for action, without going into all the processes by which those conclusions were reached.

It is expected that the reader will take the fundamental statements upon faith, just as he would take statements concerning a law of electrical action if they were promulgated by a Marconi or an Edison; and, taking the statements upon faith, that he will prove their truth by acting upon them without fear or hesitation. Every man or woman who does this will certainly get rich; for the science herein applied is an exact science, and failure is impossible. For the benefit, however, of those who wish to investigate philosophical theories and so secure a logical basis for faith, I will here cite certain authorities.

The monistic theory of the universe the theory that One is All, and that All is One; That one Substance manifests itself as the seeming many elements of the material world -is of Hindu origin, and has been gradually winning its way into the thought of the western world for two hundred years. It is the foundation of all the Oriental philosophies, and of those of Descartes, Spinoza, Leibnitz, Schopenhauer, Hegel, and Emerson. The reader who would dig to the philosophical foundations of this is advised to read Hegel and Emerson for himself.

In writing this book I have sacrificed all other considerations to plainness and simplicity of style, so that all might understand. The plan of action laid down herein was deduced from the conclusions of philosophy; it has been thoroughly tested, and bears the supreme test of practical experiment; it works. If you wish to know how the conclusions were arrived at, read the writings of the authors mentioned above; and if you wish to reap the fruits of their philosophies in actual practice, read this book and do exactly as it tells you to do.

—The Author

chapter one
The Right To Be Rich

Whatever may be said in praise of poverty, the fact remains that it is not possible to live a really complete or successful life unless one is rich. No man can rise to his greatest possible height in talent or soul development unless he has plenty of money; for to unfold the soul and to develop talent he must have many things to use, and he cannot have these things unless he has money to buy them with.

A man develops in mind, soul, and body by making use of things, and society is so organized that man must have money in order to become the possessor of things; therefore, the basis of all advancement for man must be the science of getting rich.

The object of all life is development; and everything that lives has an inalienable right to all the development it is capable of attaining. Man's right to life means his right to have the free and unrestricted use of all the things which may be necessary to his fullest mental, spiritual, and physical unfoldment; or, in other words, his right to be rich.

In this book, I shall not speak of riches in a figurative way; to be really rich does not mean to be satisfied or contented with a little. No man ought to be satisfied with a little if he is capable of using and enjoying more. The purpose of Nature is the advancement and unfoldment of life; and every man should have all that can contribute to the power; elegance, beauty, and richness of life; to be content with less is sinful.

The man who owns all he wants for the living of all the life he is capable of living is rich; and no man who has not plenty of money can have all he wants. Life has advanced so far, and become so complex, that even the most ordinary man or woman requires a great amount of wealth in order to live in a manner that even approaches completeness. Every person naturally wants to become all that they are capable of becoming; this desire to realize innate possibilities is inherent in human nature; we cannot help wanting to be all that we can be. Success in life is becoming what you want to be; you can become what you want to be only by making use of things, and you can have the free use of things only as you become rich enough to buy them. To understand the science of getting rich is therefore the most essential of all knowledge.

There is nothing wrong in wanting to get rich. The desire for riches is really the desire for a richer, fuller, and more abundant life; and that desire is praise worthy. The man who does not desire to live more abundantly is abnormal, and so the man who does not desire to have money enough to buy all he wants is abnormal. There are three motives for which we live; we live for the body, we live for the mind, we live for the soul. No one of these is better or holier than the other; all are alike desirable, and no one of the three—body, mind, or soul—can live fully if either of the others is cut short of full life and expression. It is not right or noble to live only for the soul and deny mind or body; and it is wrong to live for the intellect and deny body or soul.

We are all acquainted with the loathsome consequences of living for the body and denying both mind and soul; and we see that real life means the complete expression of all that man can give forth through body, mind, and soul. Whatever he can say, no man can be really happy or satisfied unless his body is living fully in every function, and unless the same is true of his mind and his soul. Wherever there is unexpressed possibility, or function not performed, there is unsatisfied desire. Desire is possibility seeking expression, or function seeking performance.

Man cannot live fully in body without good food, comfortable clothing, and warm shelter; and without freedom from excessive toil. Rest and recreation are also necessary to his physical life.

He cannot live fully in mind without books and time to study them, without opportunity for travel and observation, or without intellectual companionship. To live fully in mind he must have intellectual recreations, and must surround himself with all the objects of art and beauty he is capable of using and appreciating.

To live fully in soul, man must have love; and love is denied expression by poverty. A man's highest happiness is found in the bestowal of benefits on those he loves; love finds its most natural and spontaneous expression in giving. The man who has nothing to give cannot fill his place as a husband or father, as a citizen, or as a man. It is in the use of material things that a man finds full life for his body, develops his mind, and unfolds his soul. It is therefore of supreme importance to him that he should be rich.

It is perfectly right that you should desire to be rich; if you are a normal man or woman you cannot help doing so. It is perfectly right that you should give your best attention to the Science of Getting Rich, for it is the noblest and most necessary of all studies. If you neglect this study, you are derelict in your duty to yourself, to God and humanity; for you can render to God and humanity no greater service than to make the most of yourself.

chapter two
There is A Science of Getting Rich

There is a Science of getting rich, and it is an exact science, like algebra or arithmetic. There are certain laws that govern the process of acquiring riches; once these laws are learned and obeyed by any man, he will get rich with mathematical certainty.

The ownership of money and property comes as a result of doing things in a certain way; those who do things in this Certain Way, whether on purpose or accidentally, get rich; while those who do not do things in this Certain Way, no matter how hard they work or how able they are, remain poor.

It is a natural law that like causes always produce like effects; and, therefore, any man or woman who learns to do things in this certain way will infallibly get rich. That the above statement is true is shown by the following facts:

Getting rich is not a matter of environment, for, if it were, all the people in certain neighborhoods would become wealthy; the people of one city would all be rich, while those of other towns would all be poor; or the inhabitants of one state would roll in wealth, while those of an adjoining state would be in poverty.

But everywhere we see rich and poor living side-by-side, in the same environment, and often engaged in the same vocations. When two men are in the same locality, and in the same business, and one gets rich while the other remains poor, it shows that getting rich is not, primarily, a matter of environment. Some environments may be more favorable than others, but when two men in the same business are in the same neighborhood, and one gets rich while the other fails, it indicates that getting rich is the result of doing things in a Certain Way. And further, the ability to do things in this certain way is not due solely to the possession of talent, for many people who have great talent remain poor, while other who have very little talent get rich.

Studying the people who have got rich, we find that they are an average lot in all respects, having no greater talents and abilities than other men. It is evident that they do not get rich because they possess talents and abilities that other men have not, but because they happen to do things in a Certain Way.

Getting rich is not the result of saving, or "thrift"; many very penurious people are poor, while free spenders often get rich.

Nor is getting rich due to doing things which others fail to do; for two men in the same business often do almost exactly the same things, and one gets rich while the other remains poor or becomes bankrupt. From all these things, we must come to the conclusion that getting rich is the result of doing things in a Certain Way.

If getting rich is the result of doing things in a Certain Way, and if like causes always produce like effects, then any man or woman who can do things in that way can become rich, and the whole matter is brought within the domain of exact science.

The question arises here, whether this Certain Way may not be so difficult that only a few may follow it. This cannot be true, as we have seen, so far as natural ability is concerned. Talented people get rich, and blockheads get rich; intellectually brilliant people get rich, and very stupid people get rich; physically strong people get rich, and weak and sickly people get rich.

Some degree of ability to think and understand is, of course, essential; but in so far natural ability is concerned, any man or woman who has sense enough to read and understand these words can certainly get rich. Also, we have seen that it is not a matter of environment. Location counts for something; one would not go to the heart of the Sahara and expect to do successful business.

Getting rich involves the necessity of dealing with men, and of being where there are people to deal with; and if these people are inclined to deal in the way you want to deal, so much the better. But that is about as far as environment goes.

If anybody else in your town can get rich, so can you; and if anybody else in your state can get rich, so can you. Again, it is not a matter of choosing some particular business or profession. People get rich in every business, and in every profession; while their next door neighbors in the same vocation remain in poverty.

It is true that you will do best in a business that you like, and which is congenial to you; and if you have certain talents that are well developed, you will do best in a business that calls for the exercise of those talents. Also, you will do best in a business, which is suited to your locality; an ice-cream parlor would do better in a warm climate than in Greenland, and a salmon fishery will succeed better in the Northwest than in Florida, where there are no salmon.

But, aside from these general limitations, getting rich is not dependent upon your engaging in some particular business, but upon your learning to do things in a Certain Way. If you are now in business, and anybody else in your locality is getting rich in the same business, while you are not getting rich, it is because you are not doing things in the same Way that the other person is doing them.

No one is prevented from getting rich by lack of capital. True, as you get capital the increase becomes more easy and rapid; but one who has capital is already rich, and does not need to consider how to become so. No matter how poor you may be, if you begin to do things in the Certain Way you will begin to get rich; and you will begin to have capital. The getting of capital is a part of the process of getting rich; and it is a part of the result that invariably follows the doing of things in the Certain Way. You may be the poorest man on the continent, and be deeply in debt; you may have neither friends, influence, nor resources; but if you begin to do things in this way, you must infallibly begin to get rich, for like causes must produce like effects. If you have no capital, you can get capital; if you are in the wrong business, you can get into the right business; if you are in the wrong location, you can go to the right location; and you can do so by beginning in your present business and in your present location to do things in the Certain Way which causes success.

chapter three
Is Opportunity Monopolized?

No man is kept poor because opportunity has been taken away from him; because other people have monopolized the wealth, and have put a fence around it. You may be shut off from engaging in business in certain lines, but there are other channels open to you. Probably it would be hard for you to get control of any of the great railroad systems; that field is pretty well monopolized. But the electric railway business is still in its infancy, and offers plenty of scope for enterprise; and it will be but a very few years until traffic and transportation through the air will become a great industry, and in all its branches will give employment to hundreds of thousands, and perhaps to millions, of people. Why not turn your attention to the development of aerial transportation, instead of competing with J. J. Hill and others for a chance in the steam railway world?

It is quite true that if you are a workman in the employ of the steel trust you have very little chance of becoming the owner of the plant in which you work; but it is also true that if you will commence to act in a Certain Way, you can soon leave the employ of the steel trust; you can buy a farm of from ten to forty acres, and engage in business as a producer of foodstuffs. There is great opportunity at this time for men who will live upon small tracts of land and cultivate the same intensively; such men will certainly get rich. You may say that it is impossible for you to get the land, but I am going to prove to you that it is not impossible, and that you can certainly get a farm if you will go to work in a Certain Way.

At different periods the tide of opportunity sets in different directions, according to the needs of the whole, and the particular stage of social evolution which has been reached. At present, in America, it is setting toward agriculture and the allied industries and professions. Today, opportunity is open before the factory worker in his line. It is open before the business man who supplies the farmer more than before the one who supplies the factory worker; and before the professional man who waits upon the farmer more than before the one who serves the working class.

There is abundance of opportunity for the man who will go with the tide, instead of trying to swim against it. So the factory workers, either as individuals or as a class, are not deprived of opportunity. The workers are not being "kept down" by their masters; they are not being "ground" by the trusts and combinations of capital. As a class, they are where they are because they do not do things in a Certain Way. If the workers of America chose to do so, they could follow the example of their brothers in Belgium and other countries, and establish great department stores and co-operative industries; they could elect men of their own class to office, and pass laws favoring the development of such co-operative industries; and in a few years they could take peaceable possession of the industrial field.

The working class may become the master class whenever they will begin to do things in a Certain Way; the law of wealth is the same for them as it is for all others. This they must learn; and they will remain where they are as long as they continue to do as they do. The individual worker, however, is not held down by the ignorance or the mental slothfulness of his class; he can follow the tide of opportunity to riches, and this book will tell him how.

No one is kept in poverty by a shortness in the supply of riches; there is more than enough for all. A palace as large as the capitol at Washington might be built for every family on earth from the building material in the United States alone; and under intensive cultivation, this country would produce wool, cotton, linen, and silk enough to cloth each person in the world finer than Solomon was arrayed in all his glory; together with food enough to feed them all luxuriously.

The visible supply is practically inexhaustible; and the invisible supply really IS inexhaustible. Everything you see on earth is made from one original substance, out of which all things proceed.

New Forms are constantly being made, and older ones are dissolving; but all are shapes assumed by One Thing. There is no limit to the supply of Formless Stuff, or Original Substance. The universe is made out of it; but it was not all used in making the universe. The spaces in, through, and between the forms of the visible universe are permeated and filled with the Original Substance; with the formless Stuff; with the raw material of all things. Ten thousand times as much as has been made might still be made, and even then we should not have exhausted the supply of universal raw material. No man, therefore, is poor because nature is poor, or because there is not enough to go around.

Nature is an inexhaustible storehouse of riches; the supply will never run short. Original Substance is alive with creative energy, and is constantly producing more forms. When the supply of building material is exhausted, more will be produced; when the soil is exhausted so that food stuffs and materials for clothing will no longer grow upon it, it will be renewed or more soil will be made. When all the gold and silver has been dug from the earth, if man is still in such a stage of social development that he needs gold and silver, more will produced from the Formless. The Formless Stuff responds to the needs of man; it will not let him be without any good thing. This is true of man collectively; the race as a whole is always abundantly rich, and if individuals are poor, it is because they do not follow the Certain Way of doing things which makes the individual man rich.

The Formless Stuff is intelligent; it is stuff which thinks. It is alive, and is always impelled toward more life. It is the natural and inherent impulse of life to seek to live more; it is the nature of intelligence to enlarge itself, and of consciousness to seek to extend its boundaries and find fuller expression. The universe of forms has been made by Formless Living Substance, throwing itself into form in order to express itself more fully.

The universe is a great Living Presence, always moving inherently toward more life and fuller functioning. Nature is formed for the advancement of life; its impelling motive is the increase of life. For this cause, everything which can possibly minister to life is bountifully provided; there can be no lack unless God is to contradict himself and nullify his own works. You are not kept poor by lack in the supply of riches; it is a fact which I shall demonstrate a little farther on that even the resources of the Formless Supply are at the command of the man or woman will act and think in a Certain Way.

chapter four
The First Principle in The Science of Getting Rich

Thought is the only power which can produce tangible riches from the Formless Substance. The stuff from which all things are made is a substance which thinks, and a thought of form in this substance produces the form.

Original Substance moves according to its thoughts; every form and process you see in nature is the visible expression of a thought in Original Substance. As the Formless Stuff thinks of a form, it takes that form; as it thinks of a motion, it makes that motion. That is the way all things were created. We live in a thought world, which is part of a thought universe. The thought of a moving universe extended throughout Formless Substance, and the Thinking Stuff moving according to that thought, took the form of systems of planets, and maintains that form. Thinking Substance takes the form of its thought, and moves according to the thought. Holding the idea of a circling system of suns and worlds, it takes the form of these bodies, and moves them as it thinks. Thinking the form of a slow-growing oak tree, it moves accordingly, and produces the tree, though centuries may be required to do the work. In creating, the Formless seems to move according to the lines of motion it has established; the thought of an oak tree does not cause the instant formation of a full-grown tree, but it does start in motion the forces which will produce the tree, along established lines of growth.

Every thought of form, held in thinking Substance, causes the creation of the form, but always, or at least generally, along lines of growth and action already established.

The thought of a house of a certain construction, if it were impressed upon Formless Substance, might not cause the instant formation, of the house; but it would cause the turning of creative energies already working in trade and commerce into such channels as to result in the speedy building of the house. And if there were no existing channels through which the creative energy could work, then the house would be formed directly from primal substance, without waiting for the slow processes of the organic and inorganic world.

No thought of form can be impressed upon Original Substance without causing the creation of the form. Man is a thinking center, and can originate thought. All the forms that man fashions with his hands must first exist in his thought; he cannot shape a thing until he has thought that thing.

And so far man has confined his efforts wholly to the work of his hands; he has applied manual labor to the world of forms, seeking to change or modify those already existing. He has never thought of trying to cause the creation of new forms by impressing his thoughts upon Formless Substance.

When man has a thought-form, he takes material from the forms of nature, and makes an image of the form which is in his mind. He has, so far, made little or no effort to cooperate with Formless Intelligence; to work "with the Father." He has not dreamed that he can "do what he seeth the Father doing." Man reshapes and modifies existing forms by manual labor; he has given no attention to the question whether he may not produce things from Formless Substance by communicating his thoughts to it. We propose to prove that he may do so; to prove that any man or woman may do so, and to show how.

As our first step, we must lay down three fundamental propositions. First, we assert that there is one original formless stuff, or substance, from which all things are made. All the seemingly many elements are but different presentations of one element; all the many forms found in organic and inorganic nature are but different shapes, made from the same stuff. And this stuff is thinking stuff; a thought held in it produces the form of the thought. Thought, in thinking substance, produces shapes. Man is a thinking center, capable of original thought; if man can communicate his thought to original thinking substance, he can cause the creation, or formation, of the thing he thinks about. To summarize this:-

There is a thinking stuff from which all things are made, and which, in its original state, permeates, penetrates, and fills the interspaces of the universe. A thought, in this substance, Produces the thing that is imaged by the thought.

Man can form things in his thought, and, by impressing his thought upon formless substance, can cause the thing he thinks about to be created. It may be asked if I can prove these statements; and without going into details, I answer that I can do so, both by logic and experience.

Reasoning back from the phenomena of form and thought, I come to one original thinking substance; and reasoning forward from this thinking substance, I come to man's power to cause the formation of the thing he thinks about.

And by experiment, I find the reasoning true; and this is my strongest proof.

If one man who reads this book gets rich by doing what it tells him to do, that is evidence in support of my claim; but if every man who does what it tells him to do gets rich, that is positive proof until some one goes through the process and fails. The theory is true until the process fails; and this process will not fail, for every man who does exactly what this book tells him to do will get rich.

I have said that men get rich by doing things in a Certain Way; and in order to do so, men must become able to think in a certain way.

A man's way of doing things is the direct result of the way he thinks about things.

To do things in a way you want to do them, you will have to acquire the ability to think the way you want to think; this is the first step toward getting rich.

To think what you want to think is to think TRUTH, regardless of appearances.

Every man has the natural and inherent power to think what he wants to think, but it requires far more effort to do so than it does to think the thoughts which are suggested by appearances. To think according to appearance is easy; to think truth regardless of appearances is laborious, and requires the expenditure of more power than any other work man is called upon to perform.

There is no labor from which most people shrink as they do from that of sustained and consecutive thought; it is the hardest work in the world. This is especially true when truth is contrary to appearances. Every appearance in the visible world tends to produce a corresponding form in the mind which observes it; and this can only be prevented by holding the thought of the TRUTH.

To look upon the appearance of disease will produce the form of disease in your own mind, and ultimately in your body, unless you hold the thought of the truth, which is that there is no disease; it is only an appearance, and the reality is health.

To look upon the appearances of poverty will produce corresponding forms in your own mind, unless you hold to the truth that there is no poverty; there is only abundance.

To think health when surrounded by the appearances of disease, or to think riches when in the midst of appearances of poverty, requires power; but he who acquires this power becomes a MASTER MIND. He can conquer fate; he can have what he wants.

This power can only be acquired by getting hold of the basic fact which is behind all appearances; and that fact is that there is one Thinking Substance, from which and by which all things are made.

Then we must grasp the truth that every thought held in this substance becomes a form, and that man can so impress his thoughts upon it as to cause them to take form and become visible things.

When we realize this, we lose all doubt and fear, for we know that we can create what we want to create; we can get what we want to have, and can become what we want to be. As a first step toward getting rich, you must believe the three fundamental statements given previously in this chapter; and in order to emphasize them. I repeat them here:

There is a thinking stuff from which all things are made, and which, in its original state, permeates, penetrates, and fills the interspaces of the universe. A thought, in this substance, Produces the thing that is imaged by the thought.

Man can form things in his thought, and, by impressing his thought upon formless substance, can cause the thing he thinks about to be created.

You must lay aside all other concepts of the universe than this monistic one; and you must dwell upon this until it is fixed in your mind, and has become your habitual thought.

Read these creed statements over and over again; fix every word upon your memory, and meditate upon them until you firmly believe what they say. If a doubt comes to you, cast it aside as a sin. Do not listen to arguments against this idea; do not go to churches or lectures where a contrary concept of things is taught or preached. Do not read magazines or books which teach a different idea; if you get mixed up in your faith, all your efforts will be in vain.

Do not ask why these things are true, nor speculate as to how they can be true; simply take them on trust. The science of getting rich begins with the absolute acceptance of this faith.

chapter five
Increasing Life

You must get rid of the last vestige of the old idea that there is a Deity whose will it is that you should be poor, or whose purposes may be served by keeping you in poverty.

The Intelligent Substance which is All, and in All, and which lives in All and lives in you, is a consciously Living Substance. Being a consciously living substance, It must have the nature and inherent desire of every living intelligence for increase of life. Every living thing must continually seek for the enlargement of its life, because life, in the mere act of living, must increase itself. A seed, dropped into the ground, springs into activity, and in the act of living produces a hundred more seeds; life, by living, multiplies itself. It is forever Becoming More; it must do so, if it continues to be at all.

Intelligence is under this same necessity for continuous increase. Every thought we think makes it necessary for us to think another thought; consciousness is continually expanding. Every fact we learn leads us to the learning of another fact; knowledge is continually increasing. Every talent we cultivate brings to the mind the desire to cultivate another talent; we are subject to the urge of life, seeking expression, which ever drives us on to know more, to do more, and to be more. In order to know more, do more, and be more we must have more; we must have things to use, for we learn, and do, and become, only by using things. We must get rich, so that we can live more. The desire for riches is simply the capacity for larger life seeking fulfillment; every desire is the effort of an unexpressed possibility to come into action. It is power seeking to manifest which causes desire. That which makes you want more money is the same as that which makes the plant grow; it is Life, seeking fuller expression.

The One Living Substance must be subject to this inherent law of all life; it is permeated with the desire to live more; that is why it is under the necessity of creating things.

The One Substance desires to live more in you; hence it wants you to have all the things you can use. It is the desire of God that you should get rich. He wants you to get rich because he can express himself better through you if you have plenty of things to use in giving him expression. He can live more in you if you have unlimited command of the means of life. The universe desires you to have everything you want to have.

Nature is friendly to your plans. Everything is naturally for you. Make up your mind that this is true. It is essential, however that your purpose should harmonize with the purpose that is in All. You must want real life, not mere pleasure of sensual gratification. Life is the performance of function; and the individual really lives only when he performs every function, physical, mental, and spiritual, of which he is capable, without excess in any.

You do not want to get rich in order to live swinishly, for the gratification of animal desires; that is not life. But the performance of every physical function is a part of life, and no one lives completely who denies the impulses of the body a normal and healthful expression. You do not want to get rich solely to enjoy mental pleasures, to get knowledge, to gratify ambition, to outshine others, to be famous. All these are a legitimate part of life, but the man who lives for the pleasures of the intellect alone will only have a partial life, and he will never be satisfied with his lot.

You do not want to get rich solely for the good of others, to lose yourself for the salvation of mankind, to experience the joys of philanthropy and sacrifice. The joys of the soul are only a part of life; and they are no better or nobler than any other part.

You want to get rich in order that you may eat, drink, and be merry when it is time to do these things; in order that you may surround yourself with beautiful things, see distant lands, feed your mind, and develop your intellect; in order that you may love men and do kind things, and be able to play a good part in helping the world to find truth.

But remember that extreme altruism is no better and no nobler than extreme selfishness; both are mistakes. Get rid of the idea that God wants you to sacrifice yourself for others, and that you can secure his favor by doing so; God requires nothing of the kind.

What he wants is that you should make the most of yourself, for yourself, and for others; and you can help others more by making the most of yourself than in any other way.

You can make the most of yourself only by getting rich; so it is right and praiseworthy that you should give your first and best thought to the work of acquiring wealth.

Remember, however, that the desire of Substance is for all, and its movements must be for more life to all; it cannot be made to work for less life to any, because it is equally in all, seeking riches and life.

Intelligent Substance will make things for you, but it will not take things away from some one else and give them to you.

You must get rid of the thought of competition. You are to create, not to compete for what is already created. You do not have to take anything away from any one. You do not have to drive sharp bargains. You do not have to cheat, or to take advantage. You do not need to let any man work for you for less than he earns.

You do not have to covet the property of others, or to look at it with wishful eyes; no man has anything of which you cannot have the like, and that without taking what he has away from him.

You are to become a creator, not a competitor; you are going to get what you want, but in such a way that when you get it every other man will have more than he has now.

I am aware that there are men who get a vast amount of money by proceeding in direct opposition to the statements in the paragraph above, and may add a word of explanation here. Men of the plutocratic type, who become very rich, do so sometimes purely by their extraordinary ability on the plane of competition; and sometimes they unconsciously relate themselves to Substance in its great purposes and movements for the general racial upbuilding through industrial evolution. Rockefeller, Carnegie, Morgan, et al., have been the unconscious agents of the Supreme in the necessary work of systematizing and organizing productive industry; and in the end, their work will contribute immensely toward increased life for all. Their day is nearly over; they have organized production, and will soon be succeeded by the agents of the multitude, who will organize the machinery of distribution.

The multi-millionaires are like the monster reptiles of the prehistoric eras; they play a necessary part in the evolutionary process, but the same Power which produced them will dispose of them.

And it is well to bear in mind that they have never been really rich; a record of the private lives of most of this class will show that they have really been the most abject and wretched of the poor.

Riches secured on the competitive plane are never satisfactory and permanent; they are yours to-day, and another's tomorrow. Remember, if you are to become rich in a scientific and certain way, you must rise entirely out of the competitive thought. You must never think for a moment that the supply is limited. Just as soon as you begin to think that all the money is being "cornered" and controlled by bankers and others, and that you must exert yourself to get laws passed to stop this process, and so on; in that moment you drop into the competitive mind, and your power to cause creation is gone for the time being; and what is worse, you will probably arrest the creative movements you have already instituted.

KNOW that there are countless millions of dollars' worth of gold in the mountains of the earth, not yet brought to light; and know that if there were not, more would be created from Thinking Substance to supply your needs.

KNOW that the money you need will come, even if it is necessary for a thousand men to be led to the discovery of new gold mines to-morrow.

Never look at the visible supply; look always at the limitless riches in Formless Substance, and KNOW that they are coming to you as fast as you can receive and use them. Nobody, by cornering the visible supply, can prevent you from getting what is yours.

So never allow yourself to think for an instant that all the best building spots will be taken before you get ready to build your house, unless you hurry. Never worry about the trusts and combines, and get anxious for fear they will soon come to own the whole earth. Never get afraid that you will lose what you want because some other person "beats you to it." That cannot possibly happen; you are not seeking any thing that is possessed by anybody else; you are causing what you want to be created from formless Substance, and the supply is without limits. Stick to the formulated statement:

There is a thinking stuff from which all things are made, and which, in its original state, permeates, penetrates, and fills the interspaces of the universe. A thought, in this substance, produces the thing that is imaged by the thought.

Man can form things in his thought, and, by impressing his thought upon formless substance, can cause the thing he thinks about to be created.

chapter six
How Riches Come to You

When I say that you do not have to drive sharp bargains, I do not mean that you do not have to drive any bargains at all, or that you are above the necessity for having any dealings with your fellow men. I mean that you will not need to deal with them unfairly; you do not have to get something for nothing, but can give to every man more than you take from him.

You cannot give every man more in cash market value than you take from him, but you can give him more in use value than the cash value of the thing you take from him. The paper, ink, and other material in this book may not be worth the money you pay for it; but if the ideas suggested by it bring you thousands of dollars, you have not been wronged by those who sold it to you; they have given you a great use value for a small cash value.

Let us suppose that I own a picture by one of the great artists, which, in any civilized community, is worth thousands of dollars. I take it to Baffin Bay, and by "salesmanship" induce an Eskimo to give a bundle of furs worth $500 for it. I have really wronged him, for he has no use for the picture; it has no use value to him; it will not add to his life.

But suppose I give him a gun worth $50 for his furs; then he has made a good bargain. He has use for the gun; it will get him many more furs and much food; it will add to his life in every way; it will make him rich. When you rise from the competitive to the creative plane, you can scan your business transactions very strictly, and if you are selling any man anything which does not add more to his life than the thing he give you in exchange, you can afford to stop it. You do not have to beat anybody in business. And if you are in a business which does beat people, get out of it at once.

Give every man more in use value than you take from him in cash value; then you are adding to the life of the world by every business transaction.

If you have people working for you, you must take from them more in cash value than you pay them in wages; but you can so organize your business that it will be filled with the principle of advancement, and so that each employee who wishes to do so may advance a little every day.

You can make your business do for your employees what this book is doing for you. You can so conduct your business that it will be a sort of ladder, by which every employee who will take the trouble may climb to riches himself; and given the opportunity, if he will not do so it is not your fault.

And finally, because you are to cause the creation of your riches from Formless Substance which permeates all your environment, it does not follow that they are to take shape from the atmosphere and come into being before your eyes.

If you want a sewing machine, for instance, I do not mean to tell you that you are to impress the thought of a sewing machine on Thinking Substance until the machine is formed without hands, in the room where you sit, or elsewhere. But if you want a sewing machine, hold the mental image of it with the most positive certainty that it is being made, or is on its way to you. After once forming the thought, have the most absolute and unquestioning faith that the sewing machine is coming; never think of it, or speak, of it, in any other way than as being sure to arrive. Claim it as already yours. It will be brought to you by the power of the Supreme Intelligence, acting upon the minds of men. If you live in Maine, it may be that a man will be brought from Texas or Japan to engage in some transaction which will result in your getting what you want.

If so, the whole matter will be as much to that man's advantage as it is to yours.

Do not forget for a moment that the Thinking Substance is through all, in all, communicating with all, and can influence all. The desire of Thinking Substance for fuller life and better living has caused the creation of all the sewing machines already made; and it can cause the creation of millions more, and will, whenever men set it in motion by desire and faith, and by acting in a Certain Way.

You can certainly have a sewing machine in your house; and it is just as certain that you can have any other thing or things which you want, and which you will use for the advancement of your own life and the lives of others.

You need not hesitate about asking largely; "it is your Father's pleasure to give you the kingdom," said Jesus. Original Substance wants to live all that is possible in you, and wants you to have all that you can or will use for the living of the most abundant life.

If you fix upon your consciousness the fact that the desire you feel for the possession of riches is one with the desire of Omnipotence for more complete expression, your faith becomes invincible.

Once I saw a little boy sitting at a piano, and vainly trying to bring harmony out of the keys; and I saw that he was grieved and provoked by his inability to play real music. I asked him the cause of his vexation, and he answered, "I can feel the music in me, but I can't make my hands go right." The music in him was the URGE of Original Substance, containing all the possibilities of all life; all that there is of music was seeking expression through the child.

God, the One Substance, is trying to live and do and enjoy things through humanity. He is saying "I want hands to build wonderful structures, to play divine harmonies, to paint glorious pictures; I want feet to run my errands, eyes to see my beauties, tongues to tell mighty truths and to sing marvelous songs," and so on. All that there is of possibility is seeking expression through men. God wants those who can play music to have pianos and every other instrument, and to have the means to cultivate their talents to the fullest extent; He wants those who can appreciate beauty to be able to surround themselves with beautiful things; He wants those who can discern truth to have every opportunity to travel and observe; He wants those who can appreciate dress to be beautifully clothed, and those who can appreciate good food to be luxuriously fed.

He wants all these things because it is Himself that enjoys and appreciates them; it is God who wants to play, and sing, and enjoy beauty, and proclaim truth and wear fine clothes, and eat good foods, "it is God that worketh in you to will and to do," said Paul.

The desire you feel for riches is the infinite, seeking to express Himself in you as He sought to find expression in the little boy at the piano.

So you need not hesitate to ask largely. Your part is to focalize and express the desire to God. This is a difficult point with most people; they retain something of the old idea that poverty and self-sacrifice are pleasing to God. They look upon poverty as a part of the plan, a necessity of nature. They have the idea that God has finished His work, and made all that He can make, and that the majority of men must stay poor because there is not enough to go around. They hold to so much of this erroneous thought that they feel ashamed to ask for wealth; they try not to want more than a very modest competence, just enough to make them fairly comfortable.

I recall now the case of one student who was told that he must get in mind a clear picture of the things he desired, so that the creative thought of them might be impressed on Formless Substance. He was a very poor man, living in a rented house, and having only what he earned from day to day; and he could not grasp the fact that all wealth was his.

So, after thinking the matter over, he decided that he might reasonably ask for a new rug for the floor of his best room, and an anthracite coal stove to heat the house during the cold weather. Following the instructions given in this book, he obtained these things in a few months; and then it dawned upon him that he had not asked enough. He went through the house in which he lived, and planned all the improvements he would like to make in it; he mentally added a bay window here and a room there, until it was complete in his mind as his ideal home; and then he planned its furnishings.

Holding the whole picture in his mind, he began living in the Certain Way, and moving toward what he wanted; and he owns the house now, and is rebuilding it after the form of his mental image. And now, with still larger faith, he is going on to get greater things. It has been unto him according to his faith, and it is so with you and with all of us.

chapter seven
Gratitude

The illustrations given in the last chapter will have conveyed to the reader the fact that the first step toward getting rich is to convey the idea of your wants to the Formless Substance.

This is true, and you will see that in order to do so it becomes necessary to relate yourself to the Formless Intelligence in a harmonious way.

To secure this harmonious relation is a matter of such primary and vital importance that I shall give some space to its discussion here, and give you instructions which, if you will follow them, will be certain to bring you into perfect unity of mind with God.

The whole process of mental adjustment and atonement can be summed up in one word, gratitude. First, you believe that there is one Intelligent Substance, from which all things proceed; second, you believe that this Substance gives you everything you desire; and third, you relate yourself to it by a feeling of deep and profound gratitude.

Many people who order their lives rightly in all other ways are kept in poverty by their lack of gratitude. Having received one gift from God, they cut the wires which connect them with Him by failing to make acknowledgment.

It is easy to understand that the nearer we live to the source of wealth, the more wealth we shall receive; and it is easy also to understand that the soul that is always grateful lives in closer touch with God than the one which never looks to Him in thankful acknowledgment. The more gratefully we fix our minds on the Supreme when good things come to us, the more good things we will receive, and the more rapidly they will come; and the reason simply is that the mental attitude of gratitude draws the mind into closer touch with the source from which the blessings come.

If it is a new thought to you that gratitude brings your whole mind into closer harmony with the creative energies of the universe, consider it well, and you will see that it is true.

The good things you already have come to you along the line of obedience to certain laws. Gratitude will lead your mind out along the ways by which things come; and it will keep you in close harmony with creative thought and prevent you from falling into competitive thought.

Gratitude alone can keep you looking toward the All, and prevent you from falling into the error of thinking of the supply as limited; and to do that would be fatal to your hopes. There is a Law of Gratitude, and it is absolutely necessary that you should observe the law, if you are to get the results you seek.

The law of gratitude is the natural principle that action and reaction are always equal, and in opposite directions.

The grateful outreaching of your mind in thankful praise to the Supreme is a liberation or expenditure of force; it cannot fail to reach that to which it addressed, and the reaction is an instantaneous movement towards you.

"Draw nigh unto God, and He will draw nigh unto you." That is a statement of psychological truth. And if your gratitude is strong and constant, the reaction in Formless Substance will be strong and continuous; the movement of the things you want will be always toward you. Notice the grateful attitude that Jesus took; how He always seems to be saying, "I thank Thee, Father, that Thou hearest me." You cannot exercise much power without gratitude; for it is gratitude that keeps you connected with Power.

But the value of gratitude does not consist solely in getting you more blessings in the future. Without gratitude you cannot long keep from dissatisfied thought regarding things as they are.

The moment you permit your mind to dwell with dissatisfaction upon things as they are, you begin to lose ground. You fix attention upon the common, the ordinary, the poor, and the squalid and mean; and your mind takes the form of these things. Then you will transmit these forms or mental images to the Formless, and the common, the poor, the squalid, and mean will come to you.

To permit your mind to dwell upon the inferior is to become inferior and to surround yourself with inferior things. On the other hand, to fix your attention on the best is to surround yourself with the best, and to become the best.

The Creative Power within us makes us into the image of that to which we give our attention. We are Thinking Substance, and thinking substance always takes the form of that which it thinks about. The grateful mind is constantly fixed upon the best; therefore it tends to become the best; it takes the form or character of the best, and will receive the best. Also, faith is born of gratitude. The grateful mind continually expects good things, and expectation becomes faith. The reaction of gratitude upon one's own mind produces faith; and every outgoing wave of grateful thanksgiving increases faith. He who has no feeling of gratitude cannot long retain a living faith; and without a living faith you cannot get rich by the creative method, as we shall see in the following chapters.

It is necessary, then, to cultivate the habit of being grateful for every good thing that comes to you; and to give thanks continuously.

And because all things have contributed to your advancement, you should include all things in your gratitude. Do not waste time thinking or talking about the shortcomings or wrong actions of plutocrats or trust magnates. Their organization of the world has made your opportunity; all you get really comes to you because of them.

Do not rage against, corrupt politicians; if it were not for politicians we should fall into anarchy, and your opportunity would be greatly lessened. God has worked a long time and very patiently to bring us up to where we are in industry and government, and He is going right on with His work. There is not the least doubt that He will do away with plutocrats, trust magnates, captains of industry, and politicians as soon as they can be spared; but in the meantime, behold they are all very good. Remember that they are all helping to arrange the lines of transmission along which your riches will come to you, and be grateful to them all. This will bring you into harmonious relations with the good in everything, and the good in everything will move toward you.

chapter eight
Thinking in the Certain Way

Turn back to chapter 6 and read again the story of the man who formed a mental image of his house, and you will get a fair idea of the initial step toward getting rich. You must form a clear and definite mental picture of what you want; you cannot transmit an idea unless you have it yourself.

You must have it before you can give it; and many people fail to impress Thinking Substance because they have themselves only a vague and misty concept of the things they want to do, to have, or to become.

It is not enough that you should have a general desire for wealth "to do good with"; everybody has that desire. It is not enough that you should have a wish to travel, see things, live more, etc. Everybody has those desires also. If you were going to send a wireless message to a friend, you would not send the letters of the alphabet in their order, and let him construct the message for himself; nor would you take words at random from the dictionary. You would send a coherent sentence; one which meant something. When you try to impress your wants upon Substance, remember that it must be done by a coherent statement; you must know what you want, and be definite. You can never get rich, or start the creative power into action, by sending out unformed longings and vague desires.

Go over your desires just as the man I have described went over his house; see just what you want, and get a clear mental picture of it as you wish it to look when you get it.

That clear mental picture you must have continually in mind, as the sailor has in mind the port toward which he is sailing the ship; you must keep your face toward it all the time. You must no more lose sight of it than the steersman loses sight of the compass.

It is not necessary to take exercises in concentration, nor to set apart special times for prayer and affirmation, nor to "go into the silence," nor to do occult stunts of any kind. There things are well enough, but all you need is to know what you want, and to want it badly enough so that it will stay in your thoughts.

Spend as much of your leisure time as you can in contemplating your picture, but no one needs to take exercises to concentrate his mind on a thing which he really wants; it is the things you do not really care about which require effort to fix your attention upon them.

And unless you really want to get rich, so that the desire is strong enough to hold your thoughts directed to the purpose as the magnetic pole holds the needle of the compass, it will hardly be worth while for you to try to carry out the instructions given in this book.

The methods herein set forth are for people whose desire for riches is strong enough to overcome mental laziness and the love of ease, and make them work. The more clear and definite you make your picture then, and the more you dwell upon it, bringing out all its delightful details, the stronger your desire will be; and the stronger your desire, the easier it will be to hold your mind fixed upon the picture of what you want. Something more is necessary, however, than merely to see the picture clearly. If that is all you do, you are only a dreamer, and will have little or no power for accomplishment.

Behind your clear vision must be the purpose to realize it; to bring it out in tangible expression. And behind this purpose must be an invincible and unwavering FAITH that the thing is already yours; that it is "at hand" and you have only to take possession of it. Live in the new house, mentally, until it takes form around you physically. In the mental realm, enter at once into full enjoyment of the things you want. "Whatsoever things ye ask for when ye pray, believe that ye receive them, and ye shall have them," said Jesus. See the things you want as if they were actually around you all the time; see yourself as owning and using them. Make use of them in imagination just as you will use them when they are your tangible possessions. Dwell upon your mental picture until it is clear and distinct, and then take the Mental Attitude of Ownership toward everything in that picture. Take possession of it, in mind, in the full faith that it is actually yours. Hold to this mental ownership; do not waiver for an instant in the faith that it is real.

And remember what was said in a proceeding chapter about gratitude; be as thankful for it all the time as you expect to be when it has taken form. The man who can sincerely thank God for the things which as yet he owns only in imagination, has real faith. He will get rich; he will cause the creation of whatsoever he wants. You do not need to pray repeatedly for things you want; it is not necessary to tell God about it every day. "Use not vain repetitions as the heathen do," said Jesus said to his pupils, "for your Father knoweth the ye have need of these things before ye ask Him."

Your part is to intelligently formulate your desire for the things which make for a larger life, and to get these desire arranged into a coherent whole; and then to impress this Whole Desire upon the Formless Substance, which has the power and the will to bring you what you want.

You do not make this impression by repeating strings of words; you make it by holding the vision with unshakable PURPOSE to attain it, and with steadfast FAITH that you do attain it.

The answer to prayer is not according to your faith while you are talking, but according to your faith while you are working.

You cannot impress the mind of God by having a special Sabbath day set apart to tell Him what you want, and the forgetting Him during the rest of the week. You cannot impress Him by having special hours to go into your closet and pray, if you then dismiss the matter from your mind until the hour of prayer comes again. Oral prayer is well enough, and has its effect, especially upon yourself, in clarifying your vision and strengthening your faith; but it is not your oral petitions which get you what you want. In order to get rich you do not need a "sweet hour of prayer"; you need to "pray without ceasing." And by prayer I mean holding steadily to your vision, with the purpose to cause its creation into solid form, and the faith that you are doing so. "Believe that ye receive them."

The whole matter turns on receiving, once you have clearly formed your vision. When you have formed it, it is well to make an oral statement, addressing the Supreme in reverent prayer; and from that moment you must, in mind, receive what you ask for. Live in the new house; wear the fine clothes; ride in the automobile; go on the journey, and confidently plan for greater journeys. Think and speak of all the things you have asked for in terms of actual present ownership. Imagine an environment, and a financial condition exactly as you want them, and live all the time in that imaginary environment and financial condition. Mind, however, that you do not do this as a mere dreamer and castle builder; hold to the FAITH that the imaginary is being realized, and to the PURPOSE to realize it. Remember that it is faith and purpose in the use of the imagination which make the difference between the scientist and the dreamer. And having learned this fact, it is here that you must learn the proper use of the Will.

chapter nine
How to Use the Will

To set about getting rich in a scientific way, you do not try to apply your will power to anything outside of yourself.

Your have no right to do so, anyway. It is wrong to apply your will to other men and women, in order to get them to do what you wish done. It is as flagrantly wrong to coerce people by mental power as it is to coerce them by physical power. If compelling people by physical force to do things for you reduces them to slavery, compelling them by mental means accomplishes exactly the same thing; the only difference is in methods. If taking things from people by physical force is robbery, them taking things by mental force is robbery also; there is no difference in principle. You have no right to use your will power upon another person, even "for his own good"; for you do not know what is for his good. The science of getting rich does not require you to apply power or force to any other person, in any way whatsoever. There is not the slightest necessity for doing so; indeed, any attempt to use your will upon others will only tend to defeat your purpose.

You do not need to apply your will to things, in order to compel them to come to you. That would simply be trying to coerce God, and would be foolish and useless, as well as irreverent. You do not have to compel God to give you good things, any more than you have to use your will power to make the sun rise.

You do not have to use your will power to conquer an unfriendly deity, or to make stubborn and rebellious forces do your bidding.

Substance is friendly to you, and is more anxious to give you what you want than you are to get it. To get rich, you need only to use your will power upon yourself. When you know what to think and do, then you must use your will to compel yourself to think and do the right things. That is the legitimate use of the will in getting what you want-to use it in holding yourself to the right course. Use your will to keep yourself thinking and acting in the Certain Way.

Do not try to project your will, or your thoughts, or your mind out into space, to "act" on things or people. Keep your mind at home; it can accomplish more there than elsewhere.

Use your mind to form a mental image of what you want, and to hold that vision with faith and purpose; and use your will to keep your mind working in the Right Way.

The more steady and continuous your faith and purpose, the more rapidly you will get rich, because you will make only POSITIVE impressions upon Substance; and you will not neutralize or offset them by negative impressions.

The picture of your desires, held with faith and purpose, is taken up by the Formless, and permeates it to great distances-throughout the universe, for all I know. As this impression spreads, all things are set moving toward its realization; every living thing, every inanimate thing, and the things yet uncreated, are stirred toward bringing into being that which you want. All force begins to be exerted in that direction; all things begin to move toward you. The minds of people, everywhere, are influenced toward doing the things necessary to the fulfilling of your desires; and they work for you, unconsciously.

But you can check all this by starting a negative impression in the Formless Substance. Doubt or unbelief is as certain to start a movement away from you as faith and purpose are to start one toward you. It is by not understanding this that most people who try to make use of "mental science" in getting rich make their failure. Every hour and moment you spend in giving heed to doubts and fears, every hour you spend in worry, every hour in which your soul is possessed by unbelief, sets a current away from you in the whole domain of intelligent Substance. All the promises are unto them that believe, and unto them only. Notice how insistent Jesus was upon this point of belief; and now you know the reason why.

Since belief is all important, it behooves you to guard your thoughts; and as your beliefs will be shaped to a very great extent by the things you observe and think about, it is important that you should command your attention. And here the will comes into use; for it is by your will that you determine upon what things your attention shall be fixed.

If you want to become rich, you must not make a study of poverty.

Things are not brought into being by thinking about their opposites. Health is never to be attained by studying disease and thinking about disease; righteousness is not to be promoted by studying sin and thinking about sin; and no one ever got rich by studying poverty and thinking about poverty.

Medicine as a science of disease has increased disease; religion as a science of sin has promoted sin, and economics as a study of poverty will fill the world with wretchedness and want.

Do not talk about poverty; do not investigate it, or concern yourself with it. Never mind what its causes are; you have nothing to do with them.

What concerns you is the cure. Do not spend your time in charitable work, or charity movements; all charity only tends to perpetuate the wretchedness it aims to eradicate.

I do not say that you should be hard hearted or unkind, and refuse to hear the cry of need; but you must not try to eradicate poverty in any of the conventional ways. Put poverty behind you, and put all that pertains to it behind you, and "make good."

Get rich; that is the best way you can help the poor. And you cannot hold the mental image which is to make you rich if you fill your mind with pictures of poverty. Do not read books or papers which give circumstantial accounts of the wretchedness of the tenement dwellers, of the horrors of child labor, and so on. Do not read anything which fills your mind with gloomy images of want and suffering.

You cannot help the poor in the least by knowing about these things; and the wide-spread knowledge of them does not tend at all to do away with poverty.

What tends to do away with poverty is not the getting of pictures of poverty into your mind, but getting pictures of wealth into the minds of the poor.

You are not deserting the poor in their misery when you refuse to allow your mind to be filled with pictures of that misery.

Poverty can be done away with, not by increasing the number of well to do people who think about poverty, but by increasing the number of poor people who purpose with faith to get rich.

The poor do not need charity; they need inspiration. Charity only sends them a loaf of bread to keep them alive in their wretchedness, or gives them an entertainment to make them forget for an hour or two; but inspiration will cause them to rise out of their misery. If you want to help the poor, demonstrate to them that they can become rich; prove it by getting rich yourself. The only way in which poverty will ever be banished from this world is by getting a large and constantly increasing number of people to practice the teachings of this book.

People must be taught to become rich by creation, not by competition.

Every man who becomes rich by competition throws down behind him the ladder by which he rises, and keeps others down; but every man who gets rich by creation opens a way for thousands to follow him, and inspires them to do so.

You are not showing hardness of heart or an unfeeling disposition when you refuse to pity poverty, see poverty, read about poverty, or think or talk about it, or to listen to those who do talk about it. Use your will power to keep your mind OFF the subject of poverty, and to keep it fixed with faith and purpose ON the vision of what you want.

chapter ten
Further Use of the Will

You cannot retain a true and clear vision of wealth if you are constantly turning your attention to opposing pictures, whether they be external or imaginary. Do not tell of your past troubles of a financial nature, if you have had them, do not think of them at all. Do no tell of the poverty of your parents, or the hardships of your early life; to do any of these things is to mentally class yourself with the poor for the time being, and it will certainly check the movement of things in your direction. "Let the dead bury their dead," as Jesus said. Put poverty and all things that pertain to poverty completely behind you.

You have accepted a certain theory of the universe as being correct, and are resting all your hopes of happiness on its being correct; and what can you gain by giving heed to conflicting theories?

Do not read religious books which tell you that the world is soon coming to an end; and do not read the writing of muck-rakers and pessimistic philosophers who tell you that it is going to the devil.

The world is not going to the devil; it is going to God. It is wonderful Becoming.

True, there may be a good many things in existing conditions which are disagreeable; but what is the use of studying them when they are certainly passing away, and when the study of them only tends to check their passing and keep them with us? Why give time and attention to things which are being removed by evolutionary growth, when you can hasten their removal only by promoting the evolutionary growth as far as your part of it goes? No matter how horrible in seeming may be the conditions in certain countries, sections, or places, you waste your time and destroy your own chances by considering them.

You should interest yourself in the world's becoming rich.

Think of the riches the world is coming into, instead of the poverty it is growing out of; and bear in mind that the only way in which you can assist the world in growing rich is by growing rich yourself through the creative method-not the competitive one.

Give your attention wholly to riches; ignore poverty. Whenever you think or speak of those who are poor, think and speak of them as those who are becoming rich, those who are to be congratulated rather than pitied. Then they and others will catch the inspiration, and begin to search for the way out.

Because I say that you are to give your whole time and mind and thought to riches, it does not follow that you are to be sordid or mean.

To become really rich is the noblest aim you can have in life, for it includes everything else.

On the competitive plane, the struggle to get rich is a Godless scramble for power over other men; but when we come into the creative mind, all this is changed. All that is possible in the way of greatness and soul unfoldment, of service and lofty endeavor, comes by way of getting rich; all is made possible by the use of things. If you lack for physical health, you will find that the attainment of it is conditional on your getting rich. Only those who are emancipated from financial worry, and who have the means to live a care-free existence and follow hygienic practices, can have and retain health.

Moral and spiritual greatness is possible only to those who are above the competitive battle for existence; and only those who are becoming rich on the plane of creative thought are free from the degrading influences of competition. If your heart is set on domestic happiness, remember that love flourishes best where there is refinement, a high level of thought, and freedom from corrupting influences; and these are to be found only where riches are attained by the exercise of creative thought, without strife or rivalry.

You can aim at nothing so great or noble, I repeat, as to become rich; and you must fix your attention upon your mental picture of riches, to the exclusion of all that may tend to dim or obscure the vision.

You must learn to see the underlying TRUTH in all things; you must see beneath all seemingly wrong conditions the Great One Life ever moving forward toward fuller expression and more complete happiness. It is the truth that there is no such thing as poverty; that there is only wealth.

Some people remain in poverty because they are ignorant of the fact that there is wealth for them; and these can best be taught by showing them the way to affluence in your own person and practice.

Others are poor because, while they feel that there is a way out, they are too intellectually indolent to put forth the mental effort necessary to find that way and by travel it; and for these the very best thing you can do is to arouse their desire by showing them the happiness that comes from being rightly rich.

Others still are poor because, while they have some notion of science, they have become so swamped and lost in the maze of metaphysical and occult theories that they do not know which road to take. They try a mixture of many systems and fail in all. For these, again, the very best thing, to do is to show the right way in your own person and practice; an ounce of doing things is worth a pound of theorizing.

The very best thing you can do for the whole world is to make the most of yourself.

You can serve God and man in no more effective way than by getting rich; that is, if you get rich by the creative method and not by the competitive one. Another thing. We assert that this book gives in detail the principles of the science of getting rich; and if that is true, you do not need to read any other book upon the subject. This may sound narrow and egotistical, but consider: there is no more scientific method of computation in mathematics than by addition, subtraction, multiplication, and division; no other method is possible. There can be but one shortest distance between two points. There is only one way to think scientifically, and that is to think in the way that leads by the most direct and simple route to the goal. No man has yet formulated a briefer or less complex "system" than the one set forth herein; it has been stripped of all nonessentials. When you commence on this, lay all others aside; put them out of your mind altogether.

Read this book every day; keep it with you; commit it to memory, and do not think about other "systems" and theories. If you do, you will begin to have doubts, and to be uncertain and wavering in your thought; and then you will begin to make failures.

After you have made good and become rich, you may study other systems as much as you please; but until you are quite sure that you have gained what you want, do not read anything on this line but this book, unless it be the authors mentioned in the Preface.

And read only the most optimistic comments on the world's news; those in harmony with your picture. Also, postpone your investigations into the occult. Do not dabble in theosophy, Spiritualism, or kindred studies. It is very likely that the dead still live, and are near; but if they are, let them alone; mind your own business. Wherever the spirits of the dead may be, they have their own work to do, and their own problems to solve; and we have no right to interfere with them. We cannot help them, and it is very doubtful whether they can help us, or whether we have any right to trespass upon their time if they can. Let the dead and the hereafter alone, and solve your own problem; get rich. If you begin to mix with the occult, you will start mental cross-currents which will surely bring your hopes to shipwreck. Now, this and the preceding chapters have brought us to the following statement of basic facts: -

There is a thinking stuff from which all things are made, and which, in its original state, permeates, penetrates, and fills the interspaces of the universe. A thought, in this substance, produces the thing that is imaged by the thought.

Man can form things in his thought, and, by impressing his thought upon formless substance, can cause the thing he thinks about to be created. In order to do this, man must pass from the competitive to the creative mind; he must form a clear mental picture of the things he wants, and hold this picture in his thoughts with the fixed PURPOSE to get what he wants, and the unwavering FAITH that he does get what he wants, closing his mind against all that may tend to shake his purpose, dim his vision, or quench his faith.

And in addition to all this, we shall now see that he must live and act in a Certain Way.

chapter eleven
Acting in the Certain Way

Thought is the creative power, or the impelling force which causes the creative power to act; thinking in a Certain Way will bring riches to you, but you must not rely upon thought alone, paying no attention to personal action. That is the rock upon which many otherwise scientific metaphysical thinkers meet shipwreck—the failure to connect thought with personal action. We have not yet reached the stage of development, even supposing such a stage to be possible, in which man can create directly from Formless Substance without nature's processes or the work of human hands; man must not only think, but his personal action must supplement his thought.

By thought you can cause the gold in the hearts of the mountains to be impelled toward you; but it will not mine itself, refine itself, coin itself into double eagles, and come rolling along the roads seeking its way into your pocket.

Under the impelling power of the Supreme Spirit, men's affairs will be so ordered that someone will be led to mine the gold for you; other men's business transactions will be so directed that the gold will be brought toward you, and you must so arrange your own business affairs that you may be able to receive it when it comes to you. Your thought makes all things, animate and inanimate, work to bring you what you want; but your personal activity must be such that you can rightly receive what you want when it reaches you. You are not to take it as charity, nor to steal it; you must give every man more in use value than he gives you in cash value. The scientific use of thought consists in forming a clear and distinct mental image of what you want; in holding fast to the purpose to get what you want; and in realizing with grateful faith that you do get what you want.

Do not try to project your thought in any mysterious or occult way, with the idea of having it go o and do things for you; that is wasted effort, and will weaken your power to think with sanity. The action of thought in getting rich is fully explained in the preceding chapters; your faith and purpose positively impress your vision upon Formless Substance, which has THE SAME DESIRE FOR MORE LIFE THAT YOU HAVE; and this vision, received from you, sets all the creative forces at work IN AND THROUGH THEIR REGULAR CHANNELS OF ACTION, but directed toward you.

It is not your part to guide or supervise the creative process; all you have to do with that is to retain your vision, stick to your purpose, and maintain your faith and gratitude.

But you must act in a Certain Way, so that you can appropriate what is yours when it comes to you; so that you can meet the things you have in your picture, and put them in their proper places as they arrive. You can really see the truth of this. When things reach you, they will be in the hands of other men, who will ask an equivalent for them.

And you can only get what is yours by giving the other man what is his.

Your pocketbook is not going to be transformed into a Fortunata's purse, which shall be always full of money without effort on your part.

This is the crucial point in the science of getting rich; right here, where thought and personal action must be combined. There are very many people who, consciously or unconsciously, set the creative forces in action by the strength and persistence of their desires, but who remain poor because they do not provide for the reception of the thing they want when it comes.

By thought, the thing you want is brought to you; by action you receive it.

Whatever your action is to be, it is evident that you must act NOW. You cannot act in the past, and it is essential to the clearness of your mental vision that you dismiss the past from your mind. You cannot act in the future, for the future is not here yet. And you cannot tell how you will want to act in any future contingency until that contingency has arrived.

Because you are not in the right business, or the right environment now, do not think that you must postpone action until you get into the right business or environment. And do not spend time in the present taking thought as to the best course in possible future emergencies; have faith in your ability to meet any emergency when it arrives.

If you act in the present with your mind on the future, your present action will be with a divided mind, and will not be effective.

Put your whole mind into present action. Do not give your creative impulse to Original Substance, and then sit down and wait for results; if you do, you will never get them. Act now. There is never any time but now, and there never will be any time but now. If you are ever to begin to make ready for the reception of what you want, you must begin now.

And your action, whatever it is, must most likely be in your present business or employment, and must be upon the persons and things in your present environment. You cannot act where you are not; you cannot act where you have been, and you cannot act where you are going to be; you can act only where you are. Do not bother as to whether yesterday' s work was well done or ill done; do today' s work well. Do not try to do tomorrow' s work now; there will be plenty of time to do that when you get to it.

Do not try, by occult or mystical means, to act on people or things that are out of your reach. Do not wait for a change of environment, before you act; get a change of environment by action.

You can so act upon the environment in which you are now, as to cause yourself to be transferred to a better environment.

Hold with faith and purpose the vision of yourself in the better environment, but act upon your present environment with all your heart, and with all your strength, and with all your mind.

Do not spend any time in daydreaming or castle building; hold to the one vision of what you want, and act NOW.

Do not cast about seeking some new thing to do, or some strange, unusual, or remarkable action to perform as a first step toward getting rich. It is probable that your actions, at least for some time to come, will be those you have been performing for some time past; but you are to begin now to perform these actions in the Certain Way, which will surely make you rich.

If you are engaged in some business, and feel that it is not the right one for you, do not wait until you get into the right business before you begin to act.

Do not feel discouraged, or sit down and lament because you are misplaced. No man was ever so misplaced but that he could not find the right place, and no man ever became so involved in the wrong business but that he could get into the right business.

Hold the vision of yourself in the right business, with the purpose to get into it, and the faith that you will get into it, and are getting into it; but ACT in your present business. Use your present business as the means of getting a better one, and use your present environment as the means of getting into a better one. Your vision of the right business, if held with faith and purpose, will cause the Supreme to move the right business toward you; and your action, if performed in the Certain Way, will cause you to move toward the business.

If you are an employee, or wage earner, and feel that you must change places in order to get what you want, do not' project" your thought into space and rely upon it to get you another job. It will probably fail to do so. Hold the vision of yourself in the job you want, while you ACT with faith and purpose on the job you have, and you will certainly get the job you want.

Your vision and faith will set the creative force in motion to bring it toward you, and your action will cause the forces in your own environment to move you toward the place you want. In closing this chapter, we will add another statement to our syllabus :-

There is a thinking stuff from which all things are made, and which, in its original state, permeates, penetrates, and fills the interspaces of the universe. A thought, in this substance, produces the thing that is imaged by the thought.

Man can form things in his thought, and, by impressing his thought upon formless substance, can cause the thing he thinks about to be created. In order to do this, man must pass from the competitive to the creative mind; he must form a clear mental picture of the things he wants, and hold this picture in his thoughts with the fixed PURPOSE to get what he wants, and the unwavering FAITH that he does get what he wants, closing his mind to all that may tend to shake his purpose, dim his vision, or quench his faith. That he may receive what he wants when it comes, man must act NOW upon the people and things in his present environment.

chapter twelve
Efficient Action

You must use your thought as directed in previous chapters, and begin to do what you can do where you are; and you must do ALL that you can do where you are.

You can advance only be being larger than your present place; and no man is larger than his present place who leaves undone any of the work pertaining to that place. The world is advanced only by those who more than fill their present places.

If no man quite filled his present place, you can see that there must be a going backward in everything. Those who do not quite fill their present places are dead weight upon society, government, commerce, and industry; they must be carried along by others at a great expense. The progress of the world is retarded only by those who do not fill the places they are holding; they belong to a former age and a lower stage or plane of life, and their tendency is toward degeneration. No society could advance if every man was smaller than his place; social evolution is guided by the law of physical and mental evolution. In the animal world, evolution is caused by excess of life.

When an organism has more life than can be expressed in the functions of its own plane, it develops the organs of a higher plane, and a new species is originated.

There never would have been new species had there not been organisms which more than filled their places. The law is exactly the same for you; your getting rich depends upon your applying this principle to your own affairs.

Every day is either a successful day or a day of failure; and it is the successful days which get you what you want. If everyday is a failure, you can never get rich; while if every day is a success, you cannot fail to get rich. If there is something that may be done today, and you do not do it, you have failed in so far as that thing is concerned; and the consequences may be more disastrous than you imagine.

You cannot foresee the results of even the most trivial act; you do not know the workings of all the forces that have been set moving in your behalf. Much may be depending on your doing some simple act; it may be the very thing which is to open the door of opportunity to very great possibilities. You can never know all the combinations which Supreme Intelligence is making for you in the world of things and of things and of human affairs; your neglect or failure to do some small thing may cause a long delay in getting what you want. Do, every day, ALL that can be done that day.

There is, however, a limitation or qualification of the above that you must take into account.

You are not to overwork, nor to rush blindly into your business in the effort to do the greatest possible number of things in the shortest possible time. You are not to try to do tomorrow' s work today, nor to do a week' s work in a day.

It is really not the number of things you do, but the EFFICIENCY of each separate action that counts. Every act is, in itself, either a success or a failure. Every act is, in itself, either effective or inefficient. Every inefficient act is a failure, and if you spend your life in doing inefficient acts, your whole life will be a failure.

The more things you do, the worse for you, if all your acts are inefficient ones.

On the other hand, every efficient act is a success in itself, and if every act of your life is an efficient one, your whole life MUST be a success.

The cause of failure is doing too many things in an inefficient manner, and not doing enough things in an efficient manner.

You will see that it is a self-evident proposition that if you do not do any inefficient acts, and if you do a sufficient number of efficient acts, you will become rich. If, now, it is possible for you to make each act an efficient one, you see again that the getting of riches is reduced to an exact science, like mathematics.

The matter turns, then, on the questions whether you can make each separate act a success in itself. And this you can certainly do.

You can make each act a success, because ALL Power is working with you; and ALL Power cannot fail. Power is at your service; and to make each act efficient you have only to put power into it.

Every action is either strong or weak; and when every one is strong, you are acting in the Certain Way which will make you rich.

Every act can be made strong and efficient by holding your vision while you are doing it, and putting the whole power of your FAITH and PURPOSE into it.

It is at this point that the people fail who separate mental power from personal action. They use the power of mind in one place and at one time, and they act in another pace and at another time. So their acts are not successful in themselves; too many of them are inefficient. But if ALL Power goes into every act, no matter how commonplace, every act will be a success in itself; and as in the nature of things every success opens the way to other successes, your progress toward what you want, and the progress of what you want toward you, will become increasingly rapid.

Remember that successful action is cumulative in its results. Since the desire for more life is inherent in all things, when a man begins to move toward larger life more things attach themselves to him, and the influence of his desire is multiplied.

Do, every day, all that you can do that day, and do each act in an efficient manner.

In saying that you must hold your vision while you are doing each act, however trivial or commonplace, I do not mean to say that it is necessary at all times to see the vision distinctly to its smallest details. It should be the work of your leisure hours to use your imagination on the details of your vision, and to contemplate them until they are firmly fixed upon memory. If you wish speedy results, spend practically all your spare time in this practice.

By continuous contemplation you will get the picture of what you want, even to the smallest details, so firmly fixed upon your mind, and so completely transferred to the mind of Formless Substance, that in your working hours you need only to mentally refer to the picture to stimulate your faith and purpose, and cause your best effort to be put forth. Contemplate your picture in your leisure hours until your consciousness is so full of it that you can grasp it instantly. You will become so enthused with its bright promises that the mere thought of it will call forth the strongest energies of your whole being. Let us again repeat our syllabus, and by slightly changing the closing statements bring it to the point we have now reached.

There is a thinking stuff from which all things are made, and which, in its original state, permeates, penetrates, and fills the interspaces of the universe. A thought, in this substance, produces the thing that is imaged by the thought.

Man can form things in his thought, and, by impressing his thought upon formless substance, can cause the thing he thinks about to be created. In order to do this, man must pass from the competitive to the creative mind; he must form a clear mental picture of the things he wants, and do, with faith and purpose, all that can be done each day, doing each separate thing in an efficient manner.

chapter thirteen
Getting into the Right Business

Success, in any particular business, depends for one thing upon your possessing in a well-developed state the faculties required in that business.

Without good musical faculty no one can succeed as a teacher of music; without well-developed mechanical faculties no one can achieve great success in any of the mechanical trades; without tact and the commercial faculties no one can succeed in mercantile pursuits. But to possess in a well-developed state the faculties required in your particular vocation does not insure getting rich. There are musicians who have remarkable talent, and who yet remain poor; there are blacksmiths, carpenters, and so on who have excellent mechanical ability, but who do not get rich; and there are merchants with good faculties for dealing with men who nevertheless fail. The different faculties are tools; it is essential to have good tools, but it is also essential that the tools should be used in the Right Way. One man can take a sharp saw, a square, a good plane, and so on, and build a handsome article of furniture; another man can take the same tools and set to work to duplicate the article, but his production will be a botch. He does not know how to use good tools in a successful way.

The various faculties of your mind are the tools with which you must do the work which is to make you rich; it will be easier for you to succeed if you get into a business for which you are well equipped with mental tools.

Generally speaking, you will do best in that business which will use your strongest faculties; the one for which you are naturally "best fitted." But there are limitations to this statement, also. No man should regard his vocation as being irrevocably fixed by the tendencies with which he was born.

You can get rich in ANY business, for if you have not the right talent for you can develop that talent; it merely means that you will have to make your tools as you go along, instead of confining yourself to the use of those with which you were born. It will be EASIER for you to succeed in a vocation for which you already have the talents in a well-developed state; but you CAN succeed in any vocation, for you can develop any rudimentary talent, and there is no talent of which you have not at least the rudiment.

You will get rich most easily in point of effort, if you do that for which you are best fitted; but you will get rich most satisfactorily if you do that which you WANT to do.

Doing what you want to do is life; and there is no real satisfaction in living if we are compelled to be forever doing something which we do not like to do, and can never do what we want to do. And it is certain that you can do what you want to do; the desire to do it is proof that you have within you the power which can do it. Desire is a manifestation of power.

The desire to play music is the power, which can play music seeking expression and development; the desire to invent mechanical devices is the mechanical talent seeking expression and development.

Where there is no power, either developed or undeveloped, to do a thing, there is never any desire to do that thing; and where there is strong desire to do a thing, it is certain proof that the power to do it is strong, and only requires to be developed and applied in the Right Way.

All things else being equal, it is best to select the business for which you have the best developed talent; but if you have a strong desire to engage in any particular line of work, you should select that work as the ultimate end at which you aim.

You can do what you want to do, and it is your right and privilege to follow the business or avocation which will be most congenial and pleasant.

You are not obliged to do what you do not like to do, and should not do it except as a means to bring you to the doing of the thing you want to do.

If there are past mistakes whose consequences have placed you in an undesirable business or environment, you may be obliged for some time to do what you do not like to do; but you can make the doing of it pleasant by knowing that it is making it possible for you to come to the doing of what you want to do.

If you feel that you are not in the right vocation, do not act too hastily in trying to get into another one. The best way, generally, to change business or environment is by growth.

Do not be afraid to make a sudden and radical change if the opportunity is presented, and you feel after careful consideration that it is the right opportunity; but never take sudden or radical action when you are in doubt as to the wisdom of doing so.

There is never any hurry on the creative plane; and there is no lack of opportunity.

When you get out of the competitive mind you will understand that you never need to act hastily. No one else is going to beat you to the thing you want to do; there is enough for all. If one space is taken, another and a better one will be opened for you a little farther on; there is plenty of time. When you are in doubt, wait. Fall back on the contemplation of your vision, and increase your faith and purpose; and by all means, in times of doubt and indecision, cultivate gratitude.

A day or two spent in contemplating the vision of what you want, and in earnest thanksgiving that you are getting it, will bring your mind into such close relationship with the Supreme that you will make no mistake when you do act.

There is a mind which knows all there is to know; and you can come into close unity with this mind by faith and the purpose to advance in life, if you have deep gratitude.

Mistakes come from acting hastily, or from acting in fear or doubt, or in forgetfulness of the Right Motive, which is more life to all, and less to none.

As you go on in the Certain Way, opportunities will come to you in increasing number; and you will need to be very steady in your faith and purpose, and to keep in close touch with the All Mind by reverent gratitude. Do all that you can do in a perfect manner every day, but do it without haste, worry, or fear. Go as fast as you can, but never hurry.

Remember that in the moment you begin to hurry you cease to be a creator and become a competitor; you drop back upon the old plane again.

Whenever you find yourself hurrying, call a halt; fix your attention on the mental image of the thing you want, and begin to give thanks that you are getting it.

The exercise of GRATITUDE will never fail to strengthen your faith and renew your purpose.

chapter fourteen
The Impression of Increase

Whether you change your vocation or not, your actions for the present must be those pertaining to the business in which you are now engaged.

You can get into the business you want by making constructive use of the business you are already established in; by doing your daily work in a Certain Way. And in so far as your business consists in dealing with other men, whether personally or by letter, the keythought of all your efforts must be to convey to their minds the impression of increase.

Increase is what all men and all women are seeking; it is the urge of the Formless Intelligence within them, seeking fuller expression.

The desire for increase is inherent in all nature; it is the fundamental impulse of the universe. All human activities are based on the desire for increase; people are seeking more food, more clothes, better shelter, more luxury, more beauty, more knowledge, more pleasure—increase in something, more life.

Every living thing is under this necessity for continuous advancement; where increase of life ceases, dissolution and death set in at once.

Man instinctively knows this, and hence he is forever seeking more. This law of perpetual increase is set forth by Jesus in the parable of the talents; only those who gain more retain any; from him who hath not shall be taken away even that which he hath.

The normal desire for increased wealth is not an evil or a reprehensible thing; it is simply the desire for more abundant life; it is aspiration.

And because it is the deepest instinct of their natures, all men and women are attracted to him who can give them more of the means of life.

In following the Certain Way as described in the foregoing pages, you are getting continuous increase for yourself, and you are giving it to all with whom you deal. You are a creative center, from which increase is given off to all.

Be sure of this, and convey assurance of the fact to every man, woman, and child with whom you come in contact. No matter how small the transaction, even if it be only the selling of a stick of candy to a little child, put into it the thought of increase, and make sure that the customer is impressed with the thought.

Convey the impression of advancement with everything you do, so that all people shall receive the impression that you are an Advancing Man, and that you advance all who deal with you. Even to the people whom you meet in a social way, without any thought of business, and to whom you do not try to sell anything, give the thought of increase.

You can convey this impression by holding the unshakable faith that you, yourself, are in the Way of Increase; and by letting this faith inspire, fill, and permeate every action.

Do everything that you do in the firm conviction that you are an advancing personality, and that you are giving advancement to everybody.

Feel that you are getting rich, and that in so doing you are making others rich, and conferring benefits on all. Do not boast or brag of your success, or talk about it unnecessarily; true faith is never boastful.

Wherever you find a boastful person, you find one who is secretly doubtful and afraid. Simply feel the faith, and let it work out in every transaction; let every act and tone and look express the quiet assurance that you are getting rich; that you are already rich. Words will not be necessary to communicate this feeling to others; they will feel the sense of increase when in your presence, and will be attracted to you again.

You must so impress others that they will feel that in associating with you they will get increase for themselves. See that you give them a use value greater than the cash value you are taking from them.

Take an honest pride in doing this, and let everybody know it; and you will have no lack of customers. People will go where they are given increase; and the Supreme, which desires increase in all, and which knows all, will move toward you men and women who have never heard of you. Your business will increase rapidly, and you will be surprised at the unexpected benefits which will come to you. You will be able from day to day to make larger combinations, secure greater advantages, and to go on into a more congenial vocation if you desire to do so. But doing thing all this, you must never lose sight of your vision of what you want, or your faith and purpose to get what you want. Let me here give you another word of caution in regard to motives. Beware of the insidious temptation to seek for power over other men.

Nothing is so pleasant to the unformed or partially developed mind as the exercise of power or dominion over others. The desire to rule for selfish gratification has been the curse of the world. For countless ages kings and lords have drenched the earth with blood in their battles to extend their dominions; this not to seek more life for all, but to get more power for themselves.

Today, the main motive in the business and industrial world is the same; men Marshal their armies of dollars, and lay waste the lives and hearts of millions in the same mad scramble for power over others. Commercial kings, like political kings, are inspired by the lust for power. Jesus saw in this desire for mastery the moving impulse of that evil world He sought to overthrow. Read the twenty-third chapter of Matthew, and see how He pictures the lust of the Pharisees to be called "Master," to sit in the high places, to domineer over others, and to lay burdens on the backs of the less fortunate; and note how He compares this lust for dominion with the brotherly seeking for the Common Good to which He calls His disciples.

Look out for the temptation to seek for authority, to become a "master," to be considered as one who is above the common herd, to impress others by lavish display, and so on.

The mind that seeks for mastery over others is the competitive mind; and the competitive mind is not the creative one. In order to master your environment and your destiny, it is not at all necessary that you should rule over your fellow men and indeed, when you fall into the world's struggle for the high places, you begin to be conquered by fate and environment, and your getting rich becomes a matter of chance and speculation. Beware of the competitive mind!! No better statement of the principle of creative action can be formulated than the favorite declaration of the late "Golden Rule" Jones of Toledo: "What I want for myself, I want for everybody."

chapter fifteen
The Advancing Man

What I have said in the last chapter applies as well to the professional man and the wage-earner as to the man who is engaged in mercantile business.

No matter whether you are a physician, a teacher, or a clergyman, if you can give increase of life to others and make them sensible of the fact, they will be attracted to you, and you will get rich. The physician who holds the vision of himself as a great and successful healer, and who works toward the complete realization of that vision with faith and purpose, as described in former chapters, will come into such close touch with the Source of Life that he will be phenomenally successful; patients will come to him in throngs.

No one has a greater opportunity to carry into effect the teaching of this book than the practitioner of medicine; it does not matter to which of the various schools he may belong, for the principle of healing is common to all of them, and may be reached by all alike. The Advancing Man in medicine, who holds to a clear mental image of himself as successful, and who obeys the laws of faith, purpose, and gratitude, will cure every curable case he undertakes, no matter what remedies he may use.

In the field of religion, the world cries out for the clergyman who can teach his hearers the true science of abundant life. He who masters the details of the science of getting rich, together with the allied sciences of being well, of being great, and of winning love, and who teaches these details from the pulpit, will never lack for a congregation. This is the gospel that the world needs; it will give increase of life, and men will hear it gladly, and will give liberal support to the man who brings it to them.

What is now needed is a demonstration of the science of life from the pulpit. We want preachers who can not only tell us how, but who in their own persons will show us how. We need the preacher who will himself be rich, healthy, great, and beloved, to teach us how to attain to these things; and when he comes he will find a numerous and loyal following.

The same is true of the teacher who can inspire the children with the faith and purpose of the advancing life. He will never be "out of a job." And any teacher who has this faith and purpose can give it to his pupils; he cannot help giving it to them if it is part of his own life and practice.

What is true of the teacher, preacher, and physician is true of the lawyer, dentist, real estate man, insurance agent-of everybody.

The combined mental and personal action I have described is infallible; it cannot fail. Every man and woman who follows these instructions steadily, perseveringly, and to the letter, will get rich. The law of the Increase of Life is as mathematically certain in its operation as the law of gravitation; getting rich is an exact science.

The wage-earner will find this as true of his case as of any of the others mentioned. Do not feel that you have no chance to get rich because you are working where there is no visible opportunity for advancement, where wages are small and the cost of living high. Form your clear mental vision of what you want, and begin to act with faith and purpose.

Do all the work you can do, every day, and do each piece of work in a perfectly successful manner; put the power of success, and the purpose to get rich, into everything that you do.

But do not do this merely with the idea of currying favor with your employer, in the hope that he, or those above you, will see your good work and advance you; it is not likely that they will do so.

The man who is merely a "good" workman, filling his place to the very best of his ability, and satisfied with that, is valuable to his employer; and it is not to the employer's interest to promote him; he is worth more where he is.

To secure advancement, something more is necessary than to be too large for your place.

The man who is certain to advance is the one who is too big for his place, and who has a clear concept of what he wants to be; who knows that he can become what he wants to be and who is determined to BE what he wants to be.

Do not try to more than fill your present place with a view to pleasing your employer; do it with the idea of advancing yourself. Hold the faith and purpose of increase during work hours, after work hours, and before work hours. Hold it in such a way that every person who comes in contact with you, whether foreman, fellow workman, or social acquaintance, will feel the power of purpose radiating from you; so that every one will get the sense of advancement and increase from you. Men will be attracted to you, and if there is no possibility for advancement in your present job, you will very soon see an opportunity to take another job.

There is a Power, which never fails to present opportunity to the Advancing Man who is moving in obedience to law.

God cannot help helping you, if you act in a Certain Way; He must do so in order to help Himself. There is nothing in your circumstances or in the industrial situation that can keep you down. If you cannot get rich working for the steel trust, you can get rich on a ten-acre farm; and if you begin to move in the Certain Way, you will certainly escape from the "clutches" of the steel trust and get on to the farm or wherever else you wish to be.

If a few thousands of its employees would enter upon the Certain Way, the steel trust would soon be in a bad plight; it would have to give its workingmen more opportunity, or go out of business. Nobody has to work for a trust; the trusts can keep men in so called hopeless conditions only so long as there are men who are too ignorant to know of the science of getting rich, or too intellectually slothful to practice it.

Begin this way of thinking and acting, and your faith and purpose will make you quick to see any opportunity to better your condition.

Such opportunities will speedily come, for the Supreme, working in All, and working for you, will bring them before you.

Do not wait for an opportunity to be all that you want to be; when an opportunity to be more than you are now is presented and you feel impelled toward it, take it. It will be the first step toward a greater opportunity. There is no such thing possible in this universe as a lack of opportunities for the man who is living the advancing life.

It is inherent in the constitution of the cosmos that all things shall be for him and work together for his good; and he must certainly get rich if he acts and thinks in the Certain Way. So let wage-earning men and women study this book with great care, and enter with confidence upon the course of action it prescribes; it will not fail.

chapter sixteen
Some Cautions, and Concluding Observations

Many people will scoff at the idea that there is an exact science of getting rich; holding the impression that the supply of wealth is limited, they will insist that social and governmental institutions must be changed before even any considerable number of people can acquire a competence.

But this is not true.

It is true that existing governments keep the masses in poverty, but this is because the masses do not think and act in the Certain Way.

If the masses begin to move forward as suggested in this book, neither governments nor industrial systems can check them; all systems must be modified to accommodate the forward movement.

If the people have the Advancing Mind, have the Faith that they can become rich, and move forward with the fixed purpose to become rich, nothing can possibly keep them in poverty.

Individuals may enter upon the Certain Way at any time, and under any government, and make themselves rich; and when any considerable number of individuals do so under any government, they will cause the system to be so modified as to open the way for others. The more men who get rich on the competitive plane, the worse for others; the more who get rich on the creative plane, the better for others.

The economic salvation of the masses can only be accomplished by getting a large number of people to practice the scientific method set down in this book, and become rich. These will show others the way, and inspire them with a desire for real life, with the faith that it can be attained, and with the purpose to attain it.

For the present, however, it is enough to know that neither the government under which you live nor the capitalistic or competitive system of industry can keep you from getting rich. When you enter upon the creative plane of thought you will rise above all these things and become a citizen of another kingdom.

But remember that your thought must be held upon the creative plane; you are never for an instant to be betrayed into regarding the supply as limited, or into acting on the moral level of competition. Whenever you do fall into old ways of thought, correct yourself instantly; for when you are in the competitive mind, you have lost the cooperation of the Mind of the Whole.

Do not spend any time in planning as to how you will meet possible emergencies in the future, except as the necessary policies may affect your actions today. You are concerned with doing today' work in a perfectly successful manner, and not with emergencies which may arise tomorrow; you can attend to them as they come. Do not concern yourself with questions as to how you shall surmount obstacles which may loom upon your business horizon, unless you can see plainly that your course must be altered today in order to avoid them. No matter how tremendous an obstruction may appear at a distance, you will find that if you go on in the Certain Way it will disappear as you approach it, or that a way over, though, or around it will appear.

No possible combination of circumstances can defeat a man or woman who is proceeding to get rich along strictly scientific lines. No man or woman who obeys the law can fail to get rich, any more than one can multiply two by two and fail to get four.

Give no anxious thought to possible disasters, obstacles, panics, or unfavorable combinations of circumstances; it is time enough to meet such things when they present themselves before you in the immediate present, and you will find that every difficulty carries with it the wherewithal for its overcoming.

Guard your speech. Never speak of yourself, your affairs, or of anything else in a discouraged or discouraging way.

Never admit the possibility of failure, or speak in a way that infers failure as a possibility.

Never speak of the times as being hard, or of business conditions as being doubtful. Times may be hard and business doubtful for those who are on the competitive plane, but they can never be so for you; you can create what you want, and you are above fear.

When others are having hard times and poor business, you will find your greatest opportunities.

Train yourself to think of and to look upon the world as a something which is Becoming, which is growing; and to regard seeming evil as being only that which is undeveloped. Always speak in terms of advancement; to do otherwise is to deny your faith, and to deny your faith is to lose it.

Never allow yourself to feel disappointed. You may expect to have a certain thing at a certain time, and not get it at that time; and this will appear to you like failure. But if you hold to your faith you will find that the failure is only apparent.

Go on in the certain way, and if you do not receive that thing, you will receive something so much better that you will see that the seeming failure was really a great success.

A student of this science had set his mind on making a certain business combination which seemed to him at the time to be very desirable, and he worked for some, weeks to bring it about. When the crucial time came, the thing failed in a perfectly inexplicable way; it was as if some unseen influence had been working secretly against him. He was not disappointed; on the contrary, he thanked God that his desire had been overruled, and went steadily on with a grateful mind. In a few weeks an opportunity so much better came his way that he would not have made the first deal on any account; and he saw that a Mind which knew more than he knew had prevented him from losing the greater good by entangling himself with the lesser.

That is the way every seeming failure will work out for you, if you keep your faith, hold to your purpose, have gratitude, and do, every day, all that can be done that day, doing each separate act in a successful manner. When you make a failure, it is because you have not asked for enough; keep on, and a larger thing then you were seeking will certainly come to you. Remember this. You will not fail because you lack the necessary talent to do what you wish to do. If you go on as I have directed, you will develop all the talent that is necessary to the doing of your work.

It is not within the scope of this book to deal with the science of cultivating talent; but it is as certain and simple as the process of getting rich.

However, do not hesitate or waver for fear that when you come to any certain place you will fail for lack of ability; keep right on, and when you come to that place, the ability will be furnished to you. The same source of Ability which enabled the untaught Lincoln to do the greatest work in government ever accomplished by a single man is open to you; you may draw upon all the mind there is for wisdom to use in meeting the responsibilities which are laid upon you. Go on in full faith.

Study this book. Make it your constant companion until you have mastered all the ideas contained in it. While you are getting firmly established in this faith, you will do well to give up most recreations and pleasure; and to stay away from places where ideas conflicting with these are advanced in lectures or sermons. Do not read pessimistic or conflicting literature, or get into arguments upon the matter. Do very little reading, outside of the writers mentioned in the Preface. Spend most of your leisure time in contemplating your vision, and in cultivating gratitude, and in reading this book. It contains all you need to know of the science of getting rich; and you will find all the essentials summed up in the following chapter.

chapter seventeen
Summary of the Science of Getting Rich

There is a thinking stuff from which all things are made, and which, in its original state, permeates, penetrates, and fills the interspaces of the universe. A thought in this substance produces the thing that is imaged by the thought.

Man can form things in his thought, and by impressing his thought upon formless substance can cause the thing he thinks about to be created.

In order to do this, man must pass from the competitive to the creative mind; otherwise he cannot be in harmony with the Formless Intelligence, which is always creative and never competitive in spirit.

Man may come into full harmony with the Formless Substance by entertaining a lively and sincere gratitude for the blessings it bestows upon him. Gratitude unifies the mind of man with the intelligence of Substance, so that man's thoughts are received by the Formless. Man can remain upon the creative plane only by uniting himself with the Formless Intelligence through a deep and continuous feeling of gratitude.

Man must form a clear and definite mental image of the things he wishes to have, to do, or to become; and he must hold this mental image in his thoughts, while being deeply grateful to the Supreme that all his desires are granted to him. The man who wishes to get rich must spend his leisure hours in contemplating his Vision, and in earnest thanksgiving that the reality is being given to him. Too much stress cannot be laid on the importance of frequent contemplation of the mental image, coupled with unwavering faith and devout gratitude. This is the process by which the impression is given to the Formless, and the creative forces set in motion.

The creative energy works through the established channels of natural growth, and of the industrial and social order. All that is included in his mental image will surely be brought to the man who follows the instructions given above, and whose faith does not waver. What he wants will come to him through the ways of established trade and commerce.

In order to receive his own when it shall come to him, man must be active; and this activity can only consist in more than filling his present place. He must keep in mind the Purpose to get rich through the realization of his mental image. And he must do, every day, all that can be done that day, taking care to do each act in a successful manner. He must give to every man a use value in excess of the cash value he receives, so that each transaction makes for more life; and he must so hold the Advancing Thought that the impression of increase will be communicated to all with whom he comes in contact.

The men and women who practice the foregoing instructions will certainly get rich; and the riches they receive will be in exact proportion to the definiteness of their vision, the fixity of their purpose, the steadiness of their faith, and the depth of their gratitude.

—The End—

www.ingramcontent.com/pod-product-compliance
Lightning Source LLC
Chambersburg PA
CBHW052008070526
44584CB00016B/1667